The Temple Pattern

An Ancient Celebration of the Plan of Salvation

Marcus M. Ladd

Tafiat Publishing
True and Faithful in All Things

Copyright 2015 by Tafiat Publishing

First Printing

ISBN-13: 978-1512152326
ISBN-10: 1512152323

Tafiat Publishing

All rights reserved. No part of this book may be reproduced in any format or in any medium without the written permission of the publisher, Tafiat Publishing. This work is not an official publication of the Church of Jesus Christ of Latter-Day Saints. The views expressed herein are the responsibility of the author and do not necessarily represent the position of the Church.

Please send E-mail correspondence to tafiat@yahoo.com

CONTENTS

Introduction
1

One
Adam's Offering
7

Two
Ordinances as the Temple Endowment
13

Three
Doctrine of Christ – 1 Ne 31
23

Four
Three Pillars of Eternity as the Endowment
31

Five
The Holy Ghost Moves in Creation
40

Six
Steven's Defense – An Endowment Pattern
51

Seven
Stephen's Temple Built without Hands
68

Eight
Creation Concepts
72

Nine
Scripture Stories that Celebrate the Endowment Pattern
103

Ten
Nephi's Temple Endowment
121

Eleven
The Sealing Power of Elijah
130

Twelve
Song of Joseph and the Lamb
141

Thirteen
Moses 1 – Christ's Mission Prefigured in the Story of Moses
149

Fourteen
King Benjamin at the Temple – Son of the Right Hand
163

Fifteen
Mosiah 15 – Abinadi's Tree of Life
178

Sixteen
Matthew 11 – Taking Christ's Yoke, Learn of Him
193

Seventeen
Greater Than the Temple Mat 12:1-7
203

Eighteen
Matthew 25 – Three Parables in One
211

Nineteen
Perfected in Christ
The Marriage Imagery of Moroni 10 30-33
219

Conclusion
Is This Not Real?
240

APPENDIX 1
The Prodigal Son's Journey – The Endowment
246

APPENDIX 2
Paul's Endowment – A Plan of Mercy and Grace
249

APPENDIX 3
The Sacrament Prayer – Chiasmus
253

APPENDIX 4
The Holy Spirit of Promise
258

APPENDIX 5
President Monson – First Presidency Message, Aug 2015
261

APPENDIX 6
2 Cor 11:2-4, Rom 1:21, Corrupted Mind & Darkened Heart
265

APPENDIX 7
The Seven Churches of Asia – The Endowment
269

APPENDIX 8 – A
3 Nephi 11:31-41, "This is my Doctrine"
278

APPENDIX 8 – B
Malachi 3 (3 Nephi 24) – Tokens of the Bread and the Wine
Opening the Windows of Heaven
282

APPENDIX 8 – C
Christ Expounds Malachi – Message on a Parallel
3rd Nephi 26:1-10
290

APPEMDIX 8 – D
Christ's Chiasmus in 3 Nephi 27 – "This is my Gospel"
294

APPENDIX 9
Notes on Mosiah 15
311

APPENDIX 10
Sod – Mysterion – Sacramentum – Sacrament
315

APPENDIX 11
Alma's Three Sons – Three Endowments
322

APPENDIX 12
Noah – The Temple Pattern
337

PREFACE

Temple Text

Brian K. Ashton of the LDS Sunday School General Presidency recently explained that the Old Testament "is **a temple text**." He said, "As you recall what you see in the temple, you begin to understand both the Old Testament and the temple better." (Church News, Jan 2018) This is so because characteristics of one are embedded in the other. Indeed, one of the primary ways that scripture and the temple unfold each other's meaning (testify of each other) is in the pattern common to both. To be sure, when the primal temple pattern is discovered, its heptadic or sevenfold sequence is found again and again in scripture text, in iterations large and small.

Templum

The word temple, in fact, comes from the Latin root templum, which can denote a template or pattern.[1] Certainly, the temple presents an outline for our lives – how to return to our Father's presence (also known as the gospel). As this book explores, the temple's master template emanates from the first series of events in the Bible, the creation pattern in Genesis 1-2. Indeed, the cosmic creation is widely recognized as the construction of God's temple, with Eden as the Holy of Holies.[2] The ancient Mosaic sacrificial system followed this original template, as does the New Covenant sacrifice performed in the temple of the contrite heart.

Fractal

"A fractal is a shape made up of smaller versions of itself. If you zoom in on each part, you can see that it is a smaller replica of the entire object. The pattern of self-similarity continues through many layers as you zoom in."[3] The seven days of creation (God's cosmic temple) have been categorized by some scholars as the primary Bible fractal. In scripture (including the Book of Mormon) its template can underpin the structure of an entire book or chapter, but may also be found in the short iterative burst of a single verse. For instance, below is the general "shape" of the Bible – from Genesis to Revelations – a very large iteration of the creation fractal, pivoting on Christ.

    In Eden with God

        Judgment and fall of Adam

            Old Covenant – Israel   *(telestial)*

                Christ   *(terrestrial)*

            New Covenant – Gentiles   *(celestial)*

        Judgment and Resurrection of man

    In heaven with God

Temple Mirrors

The self-similarity discerned in fractals is also analogous to what we experience in the temple when we stand between two mirrors, either in the celestial room or in the sealing room – our image re-iterated over and over again, ad infinitum. These parallel mirrors are displayed in every temple and symbolize eternity. However, you may want to consider that they are placed only in the upper rooms of the temple, inferring that a vision of eternity is reserved exclusively for patrons who have covenanted to be true and faithful, clothed (endowed) in white robes of righteousness (Rev 19:8), saints who are following a template of creation which is able to beautify man\woman in God's holy image.

Pattern in All Things

Undeniably, the first pattern\template – 7 days of physical creation – is perfect. It seems natural that God would also make it the spiritual "pattern in all things" – that is, how we are also transformed from telestial chaos to a celestial creation (covered, endowed with beauty). If there is a pattern in all things, as we read in D&C 52:14-18, and if it is a true statement, then we could expect to find the same pattern in the temple as we find in creation, also common to the gospel. Identifying it one place will help us clarify it in the others.

Quotes to Contemplate

"Seeking and finding the Lord's "pattern in all things" can be, then, a rewarding and important spiritual discipline on the way to becoming, as Christ charged us to be, "even as I am" (3 Nephi 27:27). All other patterns are subordinate to this grand pattern of Jesus Christ. Brigham Young taught that "the greatest mystery a man ever learned, is to know how to . . . bring every faculty and power of the [human mind] in[to] subjection to Jesus Christ" (JD 1:46). We learn that discipline by tracing his divine pattern, which he teaches at every opportunity and in every setting, of

following and teaching all men and women, everywhere, the intensifying, incremental, and upward-spiraling pattern of faith, repentance, baptism, renewal, and—hand-in-hand with the Holy Spirit—enduring to the end in discovering more and more divine patterns through knowing and following that other grand pattern."
Divine Designs: Tracing the Lord's "Pattern in All Things"
Richard H. Cracroft Professor of English at BYU, Dec. 10, 1996, Devotional

Introduction

Nowhere in scripture are we told, "Here it is, the following is the temple endowment." None the less, elements of the modern endowment set forth a progressive framework that is distinct, which allows us to compare it to the stories of scripture and find the same series of events. It could even be called the pattern of the gospel or the plan of salvation, with the death and resurrection of Jesus Christ at its center. Based on common sequence, the temple endowment is the gospel, and the gospel is the endowment.

With such emphasis placed on the temple, which we are told is the great symbol of our religion, how is it possible that we have members of the church attending one time and never returning? Having taught the temple preparation class I suspect that the problem is with our expectation and preparation. The following quote has been used before in books about the temple, but I consider it worth repeating. President David O. McKay's describes his experience:

> "When the Los Angeles temple building program was commenced, President McKay called a meeting of the stake presidents of the temple district. During this meeting, President McKay took occasion to express his feelings about the holy endowment. He indicated how some years before, a niece of his had received her ordinances in the house of the Lord. He had learned that she only recently before that had received an initiation into a sorority at the local university. She had had the crassness to say that she found the sorority initiation superior in effect and meaning to her than the endowment. President McKay was open and frank with them

about the experience of one in his own family with the endowment. He wasn't worried about their audible gasps. With characteristic aplomb, he paused, and then said, "Brothers and sisters, she was disappointed in the temple. Brothers and sisters, I was disappointed in the temple. And so were you." Then he said something incredibly important that should be engraven on all our souls. "There are few, even temple workers, who comprehend the full meaning and power of the temple endowment. Seen for what it is, it is the step-by-step ascent into the Eternal Presence."[4]

All of which begs the question, how is it possible that "only few" comprehend the full meaning and power of the temple endowment? As others have noted, it is likely because we view the ceremony too literally, whereas we should be looking at it with spiritual eyes, seeking its symbolism and higher message (a step by step ascent into the Eternal Presence). For instance, what do the white robes represent in the endowment? Shouldn't all temple attendees be familiar with Revelation 19:8, which informs us that the white linen is the "righteousness of the saints?" And, why is it so hard for us to apply its lesson, which is that the clothing represents what we are to become within – righteous. What we actually wear in heaven therefore is considerably less significant in light of what the temple clothing figuratively represents, which is of far more importance. John A. Widstoe said, "We live in a world of symbols. No man or woman can come out of the temple endowed as he should be, unless he has seen beyond the symbol, the mighty realities for which the symbols stand.....The endowment which was given by revelation can best be understood by revelation; and to those who seek most vigorously, with pure hearts, will the revelation be greatest."[5] For us to ultimately "see beyond the symbols" of the temple, however, we have to first recognize that symbols exist. Not too surprising, the seedbed or source for temple symbolism is the scriptures, which were also given by revelation and which can also "best be understood by revelation." Indeed, the likely reason for our insensitivity to the temple symbolism starts with how we read the scriptures. Far too often we also read them without "vigorously' seeking to find and understand their symbolism. For example, we have scriptural images like the tree of life to help us understand God's love, a symbol of indescribable joy flowing into our lives like a divine river of water from the heavenly throne. And since love is something that we can't see, the tree of life represents what it might look like if we could – gloriously white; possessing beauty above all other beauty. (By the way, the tree of life is an important symbol in the temple. Does it symbolize the same thing there as it does in 1 Nephi 11?)

If a person, therefore, wants to really understand the temple then he/she needs to study the scriptures, because that is where temple symbolism comes from. In addition, understanding basic disciplines of biblical literary analysis, which is a tool for enhanced understanding of scriptural symbolism, is also highly recommended. For example, 1 Nephi is reportedly a book-wide chiasmus. (A chiasmus is a Hebrew literary form wherein elements parallel one another. The first parallels the last, the second element parallels the second to the last, and so on until a central thought is manifest.) If we consider its (1 Nephi's) literary structure, we may find that its chiasmus is also a "step by step ascent into the Eternal Presence"! Further, if that is the case then Nephi might also present us with the pattern of the ancient and modern temple endowment. One of the chapters in this book will outline this exact prospect.

In particular I have found that a good place to understand the ancient roots of the temple endowment is Acts 7, where Stephen used this literary device (the chiasmus) to present the exact model of the modern temple endowment (explored in chapter 7 of this book). Stephen stands on the temple mount and repeats it (the endowment) three times to the temple priesthood, the very people who should have understood it best, yet did not because their hearts "resisted the Holy Ghost" (Acts 7:51). Curiously, Stephen's endowment is the plan of salvation woven into the stories of the patriarchs – Abraham, Joseph, and Moses. However, as I hope you will discover, the endowment\plan-of-salvation pattern is found not just in these stories but everywhere in scripture that the Holy Ghost reveals it. D&C 93:36-40 is a very good case in point; a scripture which defines intelligence, light, truth, and eternal glory.

> The glory of God is intelligence, or, in other words, light and truth. Light and truth forsake that evil one. Every spirit of man was innocent in the beginning; and God having redeemed man from the fall, men became again, in their infant state, innocent before God. And that wicked one cometh and taketh away light and truth, through disobedience, from the children of men, and because of the tradition of their fathers. But I have commanded you to bring up your children in light and truth.

Here is a brief statement of the plan – that we were innocent (pure) in the beginning; that the evil one takes away truth and light through disobedience; that God has redeemed man from the fall; and that man became again in their infant state (pure), innocent before God. This story (a fall from and a return to purity) is the loving knowledge and truth that the evil one wants to take away. When the Lord commands us to bring up our children in light and truth, he is talking about instructing them in this wonderful redemptive plan –

which, as we are told, is the glory of God. Using the literary analysis of chiasmus (just mentioned), below is how this scripture in D&C 93 might be arranged:

A 36 The glory of God is intelligence, or, in other words, **light and truth.**

   B 37 **Light and truth** forsake **that evil one.**

      C 38 Every spirit of man was **innocent**

         D in the beginning;

            E and God having **redeemed man**

               F from the fall, (Telestial, Terrestrial, Celestial)

            E' **men** became again,

         D' in their infant state,

      C' **innocent** before God.

   B' 39 And **that wicked one** cometh and **taketh away light and truth**, through disobedience, from the children of men, and because of the tradition of their fathers.

A' 40 But I have commanded you to bring up your children in **light and truth** (or intelligence).

Notice how this plan to "redeem men" (E) and return them to "their infant state" (D') pivots on "the fall," which coincidently is also the focus of the temple endowment. I have also taken the liberty to include the three worlds that fallen man encounters in the endowment as he returns to an innocent or pure state (F). You might observe the circular nature of this plan, that it begins with the glory of God and that it returns to the same place – his glory, intelligence, and light (A, A'). Indeed, that is where you and I start and end our journey, in His glorious presence (one eternal round). So, is this just a scripture about our mortal journey, or is it also a form of the temple endowment? Is it an isolated coincidence, or do these temple-like structures happen often in scripture? Let's find out.

> *Note* – Perhaps it is no coincidence that D&C 93:35, which immediately precedes and introduces the pattern just discussed, speaks of the temple: "The elements are the tabernacle of God; yea, **man is the tabernacle of God, even temples;** and whatsoever temple is defiled, God shall destroy that temple." Clearly, whether it is the temple of man or a modern temple built of granite, the light and truth to fill and be taught in both is the glorious plan of salvation – that we were "innocent in the beginning" and that by redemption from the fall (E) we can become again "innocent before God."

1

Adam's Offering

In the book of Moses, chapter 5, we read that after Adam and Eve fell from the garden they offered sacrifices unto God. Here we discover that obedience and sacrifice are not enough; that there is something additional needed to make our offerings acceptable.

> 5 And he gave unto them commandments, that they should worship the Lord their God, and should offer the firstlings of their flocks, for an offering unto the Lord. And Adam was obedient unto the commandments of the Lord.
> 6 And after many days an angel of the Lord appeared unto Adam, saying: Why dost thou offer sacrifices unto the Lord? And Adam said unto him: I know not, save the Lord commanded me.
> 7 And then the angel spake, saying: This thing is a similitude of the sacrifice of the Only Begotten of the Father, which is full of grace and truth.
> 8 Wherefore, thou shalt do all that thou doest in the name of the Son, and thou shalt repent and call upon God in the name of the Son forevermore.

Looking forward to Jesus Christ, the Only Begotten of the Father, Adam is given saving knowledge – that obedience and sacrifices alone do not transcend. His actions need to come from a heart infused with love for his Savior. And of course, this lesson is there for us – all that we do (our obedience) should come from our hearts, with an ever-growing love for Jesus Christ; inward not outward sacrifice. After Adam is instructed, we then read the following:

> 9 And in that day the Holy Ghost fell upon Adam, which beareth record of the Father and the Son, saying: I am the Only Begotten of the Father from the beginning, henceforth and forever, that as thou hast fallen thou mayest be redeemed, and all mankind, even as many as will.

In order for Adam to do as God commanded, which is to do all in the name of Christ, he will need to have the assistance of the Holy Ghost, without which he could not do what the Lord has asked. It is the Holy Ghost which will "shed the love of God abroad in his heart" (1 Ne 11), making his sacrifice acceptable. And again, so it is with us – we cannot properly serve without feeling in our hearts that "which is most desirable and joyous" to the soul, His love.

To help us understand these profound ideas as they relate to the temple, we can arrange them in the following format, which is also coincidently a literary pattern often found in the Old and New Testament – a chiasmus.

Obedience without knowledge *telestial*

    Revelation of Only Begotten *terrestrial*

Obedience through Holy Ghost, revealer of spiritual knowledge *celestial*

You will notice that we can connect the three periods of our mortal experience (as learned in the temple) to the various stages of

Adam's experience. The hinge whereby Adam transitions (ascends) from a telestial to a celestial existence (abiding by its law) is a personal revelation of the Son of God, just as it is the spiritual hinge for our lives. These relationships help us to understand that the temple pattern is the gospel pattern, that one is enfolded within the other.[6] To break this notion down further, in the LDS Guide to the Scriptures we read a definition of the gospel:

> God's plan of salvation, made possible through the atonement of Jesus Christ. The gospel includes the eternal truths or laws, covenants, and ordinances needed for mankind to enter back into the presence of God. [7]

The gospel, therefore, is the plan of salvation, which is also what the temple communicates to us in symbol and pattern. About the temple Gordon B. Hinckley has said:

> "Here we have outlined the plan of a loving Father in behalf of His sons and daughters of all generations. Here we have sketched before us the odyssey of man's eternal journey from premortal existence through this life to the life beyond. Great fundamental and basic truths are taught with clarity and simplicity well within the understanding of all who hear" [8]

To clarify this point further – how the temple pattern is a gospel pattern – let's compare the first lesson in the LDS temple preparation course ("Endowed from on High"). Here we find an expanded chiastic pattern of the gospel plan, including what happens before and after mortality:

> With our Heavenly Father
>
> > Spiritual Death
>
> > > Mortality
>
> > Physical Death
>
> Return to our Heavenly Father

However, this often-taught pattern does not include the three phases of mortality learned in the temple. If we were to add these, we would have the exact pattern of the temple endowment, or in other words, the complete plan of salvation. Below is what this expanded pattern looks like:

> With our Heavenly Father - Eden
>
> > Spiritual Death
>
> > > Telestial
> > > > Terrestrial
> > > Celestial
>
> > Physical Death
>
> Return to our Heavenly Father

What is interesting is that we now have a pattern which takes seven periods to "complete." If you are familiar with Hebrew Bible symbolism then you know that seven is the number used to signify wholeness, completeness, or perfection, which is also what we hope to be at the end of our life's journey. Even more important, you will notice that seven is the number of days that it took to complete God's creation of the world. Of course, this is no coincidence. In fact, **the first seven days of physical creation are a type or pattern of the seven periods of our spiritual creation**, which in the temple is accomplished through making, and being true and faithful to, covenants. And indeed, this is also the order of the endowment – physical creation followed by spiritual creation.[9]

We often hear about the three degrees of glory as they relate to heaven, after we are dead and resurrected. For most it is a new idea to understand that these three kingdoms are existent on earth. Section 88 of the Doctrine and Covenants helps to makes sense of this. Here these degrees are explained:

> 21 And they who are not sanctified through the law which I have given unto you, even the law of Christ, must inherit another kingdom, even that of a terrestrial kingdom, or that of a telestial kingdom.
> 22 For he who is not able to abide the law of a celestial kingdom cannot abide a celestial glory.
> 23 And he who cannot abide the law of a terrestrial kingdom cannot abide a terrestrial glory.
> 24 And he who cannot abide the law of a telestial kingdom cannot abide a telestial glory;

It seems that where we end up in eternity is directly related to the law that we choose to abide while in mortality. If we live according to telestial law, never allowing the love of God to govern our hearts, then the telestial kingdom is where we will "remain" in the worlds to come. Hebrews 8:5 confirms this, where we read that the temple is a "shadow of heavenly things," and indeed the three kingdoms of heaven are also the pattern (shadow) of mortality as taught in the modern temple – a telestial, terrestrial, and celestial world.

In addition to the sevenfold framework discussed in this section, there are other endowment ideas and symbols (e.g. priesthood, covenants, laws) which overlay the seven basic parts of the gospel plan. For instance, in the pattern displayed on page 10, spiritual death and physical death are parallel, the first symbolized by the garment (skin) that is provided by the death of a lamb, and the physical death which is symbolized by the veil (the material and markings are the same on each). We will discuss these in more detail as we progress, but first let's look at how this pattern is repeated and enhanced elsewhere in gospel teaching, beginning with the first principles and ordinances of the gospel.

* *Note* – The prayers offered in the temple endowment are perfectly parallel. The first thing that Adam does upon entering the telestial world is to pray. The words that he uses, and the motions of his hands, are identical to those used before passing through the veil (the last thing Adam does). The difference is that Adam's first obedient prayer was offered without knowledge of the Only Begotten (Moses 5:6). This offers insight into the meaning of "the true order of prayer," which occurs only after Adam (we) has received further light and knowledge.

2

The First Principles and Ordinances as the Temple Endowment

In the following, President Harold B Lee speaks of the temple and matter-of-factly tells us that the endowment covenants are "but an embodiment" of covenants taken at baptism. Each is a depiction of the other.

> "The receiving of the endowment requires the assuming of obligations by covenants <u>which in reality are but an embodiment or an unfolding of the covenants each person should have assumed at baptism</u>, as explained by the prophet Alma to the effect that "ye are desirous to come into the fold of God, and to be called his people, and are willing to bear one another's burdens, that they may be light; Yea, and are willing to mourn with those that mourn; yea, and comfort those that stand in need of comfort, and to stand as witnesses of God at all times and in all things, and in all places that ye may be in, even until death" (Mosiah 18:8–9). Any [people] who [are] prepared to assume those obligations declared by Alma and "who humble themselves before God … and come forth with broken hearts and contrite spirits … and are willing to take upon them the name of Jesus Christ, having a determination to serve him to the end" (D&C 20:37), need have no hesitancy in going to a holy temple and receiving, <u>in connection with the covenants taken</u>, promises of great blessings predicated upon compliance therewith." (*Teachings of Presidents of the Church: Harold B. Lee*)

President Lee's use of "unfolding" also suggests a relationship where one is "nested" within, or flows out of, the other. Indeed, if we do a side-by-side comparison between the baptismal covenants and the endowment, we discover a sequence common to both – a divinely appointed hierarchy (telestial, then terrestrial, then celestial). Bruce Porter of the Quorum of Seventy has said: "these (*first*) principles and ordinances **constitute the heart** of the gospel of salvation, **being the essential requirements for entry into the celestial kingdom.**" [10] Elder Porter does not list the temple endowment or temple marriage as "essential requirements," although he later clarifies that: "Those who would enter into **the highest degree of that kingdom** and 'all that my Father hath' (D&C 84:38), must further receive the higher ordinances of exaltation found only in the holy temple." Still, the exalting temple ordinances appear to have little or no value if not continually supported by the celestializing first principles of the gospel. Confirming this idea, President Wilford Woodruff also emphasizes the preeminence of the first principles and ordinances: "The Lord has a great many principles in store for us; and the greatest principles which he has for us are the most simple and plain. The first principles of the gospel **which lead us unto eternal life** are the simplest, and yet **none are more glorious or important** to us."[11]

In a sense, then, the endowment is an outflowing of the gospel's first principles and ordinances. When we are baptized and take His name upon us, we promise to keep all His commandments; a covenant renewed each week with the sacrament (also outflowing of baptismal covenants). For this reason, when we covenant in the temple to obey the "law of the gospel," it feels second-nature, like a commitment we have already covenanted (at baptism) to keep, as do the laws of obedience, sacrifice, chastity, and consecration. In this regard, though not vocalized – faith, repentance, baptism, and the Holy Ghost (the "heart of the gospel of salvation") are fundamental components of (neatly nested within) the temple endowment.

Let's take a few samples from scripture and examine them for the gospel's first principles and ordinances as they relate to (are enfolded within) the three mortal phases of the temple endowment. As you read, keep in mind the mutual relationship that we just examined on page 9, that the **gospel** is "God's plan of salvation" and that "The Temple Presents the Plan of Salvation," which is the title of the first lesson in the gospel prep manual (i.e. the temple and the gospel represent the same thing – the plan of salvation). In 3 Nephi 27:20-21 we read the Savior's definition of his gospel (i.e. the plan of salvation, the temple). "Now this is the commandment: **Repent**, all ye ends of the earth, and come unto me and **be baptized** in my name, that ye may be **sanctified by the reception of the Holy Ghost**, that ye may stand spotless before me at the last day. Verily, verily, I say unto you, **this is my gospel**." Broken into its corresponding categories, the gospel\plan-of-salvation\temple pattern is:

Repent, all ye ends of the earth,	*Telestial*
and come unto me and **be baptized** in my name,	*Terrestrial*
that ye may be sanctified by **the reception of the Holy Ghost**, that ye may stand spotless before me at the last day.	*Celestial*

Another sample from scripture where these three divisions are apparent is Matthew's record of John's ministry (Mat 3):

1 In those days came John the Baptist, preaching in the wilderness of Judæa, 2 And saying, **Repen**t ye: for the kingdom of heaven is at hand.	*Telestial*

15

> 5 Then went out to him Jerusalem, and all Judæa, and all the region round about Jordan, 6 And were **baptized** of him in Jordan, confessing their sins.

Terrestrial

> 11 I indeed baptize you with water unto repentance: but he that cometh after me is mightier than I, whose shoes I am not worthy to bear: he shall baptize you with **the Holy Ghost,** and with fire: 12 Whose fan is in his hand, and he will throughly purge his floor, and gather his wheat into the garner; but he will burn up the chaff with unquenchable fire.

Celestial

Here it is especially apropos that we find John preaching in the "wilderness" in verse 1, which is a good representation of the telestial world; people in need of repentance who have been abiding a telestial law. Baptism (verse 5) is the terrestrial; when we take His name upon us and covenant to always remember him. In so doing we become His begotten sons and daughters, spiritually born of Christ (Mosiah 5:7). The celestial process of "baptizing with fire" ("sanctified by the reception of the Holy Ghost") is also associated with the end-time imagery of the God's kingdom, when the earth will be made new, burned in unquenchable fire (celestialized).[12]

Though we are not told here that John started his preaching with a discussion of temporal creation, in the Book of Mormon it is not uncommon to find the creation story preceding the preaching of the gospel principles (one creation establishing the pattern of the second, as in the temple). For instance, in Alma 22 we find Aaron preaching to king Lamoni's father. We read (emboldened words are for emphasis):

> 10 And Aaron said unto him: Yea, he is that Great Spirit, and **he created all things both in heaven and in earth.** Believest thou this?

11 And he said: Yea, I believe that the Great Spirit **created all things**, and I desire that ye should tell me concerning all these things, and I will believe thy words.

12 And it came to pass that when Aaron saw that the king would believe his words, **he began from the creation of Adam**, reading the scriptures unto the king—how **God created man** after his own image, and that God gave him commandments, and that because of transgression, **man had fallen**.

13 And Aaron did expound unto him the scriptures **from the creation of Adam**, laying the fall of man before him, and their carnal state and also **the plan of redemption**, which was prepared **from the foundation of the world**, through Christ, for all whosoever would believe on his name.

14 And since man had fallen he could not merit anything of himself; but the sufferings and death of Christ atone for their sins, **through faith and repentance, and so forth (baptism)**; and that he breaketh the bands of death, that the grave shall have no victory, and that the sting of death should be swallowed up in the hopes of glory; and Aaron did expound all these things unto the king.

15 And it came to pass that after Aaron had expounded these things unto him, the king said: What shall I do that I may have this **eternal life** of which thou hast spoken? Yea, what shall I do **that I may be born of God**, having this wicked spirit rooted out of my breast, and **receive his Spirit**, that I may be filled with joy, that I may not be cast off at the last day? Behold, said he, I will give up **all that I possess (consecration)**, yea, I will forsake my kingdom, that I may receive this great joy.

16 But Aaron said unto him: If thou desirest this thing, if thou wilt bow down before God, yea, if thou **wilt repent of all thy sins**, and will bow down before God, and **call on his name in faith**, believing that ye shall receive, then shalt thou receive the hope which thou desirest.

It is particularly interesting to note the sequence of Aaron's presentation of the "plan of redemption." He starts with the creation (vs 10-12), then the fall (vs 12-13), then presents the first ordinances of the gospel – faith, repentance, baptism (vs 14). True to form, this progression culminates with the celestializing concepts of eternal life – being born again, receiving the Spirit, and consecration; "giving up all that I possess" (vs 15), a series of events which mirrors the sequence of the temple endowment.

Let's now look at our seven-phase creation pattern, the unfolded endowment as a backdrop for the gospel's first principles and ordinances. (Notice faith's underlying role, lesser to greater):

God's presence

    Fall (spiritual death)

        Initial faith **Repentance** *Telestial*

            Baptism *Terrestrial*

        Spiritual **Gift of Holy Ghost** *Celestial*
        knowledge

    Veil (temporal death)

God's presence

Repentance is a telestial concept, because in the celestial kingdom there is no sin, and therefore no need to repent. Likewise, baptism corresponds to the terrestrial world, both in alignment with the taking of His name.

- **The First Principles are a Creative Process**

After the 4 Gospels, the New Testament is made up of the writings of Paul and the apostles to the various branches of the church; a membership that many times is growing and struggling in the faith. 1 Cor 3:1-2 is a good example of this. Here Paul addresses a baptized, yet telestial, church; "And I, brethren, could not speak unto you as unto spiritual, but as unto carnal, even as unto babes in Christ. I have fed you with milk, and not with meat: for hitherto ye were not able to bear it, neither yet now are ye able. 3 For ye are yet carnal: for whereas there is among you envying, and strife, and divisions, are ye not carnal, and walk as men?" Significantly, this group has apparently been baptized yet their faith is shallow, for which Paul calls them "yet carnal." They are like those members that Alma addressed in Zarahemlah, asking, "if ye have felt to sing the song of redeeming love, I would ask, can ye feel so now?" (Alma 5:26) Clearly both of these groups had faith, but it was immature faith (like milk) and had not been deepened by the trial of their faith – yielding their hearts to the Spirit (meat). Indeed, initial faith on the word will grow into a tree of life, bearing the meat of celestial fruit only if nurtured in the continuous light of God's love.[13]

We should realize that there is a plasticity or fluidity to this pattern, that is, while we may be in the third or celestialization phase of our journey, we still willfully sin (choose to abide a telestial law) because our faith is weak. When that occurs, we have fallen and of necessity return (are "introduced into") the telestial world where we must examine our faith, repent, and again call upon the name of the Son of God for forgiveness. As we renew our baptismal covenants (terrestrial), taking his name upon us to obey his commandments – we are forgiven, are cleansed by the enabling power of the Holy Ghost we can once again participate in celestialization and sanctification (consecrate our lives and hearts completely to build up the kingdom of God); where the veil is thin and our Father's presence is near.[14]

In addition, we cannot be celestial and telestial at the same time. We may think that because we obey most commandments and disobey only a few, that the good offsets the bad. However, that is not the case; for God cannot allow the least degree of sin in his presence (D&C 1:31). As he says in Rev 3:15-16, "I know thy works, that thou art neither cold nor hot: I would thou wert cold or hot. So then because thou art lukewarm, and neither cold nor hot, I will spue thee out of my mouth." Or, as we read in 1 Kings 18:21, we cannot be "halt between two opinions," but must choose Baal (the world) or God.

Abandoning this doublemindedness is taught especially well by the Savior in Mat 5:23-24, during the Sermon on the Mount, to those contemplating living the higher Law of the Gospel. He identifies the dissonance of having a foot in both kingdoms, along with how to leave the lesser (telestial) behind and enter the higher (celestial). "23 Therefore if thou bring thy gift to the altar, and there rememberest that thy brother hath ought against thee; 24 Leave there thy gift before the altar, and go thy way; first be reconciled to thy brother, and then come and offer thy gift." Here we find a man\woman, standing in a celestial place, performing a temple ordinance, bringing a physical (symbolic) offering, and discovering (revealed by the Holy Ghost) that his heart is out of alignment with the sacred place where he stands. His actions seem pure, but his heart is not. However, there is a "plan of salvation" for him. If he wants to stand in the temple (celestial) in worthiness then he must first leave (go into the world), put on his street clothes, struggle in repentance to place his carnal pride upon the altar (the real offering), call upon the name of the Lord for power to overcome, be strengthened by the Spirit and filled with God's love, seek at-one-ment with his brother, whereupon he may return to the temple, clothed in the temple robes of righteousness, and stand again before the Lord in His holy presence. (See the footnotes for this 7-part chiasmus.)[15]

In D&C the Lord speaks of his temple (and the temple of our hearts) and promises, "And inasmuch as my people build a house unto me in the name of the Lord, and do not suffer any unclean thing to come into it, that it be not defiled, my glory shall rest upon it; **Yea, and my presence shall be there, for I will come into it, and all the pure in heart that shall come into it shall see God. But if it be defiled I will not come into it, and my glory shall not be there; for I will not come into unholy temples.**" (D&C 97:17)

Certainly, we cannot expect that we "shall come to see God" if our heart is impure – good mixed with evil. Sin left unattended in our lives will keep us in the telestial realm and only repentance and reliance upon the promises of Christ's Atonement allow us to live in the joy and rest of the celestial. Indeed, as we remember our sacrament covenants and look to Him, we are promised His Spirit, which, if yielded to, will transform and purify who we are – creating a clean and holy temple. Apostle Dale Renlund, in Oct. 2018 general conference, called this an "iterative" process. He said, "After baptism, all members slip off the path—some of us even dive off. Therefore, exercising faith in Jesus Christ, repenting, receiving help from Him, and being forgiven are not onetime events but **lifelong processes**, processes that are **repetitive and iterative**. This is how we "endure to the end.""' [16] Proverbs 4:8 calls it (this iterative process) the "path of the righteous," which is "like the morning sun, shining ever brighter till the full light of day."

> * *Note* – In this chapter we have compared the 1st principals and ordinances of the gospel to the temple, assigning each principle to one of three mortal worlds (kingdoms). In particular, the gift of the Holy Ghost is associated with the celestial. Significantly, D&C 88:2-6 not only associates the Holy Ghost with the celestial kingdom, but also reveals an even greater endowment of this gift. See Appendix 4 for more information.

3

"Doctrine of Christ," 2 Nephi 31 as Temple Pattern

Consequently, whenever we encounter the sequence of the first principles and ordinances, the temple pattern is iterated, imitating and honoring creation's exquisite order. Others have also written about the temple as it relates to repentance, baptism, and the Holy Ghost. For instance, this idea is explored in an article from the Book of Mormon Central website, entitled "How Does the Doctrine of Christ Relate to the Ancient Temple." Referencing LDS scholar Shon D. Hopkin, it states:

> "Nephi's presentation of the doctrine of Christ relied 'upon imagery of the high priest's divine ascent' performed on the Day of Atonement, when the priest went 'from the east end of the Temple (at the altar of sacrifice) to its west end (in the holy of holies).' In the doctrine of Christ, Hopkin compares repentance and baptism to symbolically passing by the altar of sacrifice (repentance) and the molten sea (baptism) while entering in through the 'gate' or temple door into the 'holy place.'" [17]

In the temple endowment we are also a priest (wearing the robes of the priesthood) tracing the exact same journey as the ancient temple high priest. Symbolically we move from the telestial world (of the outer court) with the altar of sacrifice (repentance) and the molten sea of baptism (terrestrial), into the Holy Place (celestial) where the light of the candlestand represents the Holy Ghost. We pray before the veil prior to passing through into God's presence (the Holy of Holies).

Another LDS scholar, Joseph Spencer, adds that "The last three chapters of Second Nephi are saturated with the theme of the [temple] veil,"[18] even though the temple and its furnishings are never mentioned. In particular, Spencer is referring to a statement (in chapter 32) immediately after the doctrine of Christ, wherein the lord says that there will be no more doctrine given until He "manifests himself in the flesh" (seemingly a reference to the parted veil). However, what most "saturates" 2 Nephi 31, are the first principles of the gospel (i.e. repentance, baptism, and the Holy Ghost), told and retold multiple times by not just Nephi, but also by Christ and the Father. In fact, 2 Nephi 31 has one of the highest concentrations of "baptize" or "baptism" in the Book of Mormon (12 x's). To be sure, what causes the veil to part is the clearly outlined doctrine of Christ – living a life by the temple pattern, a life with power to part the veil.

When we speak of the Doctrine of Christ we generally cite only the last two verses (20 and 21), whose beauty captures our attention, with imagery of "pressing forward" in a "perfect brightness of hope" and the "love of God and all men. However, along with the other nineteen verses there is also an underlying structural creation cadence, which upon examination, is just as elegant. Nephi incorporates the entirety of the doctrine of Christ (19 verses) into a fascinating temple-like composition:

"Doctrine of Christ" (vs 2)

> **Nephi** explains – John's baptism of Christ and Holy Ghost (vs 3-10)
>
> > **Father** speaks – repent and be baptized in name of Son (vs 11)
> >
> > > The **Son** speaks – baptism and Holy Ghost (vs 12)
> > >
> > > > **Nephi** – repent, baptize, Holy Ghost, then tongue of angels (vs 13)
> > >
> > > The **Son** speaks – repent, baptize, Holy Ghost (vs14)
> >
> > **Father** speaks – confirms Son's words, endure to end (vs 15)
>
> **Nephi** explains - Repent, baptism, Holy Ghost, "endure to end" to have eternal life (vs 16-20)

"Doctrine of Christ and the Father" (vs 21)

When read in its entirety, this doctrine tell us repeatedly (7 tines) how enduring to the end, with a perfect brightness of hope, is done. It doesn't imply never committing a sin, because even those who are enduring will sin, causing a fall from the Lord's presence. Yet, as indicated, they are able to repent and take His name anew, receiving the Spirit to "always be with them" as they once more consecrate all they possess to the Lord. It is the bright plan for how we endure to end, pressing forward in the brilliant hope that we can be forgiven and made clean, prepared to worthily enter the Father's presence.

You might be pondering why Nephi is at the center of this chiasmus, a position normally reserved for Christ or the Holy Ghost (representing new birth). Indeed, he inserts himself into the discussion about baptism as if he is one of the Godhead. The key is undoubtedly what he says about now having the tongue of angels (which means messenger). To be sure, Nephi is a messenger of Jesus Christ, and is speaking with the tongue of angels, which he later explains in 1 Ne 32 is done by the power of the Holy Ghost. Nephi is (by proxy) representing the Holy Ghost in this conversation between the Godhead, each bearing witness of the others.

Incidentally, verses 20 and 21 are Nephi's reflection upon his and Lehi's earlier vision of the tree of life (found in 1 Nephi 8 and 11). In only two places in the Book of Mormon do we read the phrase "pressing forward," in Lehi's vision and here in 2 Nephi 31:20 where Nephi borrows its imagery to bring his brethren (you and me) to the "love of God," which sheds abroad in the heart of those who "know" (to whom it has been revealed by the Holy Ghost). Man's journey begins as he leaves the tree of life (like Adam and Eve), ending upon a return to it, found in the kingdom of the Father (Rev. 19), a journey which the Doctrine of Christ poetically teaches.

Until we take the time to search them out, structures such as the one woven into the Doctrine of Christ are the unseen magnificence of the Book of Mormon. Out of what seems to be muddled repetition is the beautiful rhyming of sacred and holy principles, a divine plan reverberating again and again. We might ponder - Would the Father and Son continue to repeat it, emphasizing it so many times, if it wasn't extremely important? Nephi's use of precise symmetry in creating his record pays literary tribute to God's original creation of order-out-of-chaos, a symbolic adaptation of the earliest creation account found in Genesis 1-3, the first principles and ordinances spoken of seven times, denoting its perfection. Below are these basic gospel principles with their temple equivalents, to the right in italics.

Repentance	*telestial*	*lesser life*	Repeated 7 times
Baptism	*terrestrial*	*greater light*	
Holy Ghost	*celestial*	*fruitful, beautiful*	

This holy "doctrine" is later iterated by Christ in 3 Nephi 11, after his resurrection, when he teaches the Nephites at the temple, again outlining repentance, baptism, and the Holy Ghost multiple times – declaring anew, "this is my doctrine." In fact, after the people feel the prints of the nails in his hands and in his feet, it is the first thing he teaches. Later, before leaving on the third day, he teaches it again, calling it "his gospel" (3 Ne 27), saying that "whoso shall declare more or less than this (repentance, baptism, and the Holy Ghost), and establish it for my doctrine, the same cometh of evil." (Both are wonderful chiasmi, see Appendix 8.) As we appreciate the temple for what it is, a symbolic celebration of Christ's doctrine and a plan for man's salvation, then we realize how it (the temple) doesn't declare "more or less than this." Hugh Nibley makes this clear (that what is taught inside is also taught outside) when he wrote (parenthesis mine):

"In the temple <u>we are taught by symbols and examples; but that is not the fullness of the gospel.</u> One very popular argument today says, 'Look, you say the Book of Mormon contains the fullness of the gospel, but it doesn't contain any of the temple ordinances in it, does

27

it?' Ordinances (of the temple) are not the fullness of the gospel. Going to the temple is like entering into a laboratory <u>to confirm what you have already learned in the classroom and from the text. The fullness of the gospel is the understanding of what the plan is all about—the knowledge necessary to salvation.</u> You know the whys and wherefores; for the fullness of the gospel you go to Nephi, to Alma, to Moroni. Then you will enter into the lab, but not in total ignorance. The (temple) ordinances are mere forms. They do not exalt us; they merely prepare us to be ready, in case we ever become eligible."[19]

Accordingly, the temple ordinances are "mere forms" of what you already know – the fulness of the Gospel learned from the pages of 2 Nephi 31 – repentance, baptism, and the Holy Ghost – the "knowledge necessary to salvation," whereby the Father has said, "ye shall have eternal life."

See Appendix for information on the "pattern in all things," which also outlines the first principles as the temple pattern.

- What is the "pattern in all things," in D&C 52:14-18

D&C 52 speaks of a pattern in all things, and in particular a pattern which denotes that something is from God. Most members of the church, however, could not describe what this pattern is. Yet, it is especially found in scriptures, especially in the Doctrine of Christ. Upon examination, D&C 52 has three parallel structures which work together to reveal the pattern in all things. Below is that chiasmus (words in parenthesis is mine):

14 I will give unto you a **pattern in all things, that ye may not be deceived**;

> for **Satan** is abroad in the land, and he goeth forth deceiving the nations—
>
>> 15 Wherefore **he** that prayeth,
>>> a. whose spirit is contrite,
>>>> b. the same is accepted of me (Lord)
>>>>> c. if he **obey mine ordinances.**
>>
>> 16 **He** that speaketh,
>>> a. whose spirit is contrite, whose language is meek and edifieth,
>>>> b. the same is of God (Elohim)
>>>>> c. if he **obey mine ordinances**.
>>
>> 17 And again, **he** that tembleth
>>> a. under my power shall be made strong
>>>> b. and shall bring forth fruits of praise and wisdom, praise and wisdom, according to the revelations and truths which I have given you. (Spirit)
>>>>> c. (*because he **obeys mine ordinances***)

18 And again, he that is overcome (by **Satan**) and bringeth not forth fruits, even according to this pattern, is not of me.

19 Wherefore, by **this pattern ye shall know** the spirits in all cases under the whole heavens.

We understand this to be a spiritual pattern which Satan, the deceiver, cannot duplicate (vs 14), culminating in the bearing of fruits by those yielding to the celestializing "power' of the Spirit – who have progressed through a series of events; first contrite and meek, then yielding in obedience to the Lord's ordinances (faith, repentance, baptism), until "made strong" by the Holy Ghost. The preliminary elements are the creative stages which eventuate in bearing fruit (Jn 15:8 "Herein is my Father glorified, that ye bear much fruit.") Verse 18 reaffirms this same conclusion, stating that any who are overcome (by the natural man) and do not bear fruit (of the Spirit), are not of God. (In 1835, when D&C 52 was given, there were no temple ordinances, only the "first principles and ordinances.")

Those who live by this pattern are the endowed, standing before the mirrors in the upper rooms of the temple – who have been imprinted with God's perfect creation template, whose fruitful visage is repeated eternally – perfected in Christ by a perfect gospel pattern, projecting that pattern forward forever. Again, this is the gospel pattern, the same fractal model found in the temple, and in all of scripture – a telestial, terrestrial, celestial sequence.[20]

"Then comes that most important pattern of righteousness set by Jesus Christ, "a pattern to them which should hereafter believe on him to life everlasting." (1 Tim. 1:16.) In every imaginable setting from ancient times to modern days, we see this pattern repeated – faith in the Lord Jesus Christ, repentance, baptism, the gift of the Holy Ghost.
Patterns are meant to be repeated. A pattern of righteousness is worthy of duplication, yet there are those who suppose that our righteousness involves climbing some imaginary vertical ladder. We then think we hasten our progress by trying to get above or ahead of others. Righteousness is reproduced horizontally, not vertically. When we establish a pattern of righteousness in our lives, we commit to our Heavenly Father to do all in our power to help others reproduce this pattern in their lives. This can happen over and over until, as it says in Isaiah, "the inhabitants of the world will learn righteousness." (Isa. 26:9.)"
April 1991, General Conference, A Pattern of Righteousness, Janette C. Hales

4

The Three Pillars of Eternity as the Endowment

Along these lines, there is doctrine taught in the manuals of the LDS church which was first introduced by Bruce R. McConkie. In 1981 he gave a talk at BYU entitled the "Three Pillars of Eternity" wherein he outlined the foundations upon which the plan of salvation rests.[21] He said:

> "The three pillars of eternity, the three events, preeminent and transcendent above all others, are the creation, the fall, and the atonement. These three are the foundations upon which all things rest. Without any one of them all things would lose their purpose and meaning, and the plans and designs of Deity would come to naught. If there had been no creation, we would not be, neither the earth, nor any form of life upon its face. All things, all the primal elements, would be without form and void. God would have no spirit children; there would be no mortal probation; and none of us would be on the way to immortality and eternal life."

Below is an often-seen image of this concept:[22]

Although this model of salvation is altered from the one we have been considering, it still follows the sequence of the temple endowment; the **creation** (inferring its seven parts), followed by the events of the **fall**, and finally the **Atonement** which redeems us from the fall. Although he doesn't outright mention the "temple" in his speech, it is the unspoken focus of his thoughts. In fact, when Brother McConkie presented these pillars, he explained how the *creation* includes such temple elements as Elohim, Jehovah, Michael, and the Garden of Eden. In particular, Bro. McConkie pays special attention to the *Atonement;* that it is what allows us to overcome sin and death (effects of the fall) and ascend to our Father's presence.[23] Using the Third Article of Faith, along with Mosiah 3:18-19, Bro McConkie uniquely explains how we are saved through the atonement:

> "He (the angel) said, 'Salvation was, and is, and is to come, in and through the atoning blood of Christ, the Lord Omnipotent' (Mosiah 3:18). There is no other source of salvation from the fall than that which comes through Christ. He said, 'The natural man is an enemy to God, and has been from the fall of Adam, and will be, forever and ever, unless he yields to the enticings of the Holy Spirit, and putteth off the natural man and becometh a saint through the atonement of Christ the Lord' (**Mosiah 3:19**). Thus the natural man, which is Adam, is conquered by the perfect man, which is Christ; and thus 'all mankind may be saved by obedience to the laws and ordinances of the gospel' (**Third Article of Faith**)."

To better appreciate what Brother McConkie is saying about the plan of salvation, let's view his last two statements in parallel.

A The **natural man** is an enemy to God,
    B and has been from the **fall of Adam**, and will be, forever and ever,
        C unless he **yields** to the enticings of the Holy Spirit, and putteth off the **natural man**
            D and becometh a saint (**saved**) through the atonement of Christ the Lord

A' Thus the **natural man,**
    B' which is **Adam**,
        C' is **conquered** by the **perfect man**, which is Christ;
            D' and thus 'all mankind may be **saved** by obedience to the laws and ordinances of the gospel'

The parallels in A and B are noticeably clear, and in C-C' "conquered by Christ" is wonderfully associated with "yielding to the Holy Ghost." Truly, Jesus Christ was the perfect man who came 2000 years ago and conquered sin, but as important, he now conquers our hearts and minds, which he does through the Spirit. Synthesizing Mosiah 3:19 and the Third Article of Faith, Bro. McConkie concludes that those who are being transformed by obedience to the Spirit are yielding to its enticement – to be true and faithful to the covenants contained within God's ordinances. Following the Spirit is the hallmark of saving obedience (Spirit-driven covenant keeping). We can be "true and faithful" to all laws and covenants only with the intimate assistance of the Spirit, whether taken in or out of the temple.

Brother McConkie's columns can also be expanded into the seven parts of the temple endowment. To do this we simply need to break out the fundamental elements which are unstipulated within his Atonement category – the principles and ordinances which save us, designated in the 4th Article of Faith. Below is an image of how the three pillars might look if appropriately expanded:

		ATONEMENT		
CREATION, with Father	FALL, spiritual death	Telestial – Repentance Terrestrial – Baptism Celestial – Holy Ghost	RETURN physical death	REST, with Father

(Salvation)

This more developed illustration iterates the same seven step process discussed on page 18 of the previous chapter. The center column now details the teaching that Brother McConkie uses to explain how Christ's Atonement perfects and saves us (D' above) – through the primary ordinances and principles of the gospel which "enable" us to repent from sin (telestial world), to be baptized and take His name upon us (terrestrial), and to have His celestializing Spirit to guide and ever sanctify us.

- **"Saints through the Atonement"**

As just examined, Bro. McConkie relies on Mosiah 3:19 to explain how the Atonement reverses the effects of the fall. In these verses, delivered at the temple in Zarahemla by King Benjamin, we read how the enabling power of the Atonement works to transform our lives. It is the quintessence of how we are celestialized; are "purified as he is pure" (1Jn 3:2) and overcome the world to reign with God in his throne (Rev 3:21). Referring to Adam, and using more references to "the creation" than anywhere else in the Book of Mormon (suggesting that the temple endowment and plan of salvation was on his mind), King Benjamin explains (parenthesis mine):

> 18 . . . but men drink damnation to their own souls except they humble themselves and become (**are recreated**) as little children, and believe that salvation was, and is, and is to come, in and through the atoning blood of Christ, the Lord Omnipotent.
> 19 For the natural man is an enemy to God, and has been from the fall of Adam, and will be, forever and ever, unless he yields to the enticings of the Holy Spirit, and putteth off the natural man and becometh a saint through the atonement of Christ the Lord, and becometh (**creation**) as a child, submissive, meek, humble, patient, full of love, willing to submit to all things which the Lord seeth fit to inflict upon him, even as a child doth submit to his father.

Again, this creation process is the hallmark of abiding by celestial law – which in turn has the power to make us saints (the key to the power of godliness). Our willing participation (yielding) is the catalyst which ignites the transforming power of the Atonement in our lives. We are perfected in Christ when we "deny not this power"; called sufficient grace by Moroni, being created in His image cannot happen in any other way (Moro 10:30-33). John Welch has outlined King Benjamin's thoughts in chiastic form. Notice how the fall is reversed by yielding to the Spirit:

(a) They *humble* themselves
  (b) and become as little *children*
    (c) believing that salvation is in the *atoning blood of Christ;*
      (d) for the *natural man*
        (e) is an enemy to God
          (f) and *has been* from
            (g) the fall of Adam
          (f) and *will be* forever and ever
        (e) unless he yieldeth to the *Holy Spirit*
      (d) and putteth off the *natural man*
    (c) and becometh a saint through the *atonement of Christ*
  (b) and becometh as a *child*
(a) submissive, meek and *humble* [24]

It is also important to realize that the attributes of becoming as a child (a new creation) submissive, meek, and humble – are fruit of our interaction with the Spirit (1 Cor 13). These are the outcomes of yielding our hearts to its warmth and love, not something that we do by our own willpower or strength. We become "partakers in the divine nature" (2 Pet 1:4) as we yield to the Spirit's voice, which will prompt us to "put off" the desires of the natural man within us. 1 Pet 1:22 calls this "obeying the truth through the Spirit." Obedience of any other kind does not serve God's ultimate purpose to celestialize and perfect man (Moses 5:5-8).

Many have wondered how Christ could be perfect; the spotless Lamb worthy to perform the Atonement. King Benjamin's discourse in fact helps us to understand. Christ is the Greek equivalent for Messiah, which in Hebrew means "anointed one." But we must stop to consider, what was he anointed with? Jesus answers this question himself as he begins his ministry. Standing in the synagogue he reads the words of Isaiah 61:1 which foretell of his coming, "The **Spirit** of the Lord is upon me, he has **anointed** me to preach the gospel . . ." (Luke 4:18). Having his Spirit "upon" you is having his anointing. We can also refer to John 3:34 for help, "For he (Christ) whom God hath sent speaketh the words of God: for God giveth not the Spirit by measure *unto him.*" And according to Joseph Smith, "None ever were perfect but Jesus; and why was He perfect? Because He was the Son of God, and had the **fullness of the Spirit**, and greater power than any man."[25]

Indeed, Christ received from his Father a fullness of the Spirit (D&C 93), to which he always perfectly yielded. It was not that he did not experience the natural man, for he was of a mortal mother, but he always did the will of his Father (Jn 4:34, 6:38) as directed by the Spirit. For this reason we understand that our highest calling is to do likewise, follow the Spirit. We commit to do this each week as we partake of the sacrament and renew our creation covenants (baptismal, rebirth covenants).

- **New Creation – New Offering**

When Christ visited the Nephites at the time of his resurrection (coincidently at the temple) he gave them a new commandment; a command which also speaks of re-creation ("becoming" a son of God) and putting off the natural man. Referring to the old temple sacrifice he told them:

3 Ne 9:17 And as many as have received me, to them I have given to become the sons of God; and even so will I to as many as shall believe on my name, for behold, by me redemption cometh, and in me is the law of Moses fulfilled. 18 I am the light and the life of the world. I am Alpha and Omega, the beginning and the end. 19 And ye shall offer up unto me **no more the shedding of blood**; yea, your sacrifices and your burnt offerings shall be done away, for I will accept none of your sacrifices and your burnt offerings.

20 And **ye shall offer for a sacrifice unto me a broken heart and a contrite spirit**. And whoso cometh unto me with a broken heart and a contrite spirit, him will I baptize with fire and with the Holy Ghost (celestialize).

Verse 17's mention of the "law of Moses" is a reference to the Old Covenant (a type of the telestial) and its preparatory ordinances of blood sacrifice which pointed forward to Christ [26] If you are wondering exactly what it means to offer a broken heart and contrite spirit, Elder Neal Maxwell astutely explains: "So it is, that real, personal sacrifice never was placing an animal on the altar. Instead, it is a willingness **to put the animal in us** upon the altar and letting it be consumed! Such is the "sacrifice unto the Lord … of a **broken heart and a contrite spirit**."[27] Using the same imagery Paul also indicates, "For if ye live after the flesh, ye shall die: but if ye through the Spirit do mortify (sacrifice) the deeds of the body (natural man), ye shall live" (Rom 8:13). Overcoming the natural man by yielding to the Spirit is the foremost trial of this life. It is the

Spiritual warfare that we are involved in everyday. We may be waiting for some grandiose test of our faith, but in doing that we miss the true test of mortality. Having the faith to sacrifice the selfishness and self-centeredness in ourselves to our loving Heavenly Father, is the test of Abraham. It was daily for Christ and it is for us.

"Wherefore, redemption cometh in and through the Holy Messiah; for he is full of grace and truth. Behold, he offereth himself a sacrifice for sin, to answer the ends of the law, unto all those who have a **broken heart and a contrite spirit**; and **unto none else** can the ends of the law be answered." 2 Ne 2:6-7

"Our covenants should be watershed events in our lives. They are a Great Divide, with the natural man on one side and the man of Christ on the other . . . But the simplicity of the way is also the difficulty of the way, for the natural man mightily resists its demise. The covenant-keeping process is a powerful antidote for the natural man." *(Peter B. Rawlins, "Covenants, Sacraments, and Vows: The Active Pathway to Mercy,")*[28]

5

The Holy Ghost Moves in Creation

Thus far we have examined the important role that the Holy Ghost plays in the "celestial" world; that it is essential in becoming holy and that without it we cannot overcome the natural man. Certainly, the enabling power of the Atonement is possible only through its work in our hearts. Six times in the Doctrine and Covenants we find the phrase "endow with power from on high," and each time its usage relates to the temple. However, the broadest sense of this phrase is revealed by examining its first use in Luke 24:49. "Behold, I send the promise of my Father upon you: but tarry ye in the city of Jerusalem, until ye be endued with power from on high." Here Jesus was speaking of Pentecost (Acts 2) when the Holy Ghost fell upon the disciples in the upper room. In modernity (in the "upper room" of the temple) the meaning of the phrase is still largely the same, for we cannot be true and faithful to our temple covenants (or any covenant) without this endowment – a covering of God's power and love manifest through the Spirit. Consequently, if we don't understand the Spirit, then we will never truly appreciate the temple (remember it unfolds the first principles and ordinances, one of which is the Gift of the Holy Ghost). Let's spend a few moments discussing the Spirit of God.

- **Genesis – The Spirit Moves**

Genesis 1 tells of the Spirit's participation in the creation. Before any life was formed, and simultaneous to the creation of light, we are told that:

2 And the earth was without form, and void; and darkness [was] upon the face of the deep. And the **Spirit of God moved** upon the face of the waters. 3 And God said, Let there be light: and there was light.[29]

If we look closer at the Hebrew for the word "moved" (*rachaph*) we find an interesting definition:

> רָחַף [" pr. TO BE SOFT"], TO BE MOVED, AF-FECTED (cogn. to רָחַם), specially—(*a*) with the feeling of tender love, hence *to cherish*, see Piel.—
> PIEL, *to brood over* young ones, *to cherish* young (as an eagle), Deut. 32:11; figuratively used of the Spirit of God, who brooded over the shapeless mass of the earth, cherishing and vivifying. Of far more frequent use is the Syr. ܪܚܦ, which is used of birds brooding over their young, Ephr. ii. p. 552; of parents who cherish their children, Ephr. ii. p. 419; [30]

It seems reasonable to suggest that the Christian phrase, "a move of the Spirit", originates (has its genesis) in this verse. Wonderfully, it expresses not just motion, but loving or tender movement, as a bird which broods over her young. In fact, in Deut 32:11 *rachaph* is used in that context. Speaking of his love for Israel the Lord says, "As an eagle stirreth up her nest, **fluttereth** (*rachaph*) over her young, spreadeth abroad her wings, taketh them, beareth them on her wings." Indeed, this earliest image of the Spirit gently moving or fluttering superbly expresses how we feel the soft stirring of the Spirit within our hearts.

In another memorable "act of creation", when Christ is baptized a fluttering bird again stirs over the water as the Spirit descends in the form of a dove: "And straightway coming up out of the water, he saw the heavens opened, and the Spirit like a dove descending upon him" (Mark 1:10). Christ's baptism in water with the anointing of the Holy Ghost is curiously traceable all the way back to the creation in Genesis 1, which is a pattern for all those who are newly created in the waters of baptism.

- **Noah's Dove**

There is also another story from the Old Testament where a "brooding" dove is once more a symbol of rebirth, which is the story of Noah. Noah comes from the Hebrew *nuach,* meaning rest, which is apropos since by the flood the world is given rest from mankind's iniquity. There is a pivotal moment in Noah's story when a bird, coincidently a dove, again softly moves over the water as a symbol of another creation process. Forty days after the rain stops, Noah sends out the dove for the first time:

> Genesis 8:8 Also he sent forth a dove from him, to see if the waters were abated from off the face of the ground;
> 9 But **the dove found no rest for the sole of her foot**, and she returned unto him into the ark, for the waters [were] on the face of the whole earth: then he put forth his hand, and took her, and pulled her in unto him into the ark.

Because there is found no "rest for the sole of her foot", Noah will wait seven days and then send out the dove a second time:

10 And he stayed yet other seven days; and again he sent forth the dove out of the ark;

11 And the dove came in to him in the evening; and, lo, **in her mouth [was] an olive leaf** pluckt off: so Noah knew that the waters were abated from off the earth.

This time the dove returns with an olive leaf as a sign to Noah that there would be land for inheritance and a place to raise seed. It is noteworthy that the token of the promise is a *living* **olive** branch, newly created from the receding waters of the flood. We might also consider the significance of the olive, which prefigures an even greater promise, that of the Savior's Atonement in the Garden of Gethsemane, which means the place of the **olive** press[31], where Christ was crushed and bruised for man. Indeed, the resurrected Lord has promised upon his return to stand upon the Mount of Olives as a peaceful new millennial world begins (Acts 1). We might also contemplate, that like the waters of the creation (Gen 1) or the waters of Noah (Gen 8), as we emerge from the waters of baptism, the same dove of the Spirit "moves" upon us with the promise of rebirth. Could the dove have brought a greater symbol of promise, life, or peace to Noah, or mankind? Noah will send the dove out a third time in verse 12:

12 And he stayed yet other seven days; and sent forth the dove; which returned not again unto him any more.

Finally, the dove returns no more to the ark, and we might guess that it now sojourns in the land. If we have faith we might also believe that the dove is being fruitful and multiplying in a newly born world.

In fact, at this point the story requires us to exercise faith in order to "see" that which hasn't necessarily been written, which is coincidently also how God's promises of fruitfulness are fulfilled. To be sure, without faith we never grasp the end of the story or the eternal lesson it teaches. Noah's dove also sets a symbolic pattern by the *three* times that it is sent out, which, as we have studied, is the pattern of the temple endowment, the three phases of mortality. Below is a simple chiastic diagram of this event:

Land

    Flood

        Dove performs task, but not fruitful   *telestial*

            Dove brings the promise, rebirth   *terrestrial*

        Dove fruitfully sojourns in new land   *celestial*

    Food recedes

Land

These three stages represent a process whereby fruitlessness becomes fruitfulness, hinged on a divine promise of new life. Hopefully you can see that this is a pattern of our spiritual lives as well; our spiritual fruitfulness hinges on the bright promise of our Savior's Atonement, the reality of which is revealed to us by the Spirit (dove).

- **Sign (number) of Jonah – the Dove**

In Matthew's gospel Christ is asked for a sign that he is the messiah, to which he replies: "An evil and adulterous generation seeketh after a sign; and there shall no sign be given to it, but the sign of the prophet Jonas: For as Jonas was three days and three nights in the whale's belly; so shall the Son of man be three days and three nights in the heart of the earth" (Mat 12:39-40). Because Christ identifies Jonah as a type of himself and his resurrection, he also connects himself to several other aspects of Jonah's story; e.g. the symbolic number *three* (rebirth); the status of prophet (Mat 12:41). In comparative terms, even as Jonah came forth after three days in a watery grave to save Nineveh, so Christ after three days emerged from the grave to save mankind. And symbolically, our baptism is patterned after both of these events, wherein we enter the water (like the waters of Noah, or the formless and void waters of creation) and resurrect to new life.[32] Strikingly, to this day the story of Jonah is read on Yom Kippur, the Jewish Day of Atonement.[33] In the Encyclopedia Judaica we read about Jonah:

> The book is to be understood as a lesson in Divine forgiveness and mercy --- to Jonah as well as to the people of Nineveh --- and as a lesson in obedience to God's will. As a symbol of the effectiveness of repentance it is read as the haftarah at the afternoon service of the Day of Atonement.[34]

However, the full meaning of Christ's sign becomes especially clear when we consider Jonah's remarkable connection to Noah's dove (which was used to "seek a sign" of renewal) or to the Spirit which flutters in creation, because in Hebrew, Jonah (*yonah*) means the "dove"! From Joseph Smith we learn that this sign was not chosen haphazardly but was given special significance from before the foundation of the world. He said, "The sign of the dove was instituted before the creation of the world, a witness for the Holy Ghost, and the devil cannot come in the sign of a dove."[35] Indeed, the story of Jonah (the dove) is another revelation of the Spirit's involvement in creation, for when Jonah (the dove) moves out over the waters from Joppa, creation and rebirth happens in Nineveh.

If we apply this meaning figuratively, then it was *yonah* (the dove) who descended upon Jesus while at the waters of baptism, **a sign** from the Father that he was the "anointed one." In fact, as has already been mentioned, Messiah in Hebrew and Christos in Greek, mean "anointed one." And moreover, we understand that Christ was anointed with a fullness of the Spirit (*yonah*) – "For he whom God hath sent speaketh the words of God: for God **giveth not the Spirit by measure** [unto him]" (Jn 3:34). Truly, when Christ says that the sign that he gives is the sign of Jonah (Mat 12:39), he is referring not just to the three days he will be in the earth before resurrection, but as important, he is referring to the Spirit (dove) which "signals" to the heart of man that He is the Christ. There is indeed no grander sign of his divinity that you or I could hope to experience, for our creation and rebirth (spiritual resurrection) begins when the Holy Ghost moves upon the spiritual waters of our lives. (Coincidently, the largest percentage of what we are composed of is water.[36])

When we read the story of Jonah we marvel that this entire city, so big that it took *three* days to cross, "believed God, and proclaimed a fast, and put on sackcloth, from the greatest of them to the least of them" (Jonah 3:5). Miraculous repentance on this scale, 120,000 people, is unequaled in scripture (only rivaled by its parallel – Christ who saves all repentant mankind). Why did the people of Nineveh repent? There could only ever be one reason for their "change" of heart, which is because the Holy Ghost revealed to them that Jonah's words were true. When Jonah (the dove) alights upon us to speak divine truth, it can have the same effect, which is to "overthrow" (the word that Jonah used to prophesy against Nineveh) our selfish lives. Expressed another way, the sign that Christ gives is inward, the whisper of the still small voice, the burning in the bosom, without which no one receives a witness of His love ("no man can say that Jesus is Lord except by the Holy Ghost" [1 Cor 12:3]). The heart must be stirred if faith is to grow, and a "mighty change of heart" begins to take root with Jonah.

Ultimately, though we may not connect the two, when Moroni promises that "by the power of the Holy Ghost" we can know if the Book of Mormon is true, he is confirming that by the sign of Jonah we can know it is true. Indeed, by the sign of Jonah we can "know the truth of all things" (Mor 10:4-5).

- **Nicodemus and the gentle wind**

Finally, consider how Christ personally describes this gentle moving of the Spirit (dove) which precedes creation and rebirth. During Christ's ministry there was a man named Nicodemus who was seeking a witness (testimony) that Jesus was the Messiah. Jesus tells him how the Holy Ghost works, comparing it to the way we softly hear or **feel** the wind, but don't see it (parenthesis mine).

> John 3:8 "The wind bloweth where it listeth, and thou hearest the sound thereof, but canst not tell (*eidos* – see) whence it cometh, and whither it goeth: so is every one that is born of the Spirit."

The meaning of this verse is often unappreciated because of the ambiguous phrase "canst not tell." However, what the Lord wants Nicodemus, and us, to learn is that the Spirit and the wind are very similar in that neither is seen, but both are **felt.**

Also important, the Greek word for "wind" in this verse is *pneuma,* which also serves as the primary word used in Greek for Spirit. (In Genesis 1:2 the word for Spirit is the Hebrew for wind, *ruach!*) When we look at the principal entry in the lexicon for "pneuma" (wind or Spirit), we find something remarkably consistent with how the Spirit has been described in the other scriptures we just examined:

> πνεῦμα, -τος, τό, (πνέω), Grk. writ. fr. Aeschyl. and Hdt. down; Hebr. רוּחַ, Lat. *spiritus*; i. e.
> 1. *a movement of air,* (gentle) *blast*;   a. of the **wind**: ἀνέμων πνεύματα, Hdt. 7, 16, 1; Paus. 5, 25; hence the *wind* itself, Jn. iii. 8; plur. Heb. i. 7, (1 K. xviii. 45; [37]

Notice that the Spirit is compared to "a movement of air" or "gentle" blast of air, which is a striking allusion to the way the "Spirit moved" in Genesis 1:2. The image of a dove's wings softly moving the air as it hovers certainly comes to mind. In just this way, the popular children's song suggests to us how we **feel** the presence of the Holy Ghost:

> We do not have to see
> To know the wind is here;
> We do not have to see
> To know God's love is near [38]

In our hearts then, the voice of the Holy Ghost, like a gentle breeze, tells us; Christ is real, that Joseph Smith saw God the Father and his Son, and that the Book of Mormon is true (Moro 10:5). Alma teaches this same principle in Alma 32 when talking about the small seed, which when planted begins to "swell within your breast" (like the swelling of God's unseen love). He describes this subtle movement of the seed in verse 28, "when you **feel** these **swelling motions**, ye will begin to say within yourselves – It must needs be that this is a good seed, or that the word is good, for it beginneth to enlarge my soul; yea, it beginneth to **enlighten** my understanding, yea, it beginneth to be delicious to me." Similarly, Nephi compares the still small voice of the Spirit to "feeling" his words in our hearts – "and he hath spoken unto you in **a still small voice**, but ye were past **feeling**, that ye could not **feel his words**" (in 1 Ne 17:45).

When Nephi wants to know the meaning of the vision that his father Lehi saw, he says that it will be possible through the Holy Ghost (1 Ne 10). He is shown a white and beautiful tree, the condescension of Christ, and then asked if he knows its meaning. Without anyone telling him, he answers that it represents "the love of God shed abroad in the hearts of the children of men." He is also able to describe how the fruit tastes – the most "desirable" and "most joyous to the soul." Indeed, Nephi's answer is simply what he is "feeling" in that moment as whispered to his heart by the Holy Ghost – which sensation is God's love. The reason that Nephi needed the Holy Ghost to understand the tree of life is because, with our physical eyes we cannot see love; rather it is something only "felt" in the heart. Nevertheless, it is the most powerful force in the world. If God is love (1 Jn 4:8), then certainly the most important and joyous message the Spirit can bring is an understanding of who

He is. The language the Spirit speaks, which is the language of angels, is love (2 Ne 31).

If you have ever loved or been loved, you have experienced the warmth of the Spirit. Consequently, when a member of the church bears his testimony and states that he "knows" a divine principle is true, the way he arrives at his "knowledge" is first and foremost through the subtle swelling, fluttering, or gentle motion of the Holy Ghost; i.e. what he really knows is what he has **felt**. By placing our faith in the seemingly least of sensations, Elijah's still small voice or Nicodemus' tender wind, the greatest transformation in our lives takes place.

Now let's see how this ancient sign of Jonah manifests itself in the story of Stephen in the New Testament, which is one of the foremost presentations of the modern temple endowment.

6

Steven's Defense – An Endowment Pattern

As we proceed to one of the best examples of the ancient temple pattern, where it isconcisely developed, the thoughts of the modern-day apostle Bruce R. McConkie, as he reflects upon the words of Malachi 4:5-6, are worth our consideration:

> "He shall plant in the hearts of the children the promises made to the fathers." That immediately raises the questions: Who are the *children,* who are the *fathers,* and what are the *promises?* If we can catch a vision from the doctrinal standpoint that answers those questions—who the fathers are, who the children are, and what the promises were—**we can have our understanding of the gospel and our comprehension of the plan of salvation expanded infinitely**. We shall then catch a vision of what the whole system of salvation is all about. Until we do that, really, we never catch that vision.[39]

With respect to the identities of the "fathers", M. Catherine Thomas asserts, "Elder McConkie identifies "the fathers" as Abraham, Isaac, and Jacob, the fathers of the house of Israel on the earth. The promises have to do with the Abrahamic Covenant, which is the premortal covenant of godhood, named after Abraham, because he would be one of the fathers of that great lineage."[40] These histories, largely recorded in Genesis, contain a foundation for understanding all subsequent scripture, as well as the temple endowment. We might be led to ponder if our understanding of the plan of salvation, as Bro McConkie alludes, has been "expanded infinitely" by the stories of the patriarchs. If that is not the case, isn't it important for us to get better acquainted with these sacred histories? Let's turn to the priceless story of Stephen on the temple mount as he presents the temple endowment, uniquely embedded into the stories of the patriarchs.

- **Stephen's Patriarchal\Temple Defense**

Before the apostle Stephen is stoned, he is allowed to first address the well-educated members of the Sanhedrin, at which time he recounts the ancient histories of his patriarch fathers. Sadly, these typological witnesses of Christ fall on hardened (unfeeling) hearts. In chapter 6 of Acts we read the events surrounding Stephen's trial:

> 13 And (they) set up false witnesses, which said, This man ceaseth not to speak blasphemous words against this holy place, and **the law**: 14 For we have heard him say, that this **Jesus of Nazareth shall destroy this place**, and shall **change** the customs which Moses delivered us. 15 And all that sat in the council, looking stedfastly on him, saw his face as it had been the face of an angel.

Stephen here is talking about change; that the failing temple priesthood has been rejected, and that the lifeless customs of the law need to be transformed to heart-felt love for God and others. In many ways, Stephen comes to the temple with the same message that Jonah delivered to Nineveh. (Intriguingly, in forty years [not days] the temple and unrepentant Jerusalem is destroyed). The heading in the LDS scriptures for Acts 6 reads, "Stephen transfigured before the Sanhedrin," and verse 15 tells us that Stephen's face was like an angel's. We might therefore anticipate that Stephen's words on such an inspired occasion will be amazing. Consider for a moment the place where Stephen stands. It is very near the exact spot that Christ stood before the Sanhedrin; it is also Mt. Moriah where father Abraham took Isaac his only son in similitude to be sacrificed; it is the threshing floor of Ornan where the pure wheat is separated from the chaff; the same floor that David bought for a price, insisting that "I will surely buy [it] of thee at a price: neither will I offer burnt offerings unto the LORD my God of that which doth cost me nothing" (1 Chr 21:24); and it is fittingly a symbolic foundation upon which all temple and Godly worship is built; a sacrificial place where Christ has promised to return and reign in glory. Surely the significance of that place and its sacred history (and future) was not lost to Stephen. Filled with the power of the Holy Ghost, so much so that his very countenance changed, Stephen is divinely guided as he testifies before the same men that had so callously sacrificed the promised Messiah. (Similar to 1 Ne 17:48 when the Spirit filled Nephi "unto the consuming of his flesh.")

Stephen narrates the patterned lives of the patriarchs, which testify of Christ and his atoning plan, and which simultaneously reveal the temple endowment. And, as evidence that these patriarchal stories are connected to the temple, when Stephen finishes speaking about Abraham, Joseph, and Moses, he will list three temples; the temples\tabernacles built by Moses, Solomon, and the temple made with no hands (of the heart). Below is the first of Stephen's *three* chiastic (endowment) stories (parenthesis mine):

A 2 And he said, **Men, brethren,** and **fathers,** hearken;
  B The **God of glory** appeared unto our father **Abraham** (covenant), when he was
    C **in Mesopotamia,** before he dwelt in Charran,
      D 3 **And said** unto him, **Get thee out of** thy country, and from thy kindred, and **come into** the land which I shall shew thee. 4 Then came he out of the land of the Chaldaeans,
        E and dwelt in **Charran**: and from thence, when his **father was dead,**
          F he **removed him into** this land, wherein ye now dwell.
            G 5 And **he gave him none inheritance in** it, no,
              H **not [so much as] to set his foot on**:
                I yet **he promised** that he would give it
                  J to **him** for a **possession,**
                  J' and to **his seed** after **him,**
                H' when [as yet] **he had no child**.
              I' 6 And **God spake** on this wise,
            G' That **his seed should sojourn in** a strange land;
          F' and that they should **bring them into** bondage, and entreat [them] evil four hundred years.
        E' 7 And the nation (**Egypt**) to whom they shall be in bondage **will I judge** (**death** of firstborns),
      D' **said God**: and after that shall **they come forth**, and serve me
    C' **in this place (Mt Sinai** and Mt Zion).
  B' 8 And **he (the God of glory)** gave **him (Moses)** the covenant of circumcision:
A' And so [Abraham] begat **Isaac**, and circumcised him the eighth day; and Isaac [begat] **Jacob**; and Jacob [begat] the **twelve patriarchs**.

This chiasmus could be simplified and distilled to the following 7 period endowment outline. It is also the template for

Stephen's next two chiasmi, and will make it easier to compare them side by side:

> God's glory in Mesopotamia
>   Charan – death of father
>   No inheritance, no foot to stand on *(telestial)*
>   Promise of possession *(terrestrial)*
>   Sojourn in land of inheritance *(celestial)*
>   Egypt – death of firstborns
> God's glory on Sinai\Mt Zion

Notice that this first of three chiastic structures in Acts 7 covers the entire cycle of all the early patriarchs, starting with Abraham through Moses, coming full circle to the current Sanhedrin! Stephen even parallels Abraham to Moses, both given a covenant by the "God of glory" (B,B'). Let's look at some other items in this scintillating first chiasmus.

Stephen starts out in verse 2 boldly addressing his audience, the Sanhedrin, as "Men, brethren, and fathers." If we look across the chiasmus to its parallel verse 8, we see the fathers who the Sanhedrin should reflect, yet sadly seem to be the antithesis – Abraham, Isaac, Joseph. Stephen then speaks of how father Abraham set the example, leaving Mesopotamia, which in the Hebrew is *'Aram Naharayim*, which means *exalted place* of two rivers[41], and enters Charan a hot or parched place[42]. If we apply a figurative significance to these verses, leaving Mesopotamia is symbolic of leaving the exalted place of heaven, dying spiritually and entering mortality. Abraham's father dies in Charan as a figure of all mankind (E) who die spiritually as they enter mortality, leaving their Father behind. At first carnal man has no inheritance (G), or no foot to stand on until he receives the divine promise of seed and possession (I-J). After obtaining this divine promise, Israel (as a figure of mankind) must sojourn for 400 years (F')[43], after which the world (Egypt) will be judged (E'). Finally, Israel (covenant man) is brought forth and once again exalted, to serve God "in this place", the exalted and eternal mountain of the Lord (C').

In addition, at the center of this first chiasmus there is also a direct allusion to the verses in Noah's story that we previously looked at! The unique phrase, "not so much as to set his foot on" is borrowed here by Stephen to describe Abraham's situation, which he cleverly compares to Noah's dove! (Stephen conflates two stories, Abraham and Noah's.) Below is a side by side assessment of the center of Abraham's story contrasted with Noah's dove:

Noah's Dove (Gen 8:8-12)	Abraham's Promise (Acts 7:5-6)
Returns to ark with nothing No rest for sole of foot *Telestial*	Abraham enters Canaan with No foot to stand on *Telestial*
Returns with Promise Olive Branch *Terrestrial*	Receives promise of Inheritance and seed *Terrestrial*
Does not return to ark Sojourns in the earth (fruitful) *Celestial*	Abraham sojourns in new land Walks in faith (fruitful) *Celestial*

As we discussed earlier, the *three* stages of Noah's dove represent a process whereby fruitlessness (telestial) becomes fruitfulness (celestial), hinged on a divine promise of new life (terrestrial). Abraham's story, as Stephen's alludes, communicates this same message of rebirth. Poignantly, the Sanhedrin could only understand these promises of renewal if they were spiritually reborn (of the dove) themselves. Using the very sign that Christ instituted, Stephen's embedded allusion provides extra special testimony to all who seek confirmation that Jesus is the Christ. Only by this sign – the dove that brings the promise of Christ – can anyone know the truth of Stephen's words.

Augustine, the early church leader, is noted for saying that the Old Testament *conceals* the New Testament and the New Testament *reveals* the Old Testament.[44] Noah's, Jonah's, and Abraham's ancient stories are examples of an Old Testament pattern which is a New Testament outline of the gospel plan of spiritual renewal.[45] And as we will continue to see, it is also the endowment pattern, repeated in the lives of the other patriarchs.

- **Second of Three Chiasmus- Descent into Egypt**

Next, let's look at Acts 7: 9-16. Here Stephen recounts the events of the patriarch Joseph, which has the same parallel features found in the last chiasmus (it starts in verse 9 and ends in 17). Remember, that Stephen's reason for telling these patriarchal stories is to convince the Sanhedrin that Christ was the Messiah. In each story he leads them to Christ, which is also the center of the endowment (parentheses are mine):

Joseph – Into and Out of Egypt

A 9 And the **patriarchs**, moved with envy (at **Sychem**), **sold** Joseph into Egypt:
  B but **God was with him, 10 And delivered him out of all his afflictions**, and **gave him favour and wisdom in the sight of Pharaoh king of Egypt**; and made him governor over Egypt and all his house.
    C 11 Now there came a **dearth over all the land of Egypt** and Chanaan,
      D and great affliction: and **our fathers** found **no sustenance**.
        E 12 But when **Jacob** heard that there was corn (**seed**) in Egypt,
          F he **sent out our fathers** first.
            G 13 And at the second [time] **Joseph** was **made known to his brethren**;
            G' and **Joseph's kindred** was **made known unto Pharaoh**.
          F' 14 Then **sent Joseph, and called his father**
        E' **Jacob** to [him], and all his kindred (**seed**), threescore and fifteen souls.
    C' 15 So Jacob went down **into Egypt**, and **died, he,**
      D' **and our fathers,**
A' 16 And were **carried over into Sychem**, and laid in the sepulchre that Abraham **bought for a sum** of money of the sons of Emmor [the father] of **Sychem**.
  B' 17 But when the **time of the promise** drew nigh, which **God had sworn to Abraham,** the **people grew and multiplied in Egypt,**

These verses give the story of Jacob and Joseph's descent into Egypt, and Israel's return to Canaan. Below is a simplified chiasmus formed within these verses, with my comments included:

Joseph in land of Promise, (sold) – near Sychem in Canaan

  Dearth over Egypt – Famine, Death – fathers found no Sustenance

    Brothers first sent for wheat (seed), meet but do not know Joseph *telestial*

      Brothers sent second time; Joseph is made known, (their Savior)*terrestrial*

    All of the kindred (seed) sent for by Joseph, are fruitful in new land *celestial*

  Jacob and fathers, all die in Egypt

Joseph returned to Abraham's tomb (bought) – Sychem in Canaan

As you can see, Stephen has given us a near duplicate pattern of his first (and historically broader) chiasmus, again with a revelatory event in the middle. I should point out that there is some historical data that is helpful when identifying some of these parallel verses which Stephen's audience, the Sanhedrin, would have readily known, but we may not. Though Sychem is not specifically mentioned in verse 9, it is parallel to verse 16 because Sychem is not only the place where Joseph is buried in a *purchased* sepulcher (vs 16), but it is also the place to where young Joseph was sent when he was initially *sold* into bondage (vs 9) by his brothers; the beginning and ending point of Israel's descent into and out of captivity. (Sychem in the Greek, or Shechem in the Old Testament [Gen 37:13]). Shechem is also significant because it is the first place that Abraham stayed when he entered Canaan, and it was there that the Lord promised the land to his posterity (Gen 12:6-7). [46]

Jacob's family goes into Egypt to be saved as a nation, which interestingly becomes a two-edged sword, a blessing and a curse. Egypt paradoxically saves the covenant seed of Abraham, yet it also introduces a 400-year period of oppression and bondage. As

God's plan would have it, like mortality, the medium which gives life later becomes bondage and death, necessitating the need for rebirth or restoration. Equally, we might observe that water at the time of Noah, which cleansed the earth, was an instrument of salvation; on the one hand to destroy evil, and on the other hand to create a new beginning. (Fire is such a biblical two-edged instrument as well.)

Following this eternal covenant pattern, the road we travel in mortality is the same as the endowment pattern that Stephen presents to the Sanhedrin. When we compare the center of this chiasmus about Joseph, to that of the first (Abraham and Noah's conflated dove), the names are different but the message discovered is the same – at its center there is a promise of salvation. If you recall, Joseph weeps and lovingly embraces his brothers when he reveals his identity – their forgiving brother who is able to save them (Gen 45:3). Such powerful emotion and comfort perhaps you have also felt, embraced by the Spirit as the promise of your Savior has been gently spoken to you. Like Joseph's brothers who sought sustenance, as we hold Him close, our welfare is also assured through a plan of provision; a storehouse of heavenly bread in the midst of a spiritually famished world.

- **Stephens Third Narration – Ascent out of Egypt**

Stephen's third narration is the life of Moses. Importantly, it repeats for a *third* time the same cycle as the first two narrations. Below is Acts 7: 17-37 (parenthesis mine):

A 17 But when the time of the promise drew nigh, which God had sworn to Abraham, the people grew and **multiplied in Egypt,**
  B 18 Till another king arose, which knew not Joseph. 19 The same dealt subtilly with our kindred, and evil entreated our fathers, so that they **cast out their young children, to the end they might not live.**
    C 20 In which time **Moses** was born, and was exceeding fair, and **nourished up** in his father's house three months. 21 And when he was cast out, Pharaoh's daughter **took him up, and nourished him** for her own son.
      D 22 And **Moses** was learned in all the wisdom of the Egyptians, and was m**ighty in words and in deeds** (signs and wonders).
        E 23 And when he **was full forty years old**, it came into his heart to visit his brethren the children of Israel.
          F 24 And seeing one of them suffer wrong, he defended him, and avenged him that was oppressed, and smote the Egyptian: 25 For he supposed his brethren would have understood **how that God by his hand would deliver them**: but they understood not.
            G 26 And the next day he shewed himself unto them as they strove, and would have set them at one again, saying, Sirs, ye are brethren; why do ye wrong one to another? (Moses acts as ruler)
              H 27 But he that did his neighbour wrong thrust him away, saying, **Who made thee a ruler and a judge over us?** 28 Wilt thou kill me, as thou diddest the Egyptian yesterday?
                I 29 Then **fled** Moses at this saying, and was a stranger **in the land of Madian,** where he begat two sons.
                  J 30 And when forty years were expired**,** there appeared to him in the wilderness **of mount Sina**
                    K an **angel of the Lord** in a flame of fire in a bush.
                      L 31 When **Moses** saw it, he **wondered** at the sight: and
                        M as he **drew near to behold** it,
                          N the **voice** of **the Lord** came unto him,
                          N 32 **Saying**, I am **the God** of thy fathers, the God of Abraham, and the God of Isaac, and the God of Jacob.
                      L Then **Moses trembled,**
                        M and **durst not behold**.
                    K 33 Then said **the Lord** to him,
                  J Put off thy shoes from thy feet: for the **place where thou standest** is **holy ground.** (mount Sina)
                I 34 I have seen, I have seen the affliction of my people which is in Egypt, and I have heard their groaning, and am come down to deliver them. And now **come**, I will **send** thee **into Egypt**.
              H 35 This Moses whom they refused, saying, **Who made thee a ruler and a judge?**
            G the same did God send to be a ruler
          F and a **deliverer by the hand of the angel** which appeared to him in the bush.
        D 36 He brought them out, after that he had shewed **wonders and signs** in the land of Egypt, and in the Red sea (mighty in words and deed),
      E and **in the wilderness forty years.**
    C 37 This is that **Moses**, which said unto the children of Israel, A prophet shall the **Lord your God raise up** unto you of your brethren, like unto me; him shall ye hear.
  B Missing Element – all the old die in wilderness ("to the end that they might not live")
A Missing Element - new generation enters Promised Land, people grow, are multiplied as God swore to Abraham

This third narration, Israel's ascent out of Egypt (verses 20-37), also forms the same simple and familiar chiastic endowment pattern:

Multiply in Egypt (initially a land of promise)
    Death of babies in the land
        Moses accused of trying to rule, people
        confused, not known as deliverer – **40 years** *(telestial)*
            In Midia (Madian), speaks with the Lord on Sinai – **40 years**
        Moses leads in the wilderness, sent   *(terrestrial)*
        by God to be deliverer - **40 years** *(celestial)*
    All die in the wilderness
Enter land of promise - Canaan

As a baby, Moses is saved and "comes forth out of water" (the Nile), which is the likely meaning of Moses' name[47], and which we understand to foreshadow events to come, when later he will lead Israel through and out of the waters of the Red Sea; a symbol of rebirth (1 Cor 10:2). In this chiasmus Stephen compares such "wonders and signs" done by Moses in Egypt (C-D), to one "like unto Moses", who was also mighty in "word and deed" (C'-D'), who he suggests to the Sanhedrin is Christ! However, Stephen doesn't actually include the last 2 patterned legs in his narration, though no doubt his Jewish audience easily fills in the necessary historical information, which is that all of old Israel dies before the newly born generation enters Canaan.

As evidence that these three narratives are temple themed, Stephen immediately discusses the temple – first, three pagan temples (telestial) and then three righteous temples (celestial). Acts 7:38-43 relates how Israel sacrificed to other Gods and built tabernacles (temples) to *three* pagan deities – the golden calf, Moloch, and Remphan. Then, in Acts 7:44-50 Stephen alternately lists *three* holy temples or tabernacles that Israel would build for the God of Jacob. (See chapter 7 in this book for a fascinating discussion of these three temples.)

Finally, Stephen reveals to the Sanhedrin the reason for their inability to understand – a denial of the divine endowment of the Holy Ghost, upon which rests a comprehension of the gospel, the plan of salvation, and temple:

> 51 Ye stiffnecked and uncircumcised in heart and ears, **ye do always resist the Holy Ghost: as your fathers [did], so [do] ye.**
> 52 Which of the prophets have not your fathers persecuted? and they have slain them which shewed before of the coming of the Just One; of whom ye have been now the betrayers and murderers:
> 53 Who have received the law by the disposition of angels, and have not kept [it].

Indeed, when they resist the Holy Ghost (Jonah), the Sanhedrin overlooks the only means by which they could recognize Jesus as the Messiah, the soft voice which forever affirms the Lord as the saving promise at the heart of these patriarchal stories. Just as their fathers had slain all those prophets that spoke of "the coming of the Just One", Stephen accuses them of something even worse, murdering the promised Messiah (vs 52) who was the very focus of the patriarchal stories, the hope for which all of Abraham's seed, by the timeless prompting of the Holy Ghost, had waited.

Stephen's wonderful words before the council have *three* times expounded, through ancient patriarchal pattern, the plan of salvation fulfilled in Christ. In his final chiasmus Stephen's main point to his listeners (at the center of this structure) is that the "Lord" who spoke to Moses, is Jesus Christ (vs 32). In a poignant and poetic twist, Stephen will be the means by which his unfinished chiasmus is completed; for he will die, as the patriarchal story pattern says all must, slain outside the city walls in similitude of his beloved Savior of whom he fearlessly testified. By Luke's account in Acts 7 we read:

> 54 When they heard these things they were cut to the heart, and they gnashed on him with their teeth.
> 55 But he, being **full of the Holy Ghost**, looked up stedfastly into heaven, and saw the glory of **God, and Jesus** standing on the right hand of God,
> 56 And said, Behold, I see the heavens opened, and the Son of man standing on the right hand of God.

His life imitating scripture, Stephen personally completes the last legs of the pattern, dying at the hands of intellectually knowing, but spiritually unfeeling, Jewish leaders. With the Dove alight upon his shoulder (vs 55), filling his soul, Stephen crosses into the Land of Promise, the exalted Father and the Son both welcoming him; just as he illustrated in prophetic pattern to the Sanhedrin they would (vs 56)! Fittingly, Luke's account in Acts squarely unites Stephen with the honored patriarchs of old, all of whom were purposed types of the Savior. (His dying words even reflect those of Jesus upon the cross, "lay not this sin to their charge." [vs 60])

- **Jacob in Haran – An Endowment**

Stephen does not provide the Sanhedrin with a narration of the patriarch Jacob's life, though he could easily have done so using the same outline. In fact, because Jacob is a patriarch, we can safely predict that his history will contain the same patterned elements. Below is the life of Jacob in chiastic form from Genesis 29-31:

With father Isaac in Canaan
   Goes to Haran (in Hebrew - parched place) pursued by Esau - death
      7 years- marries Leah *(telestial)*
         7 years- marries beloved Rachel (Lamb in Hebrew) *terrestrial*
      7 years- gathers flocks *(celestial)*
   Leaves Haran with flocks – pursued by Laban - death
Returns to father's presence in Canaan

Amid Jacob's story are the same three periods that typify the lives of the other patriarchs. Esau and Laban represent death in this story because both pursued Jacob in order to kill him. As an indication of how his journey has transformed him, when Jacob later returns to his father's house (Gen 33:10) he meets his brother and displays the divine nature of someone celestialized. He says, "I have seen thy face, as though I had seen the face of God, and thou wast pleased with me." Jacob, who initially was at such odds with Esau, now expresses love for him, as if he were God. Below is a side-by-side comparison of the mortal endowment phases (telestial, terrestrial, celestial) of the lives of three patriarchs:

Jacob	Joseph	Moses
7 Years – Marries Leah, not his beloved	Brothers don't know who Joseph is	40 years in Egypt - Moses serves Pharaoh, not God
7 Years – His beloved Rachel (means lamb) is known to Him	Joseph reveals his identity as savior to his brothers	40 years in Midia - God revealed to Moses on Sinai
7 Years – Jacob is fruitful in flocks, his seed multiplied, has 12 sons, spiritual Joseph is born	All of Abraham's seed move to Egypt, covenant preserved, multiply	40 years in wilderness. Moses and Abraham's seed are tested refined, multiplied

- **We are his type – The Sign of Jonah is also our sign**

The patterns of Jacob, Joseph, or Moses are all identical examples of the covenant plan of salvation since before the world's creation. Christ spends three days in the earth as a fulfillment of this three-part pattern or rebirth, and like the patriarchs, our lives are a type of Christ's. Coming to earth we all descend below the heavens to experience a trial of faith, to be reborn, to walk in the Spirit, reflect His redeeming love, and bear its spiritual fruit. Anointed with the Holy Ghost's companionship, our impurities are removed as we prepare to inherit a promised heavenly kingdom.

Genesis 6:3 tells us that the life of man, like Moses', is 120 years, or 3 X 40. The three "days" we are on the earth is a symbolic time frame, slightly different, longer or shorter for everyone. The three 40-year periods of Moses are long, whereas Jacob's three seven year periods are much shorter, yet they are both a type of the same thing. With the endowment blueprint in mind, consider the prophetic significance of some additional three period patterns:

Telestial	Terrestrial	Celestial
Adam-Abraham	Abraham-Christ	Christ-Millennium
2000 years	2000 years	2000 years
40 Jubilee Years (40X50)	40 Jubilee Years	40 Jubilee Years
40 Years in Egypt	40 Years in Midia	40 years in Sinai
Passover - 1st Feast	Pentecost - 2nd Feast	Tabernacles - 3rd
Noah's 1st Dove	Noah's 2nd Dove	Noah's 3rd Dove
Outer Courtyard	Holy Place	Holy of Holies

Notice that these patterns project where we are historically - see the second line of the chart above which indicates that we are at the end of 6,000 years, and on the cusp of the millennial age – the 7th and final period of 1,000 years!

- From the LDS Bible Dictionary we read how the jubilee year is symbolic of the Atonement - "A name given to every fiftieth year. It got its name from the fact that the beginning of the year was announced by the blowing of a trumpet on the Day of Atonement. In it, land that had changed hands reverted to the family to which it had belonged at the original settlement, and all bondmen of Israelitish birth were set free (Lev. 25:8–16, 23–55; 27:16–25)."[48]

7

Stephen's Temple Built without Hands

For a moment let's examine the end of Stephen's temple instruction in Acts 7. Upon completing the endowment pattern, interwoven three times in the histories of the patriarchs, Stephen finishes by talking about three different Israelite temples - an indicator that his patriarchal stories and the temple are interrelated.

> 44 Our fathers had **the tabernacle** of witness in the wilderness, as he had appointed, speaking unto Moses, that he should make it according to the fashion that he had seen.
> 45 Which also our fathers that came after brought in with Jesus (Joshua) into the possession of the Gentiles, whom God drave out before the face of our fathers, unto the days of David;
> 46 Who found favour before God, and desired to find a tabernacle for the God of Jacob.
> 47 But **Solomon** built him an house.
> 48 Howbeit the most High dwelleth not in **temples made with hands**; as saith the prophet,
> 49 Heaven is my throne, and earth is my footstool: what house will ye build me? Saith the Lord: or what is the place of my rest? (Isa 66:1-2)
> 50 Hath not **my hand made** all these things? 51 Ye stiffnecked and uncircumcised in **heart** and ears, ye do always resist the Holy Ghost: as your fathers did, so do ye.

Notice that the *third* temple on Stephen's list is a temple not "made with hands," signifying that all of the physical manifestations of the temple are irrelevant if we are not also a temple, a holy place fashioned (created) by God himself, where he can dwell. Stephen suggests that only the circumcised of heart can experience this most important temple; those who "resist not" the Holy Ghost (the divine agent that makes a temple holy). Stephen's use of circumcision here is also significant. If you recall, circumcision was given by God as an outward token of Abraham's covenant (Gen 17:11), which foreshadowed the inward sign of the New Covenant, a spiritual circumcision of the heart. Borrowing from Stephen's temple made without hands, in Col 2:11 Paul calls this new circumcision the "circumcision made without hands" or the "circumcision of Christ", wherein the "sins of the flesh" (natural man) are cut off.

Moreover, Stephen's final words about this third temple (vs 49-50) originate from Isaiah 66:1-2. However, Stephen uses only the first part of Isaiah's words, requiring us to complete them if we want to fully understand the temple not "made with hands." In Isaiah 66:1-2 we can read the entirety: "Thus saith the LORD, The heaven is my throne, and the earth is my footstool: where is the house (temple) that ye build unto me? And where is the place of my rest? For all those things hath mine hand made, and all those things have been, saith the LORD: **but to this man will I look, even to him that is poor and of a contrite spirit,** and trembleth at my word." As the Lord looks down from heaven's created splendor to locate an earthly temple that is comparable, he finds it in the man "that is poor and of a contrite spirit." Remarkably the Lord is comparing the beauty of his creation to the beauty of such a man's heart, a place where he can in holiness dwell. This is the heart that Christ mentions in 3 Nephi 9:20, and that King Benjamin also identifies in Mosiah 3:19 – which puts off (sacrifices\cuts off) the carnal man and yields to the Spirit's enticing; producing the fruit of love, meekness, humility, and patience (see pgs 35-37). In addition, in 2 Ne 2:7 Lehi specifies that

Christ "came to answer the ends of the law, unto all those who have a broken heart and a contrite spirit, and **unto none else** can the ends of the law be answered;" i.e. the power of the Atonement is accessible only to those whose heart is such a holy temple

Jesus himself talked about his body as a temple in Jn 2:19-20: "Destroy this temple, and in three days I will raise it up. Then said the Jews, Forty and six years was this temple in building, and wilt thou rear it up in three days? 21 But he spake of the temple of his body." Likely the very reason that Stephen is about to be stoned is because he earlier repeated this quote! Remember, he is accused of saying in Acts 6:14, "For we have heard him say, that this Jesus of Nazareth shall destroy this place, and shall change the customs which Moses delivered us."

In 1 Cor 3:16-17 Paul also recognizes this special inner temple, "Know ye not that ye are the temple of God, and that the Spirit of God dwelleth in you? If any man defile the temple of God, him shall God destroy; for the temple of God is holy, which temple ye are." Paul further explains that this temple is built on the foundation of Jesus Christ (3:11), by those who possess the mind of Christ, to whom the deep things of God (his love) have been revealed, but unknown to the natural man (1 Cor 2:10-16). Paul repeats this concept a few chapters later, "Know ye not that your body is the temple of the Holy Ghost which is in you, which ye have of God, and ye are not your own? For ye are bought with a price: therefore glorify God in your body, and in your spirit, which are God's." (1 Cor 6:19-20) The idea of a spiritual temple also ties together nicely with Peter's remarks concerning a spiritual priesthood, chosen to offer spiritual sacrifices (1 Pet 2:5, 9) in that temple. [49]

Neal A Maxwell is remembered for saying that members of the church may "pass through our holy temples, but, alas, they do not let the holy temples pass through them."[50] This expression would aptly apply to the ancient Sanhedrin, fixated on the outward temple, not understanding that it symbolized the inward. In our LDS Hymnal we have a hymn (pg 132 of LDS hymnal) which beautifully expresses this thought, "God is in his Holy Temple."

> God is in his holy temple,
> In the pure and holy mind,
> In the rev'rent heart and simple,
> In the soul from sin refined.
> Banish then each base emotion,
> Lift us up, O Lord to thee,
> Let our souls, in pure devotion,
> Temples for thy worship be.

Holiness to the Lord is engraved upon each temple, has it been engraved upon the temple of our hearts? The following verses from D&C 88:66-68 also talk about our bodies as temples, and how the Spirit fills them with light (sanctified by His love) until the day will come, "that you shall see him."

> 66 . . . because my voice is Spirit; my Spirit is truth; truth abideth and hath no end; and if it be in you it shall abound.
> 67 And if your eye be single to my glory, your whole bodies shall be filled with light, and there shall be no darkness in you; and that body which is filled with light comprehendeth all things.
> 68 Therefore, sanctify yourselves that your minds become single to God, and the days will come that you shall see him; for he will unveil his face unto you, and it shall be in his own time, and in his own way, and according to his own will.

8

Creation Concepts

In addition to the 7-period creation (patriarchal\endowment) pattern, there are other important elements in the temple endowment which deserve our attention. Let's examine these using the scriptures and the ancient Hebrew and Greek lexicons, which will help us better understand their symbolism and meaning.

- **Michael**

A great example of how using the Hebrew Lexicon increases our temple understanding is the word "Michael," which in Hebrew means "who is like God." In fact, it can also be a question, "Who is like God?" Those who have been to the temple know that Michael participates in the creation of the earth and then becomes Adam, which in Hebrew means "man". This is especially poignant and informative when you apply their translated meanings, because the question "Who is like God" is answered "Man." And indeed that is what the temple and the plan of salvation is all about – "becoming" (being created) in the image of our Father in Heaven; holy as he is holy.

- **Bara and Berith, Creation and Covenant**

As has been mentioned, the temple endowment is patterned in such a way that the physical creation is first presented, followed by instruction for our spiritual creation, accomplished through covenants. We discover that we must make and then be faithful to covenants if we desire to return to the presence of our Father. By and through these covenants our spiritual creation occurs. Rightly so, covenants test our inner resolve and obedience, revealing and unfolding our love for God (Jn14:15, 15:10). Genesis 1 tells us that, "in the beginning God created the heavens and the earth. The Hebrew word for "create" is *bara*, which is important because the Hebrew word for covenant (*berith*) comes from *bara*! This is what covenants do; they are the means to create who we "become". By a more traditional definition, they also create relationship between two parties: in this case God and man. Purposed to bring to pass the eternal life of man, through covenant an abiding bond is forged as man is transformed (created) spiritually, drawn ever close to the Savior and the Father. John 17:21 speaks of this bond's purpose; "That they all may be one; as thou, Father, *art* in me, and I in thee, that they also may be one in us" (At-one-ment).

Psalm 33 is an example of the Lord's physical creation, followed by spiritual creation. First we read of the physical: "4 For **the word of the Lord** is right; and all his works are done in truth. 5 He loveth righteousness and judgment: the earth is full of the goodness of the Lord. 6 **By the word of the Lord were the heavens made**; and all the host of them **by the breath of his mouth**. 9 For **he spake**, and it was *done;* he commanded, and it stood fast." We notice that by the breath (spirit-*ruach*) of his mouth the Lord created the physical heavens and earth. Significantly, by his word, spoken in covenants, laws, and commandments, we are also spiritually created. Continuing in Psalm 33 we read how this parallel creation happens: "11 **The counsel** (word) of the LORD standeth for ever, **the thoughts of his heart** to all generations. 13 The Lord looketh from heaven; he beholdeth all the sons of men. 14 From the place of his habitation (his temple) he looketh upon all the inhabitants of the earth. 15 **He fashioneth their hearts** alike; he considereth all their works." How does the Lord get into our hearts to "fashioneth" them? Certainly it is by his "counsel" or covenant word which expresses the righteous "thoughts of his heart." Significantly, in the temple we covenant to obey the law of the gospel as contained in the scriptures, which is his word. We therefore need to read them in order to fulfill this covenant obligation, which in turn will change and fashion our hearts. This is because his covenant word is Spirit infused; is the sword of the Spirit (Eph 6:17, Heb 4:12) which cuts the soul asunder, sanctifying and changing who we are as it abides in our hearts. ("Sanctify them through thy truth. Thy word is truth." Jn 17:17) Coincidently, the Hebrew word for create (*bara*), which we just examined, comes from the more fundamental root *bar*, which means to **cut** or separate. We become pure as he is pure, and are changed (fashioned, **cut**) into his image as we are true and faithful to its enticings (the word and the Spirit). Truly, it is by his covenant word that he creates the earth and man, both formed to be "full of goodness" and righteousness.

- **Priesthood**

The temple is called the place where heaven and earth meet. (Jacob calls it the gate of heaven, Gen 28:17.) A righteous priesthood was and is still needed to make this "link" happen. Anciently the priests were in charge of sacrificing the animals, performing the atonement for Israel. Through sacrifice (which looked forward to Christ's great offering) heaven and earth were joined (reconciled, made at-one). Today we still have a Levite priesthood which administers the sacrament, which are the emblems of sacrifice (our Savior's). Covenant renewal, administered by a righteous priesthood, brings heaven and earth together, and by it (renewing our covenant to remember Him and have his Spirit) the Atonement works in the lives of modern Israel. Its not too surprising that Levite, in Hebrew, gets its meaning from the verb *lavah*, which means to join or bring together. Also, the Hebrew word for priest (*kohen*) comes from *kahan*, which means to intermediate, which is evocative of our Great High Priest who mediates on our behalf before the Father. Anciently the high priest (as a type of Christ) would enter the temple holy of holies on the Day of Atonement and on behalf of Israel perform an atonement (removing sin and reconciling to God) with blood from the sacrificial lamb; a similitude of Christ (the Lamb who would ultimately intermediate and remove sin for all mankind). As mentioned, this is what happens today when the priests bless the sacrament – provide the means to remove sin through the tokens of His sacrificial atoning blood (Mat 14:22-24).

In 1 Pet 2 we read more about priesthood symbolism. "5 But also, as lively stones, are built up a spiritual house, an holy priesthood, to offer up spiritual sacrifices, acceptable to God by Jesus Christ." What Peter means by "lively stones" and "built up a spiritual house", is that we are the stones which make up the spiritual temple of God; that by baptism and the Holy Ghost all members are called to act as figures of the ancient priests, offering up not animal sacrifices, but "spiritual sacrifice" – which brings heaven and earth together in our lives. Certainly, this reminds us of King Benjamin's teaching to put off the natural man (sacrifice him) and yield to the enticings of the Spirit (the offering of the broken spirit and contrite heart). Additionally, in 1 Pet 2 we read: "9 But ye are a chosen generation, a royal priesthood, an holy nation, a peculiar people; that ye should shew forth the praises of him who hath called you out of darkness into his marvelous light." This verse is widely acknowledged as a reference to Exodus 19:5 where God covenanted with Israel on Mt Sinia: "6 Now therefore, if ye will obey my voice indeed, and keep my covenant, then shall ye be a peculiar treasure unto me above all people for all the earth is mine: 6 And ye shall be unto me **a kingdom of priests**, and an holy nation." At that time the Lord desired that all Israel would hold the priesthood, all offering sacrifices. Though they rejected God's wish for them (D&C 84:23-24), this is still God's desire for his children – to have a personal relationship with him, even to see his face (D&C 84:22). As Peter informs us, in order to be a "holy nation" this priesthood must now offer "spiritual sacrifices", which implies yielding to the Spirit who prompts us to be true and faithful to our covenants and God's commands. Ancient priesthood temple sacrifice was therefore symbolic of the daily spiritual offering now made in the temple of our bodies (1 Cor 6:19, D&C 93) upon the altar of our hearts. Moreover, just as Christ the high priest became the sacrifice, as a priest (after the order of Melchizedek) we are also the sacrifice; it is the high calling of the priesthood (laying the animal within us on the altar). "Melchizedek" in Hebrew means King of Righteousness, which is a reference to Christ. Those who hold Christ's priesthood fulfill its symbolic meaning as they surrender their natural man, i.e. you cannot be a king of righteousness without such priestly sacrifice.

    It should also be noted that the Aaronic priesthood was given father to son (a patriarchal order by lineage and birth), and is a type (foreshadow) of the Melchizedek, which requires that you be spiritually born in order to receive it. Only those who are adopted sons, spiritually begotten of our spiritual father who is Christ, may truly participate or serve in its ranks (See D&C 121:36-37).[51]

- **Beauty**

The first event that we see in the endowment is the creation of the earth. It begins as a scene dark and void of life, but with each successive day becomes more stunning. Upon completion it is pronounced beautiful. In Genesis we read something slightly different; that God saw it (his creation) that it was good. The word "good" used here in Genesis is *tov*, which can also mean beautiful![52] Beauty is therefore an important concept in understanding the temple, because the goal of the temple is to make us beautiful in righteousness (Rev 19:9). Indeed, the temple itself is beautiful because it a great symbol of Jesus Christ, built on a hill beckoning all men to come into its gates. No shortcuts are taken, and no expense is spared to give our temples impeccable beauty. The reason for this is also symbolic, a reminder that God wants a heart of impeccable beauty, to which there are no shortcuts, and which requires all within us; no expense spared.

Consistent with this idea, Nauvoo is a Hebrew word meaning beautiful, coming from the phrase in Isaiah with alludes to the beauty of the mountain of the Lord, "How beautiful upon the mountains are the feet of him that bringeth good tidings, that publisheth peace; that bringeth good tidings of good, that publisheth salvation; that saith unto Zion, Thy God reigneth!" (Isaiah 52:7). In this verse we find a brief celebration of the temple – a mountain where "good tidings" (the gospel) and "publishing salvation" (the plan of salvation) is taught. In addition, Isaiah associates beauty with the messenger, the temple mount, as well as to the plan (good\beautiful tidings of salvation). Moreover, in the verses that follow (52:8-12) Isaiah provides the detail of this beauty – the redemption of Israel; that they will be comforted as they come out of Babylon (the world), and that a Savior will come to bear their sins and grief, a lamb to the slaughter, an offering (sacrifice) for their sins.

In 2 Chronicles we find a similar sentiment, written for the dedication of Solomon's temple: "23 Sing unto the Lord, all the earth; shew forth from day to day his salvation. 26 For all the gods of the people are idols: but the Lord made the heavens. 29 Give unto the Lord the glory due unto his name: bring an offering, and come before him: worship the Lord in **the beauty of holiness**." Here we can make out the celebration of salvation, elements of the creation, followed by an invitation to come to the temple and "worship in the beauty of holiness." As before, beauty of holiness doesn't just refer to the temple, but to the disciple that brings an offering of true worship, an offering of the heart.

Nephi also tells us that the tree of life "was exceeding of all beauty" (1 Ne 11:8), which seems only fitting since it's located in the heavenly temple. Moreover, we know that it represents the love of God shed abroad in our hearts, most desirable and most joyous to the soul. Nephi's vision celebrates the condescension of Jesus Christ; that he "**went forth** among the children of men" (parallel to the love of God that is "**shed forth**") ministering to mankind, healing the sick, and that he was hung on a tree for their sins. This is the plan of salvation, and it is also beautiful beyond all other beauty. Integral to the tree of life's symbolism is the cross upon which Christ suffered for us; and while Christ's crucifixion is difficult to look upon, it is the glorious and beautiful gospel news. It is worth noting that many of the temples are now being built with an image of the tree of life in the celestial room. Indeed, our temple journey starts in Eden with the tree of life and ends in the presence of that same tree.

Tree of Life in celestial room of Palmyra LDS Temple

"That I may dwell in the house of the LORD All the days of my life, To **behold the beauty of the LORD, And to inquire in His temple**." Psa 27:4

- **Garment and Veil**

The garment is a symbol of Christ and his atoning sacrifice – In Gen 3:5 we read that the blood of an innocent animal (likely a lamb) was shed to provide coats for Adam and Eve, to cover their nakedness. Whereas they were at first innocent and unashamed by their nakedness, once they partake of the forbidden fruit and are fallen, their nakedness is a symbol of shame. This death (the first recorded of any living thing) foreshadows and is a symbol of Christ's atoning sacrifice for fallen man (a covering for his shame).

The veil is also a symbol of Christ and his atoning sacrifice – in Heb 10:19-20 we read (parenthesis mine): "Having therefore, brethren, boldness to enter into the holiest by the blood (sacrifice) of Jesus, By a new and living way, which he hath consecrated for us, **through the veil**, that is to say, his flesh (sacrifice)." Rightly so, our only access into God's holy presence is because of and "through" the blood of His sacrifice, which here we are told is symbolized by the rent veil (through which we enter).

This parallel of the garment and the veil suggests that we enter mortality with the promise of Christ's atonement (garment), and that by the same atoning sacrifice (veil), the law of justice is satisfied,[53] enabling us to return spotless back into our Father's presence. Indeed, in the temple the fabric and the markings found on one are found on the other. When we receive instruction concerning the markings on the veil it primarily concerns the markings also found on the garment. In addition, a new name is given when Adam and Eve receive their garments, just as a new name is learned at the veil. (See pg 18 or pg 83 for parallel diagram.)

- **Putting On – Endow – Covering**

As mentioned previously, in the temple endowment the seven days of creation show us how the earth is clothed with beauty. And though temporal creation is important, it is only a reflective prelude to the purpose of all creation – man's spiritual beautification\creation. Very apropos, in Hebrew the word for Atonement is *kaphar*, which means to cover. Connected to this idea, consider the words of Paul in Romans 13:11-13, "let us therefore cast off the works of darkness, and let us **put on (*enduo*)** the armour of light. Let us walk honestly, as in the day; not in rioting and drunkenness, not in chambering and wantonness, not in strife and envying. But **put ye on (*enduo*) the Lord Jesus Christ**, and make not provision for the flesh, to [fulfil] the lusts [thereof]." The highlighted word in these verses is the original Greek word which means to endow, or to clothe! Certainly, the garment is an "endowment" of light which symbolizes putting on Christ, and "casting off" (putting to death) the natural man (Mosiah 3:19).

In Ephesians 4:22-24 Paul again speaks of the endowment (*enduo*), and relates that through it (putting on the new man) we are spiritually created and beautified: "That ye **put off** concerning the former conversation the old man, which is corrupt according to the deceitful lusts; And be renewed in the spirit of your mind; And that ye **put on *(enduo)*** the new man, which after God **is created** in **righteousness** and true holiness." Paul's conclusions that the endowment's creative goal is righteousness and holiness is supported by John's description of the splendid clothing worn by those who enter God's presence: "Let us be glad and rejoice, and give honour to him: for the marriage of the Lamb is come, and his wife hath made herself ready. 8 And to her was granted that she should be arrayed in fine linen, clean and white: for the **fine linen is the righteousness of saints**" (Rev 19:7-8). As it relates to us, "putting on the new man" is how "holiness to the Lord" – the inscription on every temple – is "honoured." It is also the "new and living way," which is to yield to the enticings of the Spirit, whereby we have access to "the holiest"; the presence of God. We cannot be true and faithful to the covenants made in the temple or at baptism in any other way. In 2 Ne 9:14 Jacob speaks of the resurrection and confirms the meaning the robes worn by the bride, "Wherefore, we shall have a perfect knowledge of all our guilt, and our uncleanness, and our nakedness; and the righteous shall have a perfect knowledge of their enjoyment, and their righteousness, being **clothed with purity, yea, even with the robe of righteousness**."

In Exodus the Lord gives Moses the reason for covering the sons of Aaron in priesthood robes, "And for Aaron's sons thou shalt make coats, and thou shalt make for them girdles, and bonnets shalt thou make for them, **for glory and for beauty**. And thou shalt put them upon Aaron thy brother, and his sons with him; and shalt anoint them, and consecrate them, and sanctify them, that they may minister unto me in the priest's office" (Ex 28:40-41). If you have been to the temple you will readily make out the various articles by which you are also beautified. Significantly, the "coats" mentioned here is the same Hebrew word found in Genesis 3:21, "Unto Adam also and to his wife did the LORD God make coats (*kethonet*) of skins, and clothed them." The meaning for those priests is the same for us; the "coats" are the garment that symbolized the sacrifice of the Lamb of God. As well, the anointing oil that sanctifies and consecrates is a symbol of the Holy Ghost, the divinely appointed agent to purify and beautify the priest's heart.

These priesthood\wedding robes which represent righteousness are also celebrated in Isa 61:10, "I will greatly rejoice in the LORD, my soul shall be joyful in my God; for he hath **clothed me with the garments of salvation, he hath covered me with the robe of righteousness**, as a bridegroom decketh himself with ornaments, and as a bride adorneth herself with her jewels." (For more information on wedding imagery and God's covenant, see chapter 19.)

- **Endowment Pattern, with Priesthoods and Covenants**

If we put all of the elements of the seven-phase temple endowment together, along with the location of each related priesthood and covenant, we have an endowment master template. It is interesting that when we enter the celestial kingdom it is not announced, unlike the telestial and terrestrial where it is. For this reason, many participants don't immediately realize that they have entered a new world. However, the message is clear, that we enter the celestial realm on this side of the veil; i.e. the celestial process starts here.

Eden with Father
Dominion over Earth, 1st Aaronic Priesthood
Law of Elohim, Obedience, Sacrifice

    Garment, New Name, Sacrificial Death of Lamb

        Telestial
        2nd Aaronic Priesthood
        Law of Gospel
        Name while in mortality

            Terrestrial
            1st Melchizedek Priesthood
            Law of Chastity
            Name

        Celestial
        2nd Melchizedek Priesthood
        Law of Consecration
        Name mentioned but not given until veil

    Veil, New Name, Sacrificial Death of Christ (Heb 10:19)

Celestial Kingdom with Father
Dominion – Reign with power in priesthood as kings (Rev 1:6, 5:10)
Law of Christ (love, sacrifice, and obedience) D&C 88:21-22

I do not include an overlay of signs and tokens here but discuss them in a later section. However, there is a unique gospel idea emphasized by these parallels. I notice that Adam came to the earth with priesthood.[54] When Adam was placed in the garden he was told to "dress and keep" the garden, which in Hebrew is *abad* and *shamar*. These same Hebrew words are used of the priests of Aaron in Num 3:7 when they are commissioned to "work" in the temple. Many commentators draw comparisons between the instructions given to Adam and the instructions given to Moses' priests. In fact, it is widely understood that Eden was the first temple and Adam the first priest.[55] Indeed, in order to do God's "work" you must be created in His holy image (Adam), and you must have his priesthood (authority to "work" as an image of Him; in His name). Eden sets a pattern for all future priesthood.

Also, notice that the very first commandment given is the Law of Elohim. Of this law David O McKay said, "You will first be asked if you are willing to obey the law of Elohim; are you willing to take upon yourself the responsibility of making God the center of your lives? That is what it means."[56] In other words, the Law of Elohim (God) is to love him; make him the center of our devotion. When Christ was asked the greatest commandment (law) he replied that it was to "love the Lord thy God with all thy heart, and with all thy soul, and with all thy mind" (Mat 22:36-38). This eternal law was set in place before the world began. Indeed, God is love (1 Jn 4:16), and his law is to love.

- **Adam and Eve – a Love Story**

The great lesson of life is learning to love; it is why we are here. President Deiter Uchtdorf has said: "Love is what inspired our Heavenly Father to create our spirits; it is what led our Savior to the Garden of Gethsemane to make Himself a ransom for our sins. Love is the **grand motive of the plan of salvation**; it is the source of happiness, the ever-renewing spring of healing, the precious fountain of hope."⁵⁷ Indeed, of all beauty, love is the most beautiful (see 1 Nephi 11:8,22). And, because God is love (1 Jn 4:7-8), to be with him eternally we must become like him (pure as he is pure, full of charity, which is the love of Christ, Moroni 7:47-48). One of the most widely discussed aspects of the temple has to do with Adam and Eve's motivation; what they possibly knew, or didn't know, when they partook of the forbidden fruit. These kinds of questions are surely best answered by attempting to examine the inner workings of their hearts; their story is a love story, as is ours.

When Adam was told to cleave (become one) with his wife, in essence he was told to love her (that is how we become one). As a result, when Adam later decides to partake of the fruit in order to remain with Eve his actions are a similitude of Christ's who also gave himself for the ones he loves (his bride – those who have taken his name). Indeed, Christ (the second Adam) would later take sin upon himself in the name of love and mercy, which Adam's actions prefigure. In fact, 1Timothy 2:14 says that though Eve was deceived, Adam was not. One of the implications here is that Adam *consciously* chose love; to remain with Eve in spite of the punishment he knew would follow. And, as God indicated, from the time that Adam and Eve partook of the forbidden tree they began to be conscious (had knowledge)[58] of the consequences of their actions. However, they also began to comprehend and appreciate the power, beauty, and majesty of God's love. Good mixed with evil will bring only death just as God said, yet ironically and paradoxically it is also the means to obtain a deeper appreciation of redemptive love and mercy.

Consider for a moment the two plans in the preexistence: that of Christ's and that of Satan's. When you boil it down to what really differentiated them – it was love. Satan's plan to take away our agency would have also effectively eliminated the possibility for us to act on our feelings (good or bad). Forced obedience is empty, just as sacrificing without love could not fundamentally change Adam's fallen nature (see chapter 1). To be genuine, obedience and sacrifice must be a willing response from a heart that is free to choose.

In Moses 5 we read, "And Satan put it into the heart of the serpent, (for he had drawn away many after him,) and he sought also to beguile Eve, for he knew not the mind of God, wherefore he sought to destroy the world." We might ask, what does it mean, that he "knew not the mind of God"? The answer is that "the mind of God" is love (1 Jn 4:16), and that is something Satan cannot understand because it is felt and comprehended in the heart. To the extent that we intellectually know God's plan but fail to respond to it in our hearts, we are just like Satan, outside of God's love, "past feeling" (as Laman and Lemuel). At-one-ment, in some fashion, is when our hearts and minds work in concert, each equally guided by love.

After Eve partook of the forbidden fruit, we can imagine the inner conflict that existed as Adam wrestled with what to do – love God, or love his wife. Choosing to obey God's command (to not eat the forbidden fruit) he seemingly is breaking the command to "remain with" Eve (Moses 4:18). And, because charity is the pure love of God (Moroni 7), obeying God's command to not eat shows a lack of compassion for Eve (she will be cast out). Logic is backed into a corner – both choices appear to be simultaneously right and wrong, good and evil.

As Adam wrestles with the bounds of love, obedience, justice, and mercy, we are reminded again of Christ's later agony in another garden, Gethsemane. Adam's choice to "cleave" to his wife; love her at all costs – even suffer the wrath of the Father – is surely a type of Christ's complete sacrifice for his bride (the church). However, consider for a moment God's marriage covenant and how it works. Adam had been given the covenant to not eat of the tree first, but with Eve's arrival he was given a secondary command to love and cleave to her (Gen 2:17-24)[59]. This chronology establishes a covenant hierarchy – to obey (love) God first and then man or womankind (see Mat 12:30-31). Many fail to recognize that when we are married celestially our primary relationship is with God first and our spouse second. In fact, **our bridegroom is Jesus Christ before it is our mortal spouse.** In a successful covenant marriage, each spouse is married to Him as surely as they are to their earthly partner. Whenever we by-pass this primary love relationship (with the Creator) we undermine our capacity to truly love our partner. We can only celestially interact with our earthly spouses when we have His love shed abroad in our hearts first.

This hierarchy is evident in God's assessment of *Adam's transgression* in Genesis 3:17 and Moses 4:23. "And unto Adam, I, the Lord God, said: **Because thou hast hearkened unto the voice of thy wife** (and not to me), **and hast eaten of the fruit of the tree of which I commanded thee, saying—Thou shalt not eat** of it, cursed shall be the ground for thy sake; in sorrow shalt thou eat of it all the days of thy life." The implication here is that Adam should have listened to God first (not his wife) – who would have told him what to do. (Adam knew that God came in the cool of the day. Why didn't he wait to converse with him before disobeying?) God's desire was then, and is now, that we would love and obey him before all else, which is the only way to assure happiness. This is one of Eden's (and life's) greatest love lesson. Moreover, one of the means that God provides all men to hear His voice is the gift of conscience. Indeed, how man came to have an active conscience, or be conscious of good and evil (know the pangs of a guilty conscience), is a primary purpose of Eden's story. And surely, just before or right after he partook, Adam experienced a flash of conscience. (In LDS thought, "conscience" is manifest by the light of Christ – see Moroni 7:15-19.) [60] In fact, conscience (also consciousness) is a compound word from the Greek meaning, **with** (*con*) **knowledge** (*science*). Somewhere in that instant of time (as he partook), Adam knew (had knowledge) that he either was about to, or just had, disobeyed God. I personally think that it was just before, because a conscience also warns when we are about to transgress – something that Adam was about to do for the first time.[61] As a consequence, in his heart Adam newly sensed that his relationship with God was about to be, or already had, changed. Satan later seizes on this (a new consciousness of shame) when he tells Adam and Eve to hide.

- **Eve**

Let's now reflect on the voice that Eve hearkened to. (I realize that some of these views, though supported by modern prophets, are a counterpoint to the ideas of some church members.) Consider for a moment what Abinadi said about Satan's role in the garden, that he "did beguile (deceive) our first parents, which was the cause of their fall" (Mosiah 16:3). Notice that Abinadi believes that Satan said something deceptive (beguiling) to "cause" the fall.

Affirming this, Harold B. Lee explains: "Eve partook because she was deceived by Satan, the scriptures tell us. She was deceived. It wasn't because she understood that the great purpose of God would be realized if she did partake. She didn't understand that. She was deceived by Satan, and so she was in transgression of that law." [62]

So, what was Satan's deception which preceded Eve's decision to partake? Satan's exact conversation with her is duplicated for us three times in the standard works – Genesis 3:4-5, Moses 4:10-12, and 2 Ne 2:18. However, in the temple presentation Eve's exchange with the serpent has been altered, unfortunately creating some confusion concerning the cause of Eve's transgression. There (in the temple), we only hear Satan's assertion to Eve that she needs to partake of the forbidden fruit so that she can know good from evil, pleasure from pain, and joy from sorrow, which is seemingly true. But, according to scripture, Satan tells her something else. For example, 2 Ne 2:18 gives us the **single** deception which caused her fall. "Wherefore, he said unto Eve, yea, even that old serpent, who is the devil, who is the father of all lies, wherefore he said: Partake of the forbidden fruit, **and ye shall not die**, but ye shall be as God, knowing good and evil. And after Adam and Eve had partaken of the forbidden fruit they were driven out of the garden of Eden, to till the earth." (See also Gen 3:4-5 or Moses 4:10-12.) Apostle James Talmage concurs with Lehi. He writes, "Eve was fulfilling the foreseen purposes of God by the part she took in the great drama of the fall; yet she did not partake of the forbidden fruit with that object in view**, but with intent to act contrary to the divine command, being deceived by the sophistries of Satan** . . . declaring that **death would not follow** a violation of the divine injunction; but that, on the other hand, by doing that which the Lord had forbidden she and her husband would become like unto the gods, knowing good and evil for themselves. **The woman was captivated by these representations; and, being eager to possess the advantages pictured by Satan, she disobeyed the command of the Lord, and partook of the fruit forbidden.** She feared no evil, for she knew it not." [63] The deception, therefore, which initiated the fall was rooted in uncertainty concerning "being as God" without dying, which is a key feature distinguishing God's plan from Satan's. Eve seemed to contemplate this "advantage" and perhaps even hoped that "becoming as God" without dying was possible. Like Eve, we might also wonder how happiness and death go hand in hand. Why not joy without suffering? It can be a difficult concept to square.

Once again, let's use the backdrop of love to contextualize Eve's actions in the garden. Without a doubt, love is inseparably interlaced with the principle of sacrifice (wherein something dies to give life). This idea is wonderfully expressed by David Paul Trip in his book *What Did You Expect?* – "There is no such thing as love without sacrifice. Love calls you beyond the borders of your own wants, needs, and feelings. Love calls you to be willing to invest time, energy, money, resources, personal ability, and gifts for the good of another. Love calls you to **lay down your life** in ways that are concrete and specific. Love calls you to serve, to wait, to give, to suffer, to forgive, and to do all these things again and again." Because God's love and sacrifice are so closely related, the "law of sacrifice" found in the endowment could also be called – the law of love.[64] Certainly we see in Christ's sacrificial death the ultimate expression of true love, a sacrifice which makes eternal life possible. However, Satan's shortcut to love and eternal life circumvents the plan of salvation's most fundamental principle – sacrifice, which love unavoidably requires. Indeed, as Christ tells us in John 3:16, God **loved** us so much he sent his Son to be **sacrificed**, that those who believe on Him (will pattern their lives after His great sacrifice), will have eternal life. Just as the tree of life represents God's love shed abroad in the hearts of the children of men, Satan's tree represents a loveless plan from the beginning – that we would come to earth, be forced to obey (not out of heart-felt love), and consequently never die because we could never sin (sin is death, Rom 6:23). Feeling and growing in love would be irrelevant under such an obligatory plan, because regardless of what you truly felt your obedience would nonetheless be compulsory. To be sure, Satan still tempts us in the same fashion, by promising happiness without sacrifice or consequence. However, Christ explains in Jn 12:24 that the opposite is true; that in a spiritual sense we must die (be sacrificed) in order to bring forth the fruit of joy and love. This eternal law is the pattern of love and is the essence of who God is; as who we desire "to become" (celestialized). Eve's transgression (and often ours) stems from her contemplation of Satan's plan as a possible option to God's plan of love (as represented by the tree of life). Like Eve, when we consider any other gospel which perhaps seems easier or less painful, we are also open to Satan's deception. The "narrow way" which leads to love (eternal life) requires a sacrifice, the death of the natural man and his prideful desires – the sacrifice of the broken heart and contrite spirit.

- **The Tree of Knowledge of Good and Evil**

In 2 Ne 2:15-16 we read about the tree of knowledge of good and evil: "it must needs be that there was an opposition; even the forbidden fruit in opposition to the tree of life; the one being sweet and the other bitter. Wherefore, the Lord God gave unto man that he should act for himself. Wherefore, man could not act for himself save it should be that he **was enticed by the one or the other**." These verses indicate that the tree of knowledge of good and evil is still existent, and that it continues to "entice" us (in opposition to the enticings by the Spirit). Because this is so, we shouldn't have any problem empathizing with what happened to Eve; she surrendered to temptation in the same way we do.

James 1:12-18 confirms this idea, significantly using creation (fruit bearing) imagery to draw our minds to the temple and to Eve. "Blessed is the man that endureth temptation: for when he is tried, he shall receive the crown of **life** (eternal life), which the Lord hath promised to them that **love** him. 13 Let no man say when he is tempted, I am tempted of God: for God cannot be tempted with evil, neither tempteth he any man: 14 But every man is tempted, when he is drawn away of his own lust (desire), and **enticed**. 15 Then when lust hath **conceived**, it **bringeth forth** sin: and sin, when it is finished, bringeth forth death. 17 Every good gift (of the Spirit) and every perfect gift is from above, and cometh down from the Father of lights, with whom is no variableness, neither shadow of turning. 18 Of his own **will begat he us** with the word of truth, that we should be a kind of firstfruits of his **creatures** (creation)." Clearly, by "the word of truth" men are "begat" (born) of God unto life, while conversely through temptation they are "conceived" (born) of lust, which "brings forth" the fruit of death. This is very much like what happened to Eve; the word of Satan's tree "became" pleasant and her "desires" began to change.[65]

In fact, this is what we find in Moses 4:12; that Eve saw that, "the tree was good for food, and that it **became** pleasant to the eyes, and a tree to be desired to make her wise." Notice the emboldened word "**became**", which denotes that during her temptation something was altered in her thinking; i.e. Satan's lie "became" more palatable or delicious. (In the Genesis 3:6 account this is not apparent. It states, "the woman saw that the tree was good for food, and that it was pleasant to the eyes, and a tree to be desired to make one wise.") Whereas moments before Eve's heart and mind had a singular focus, influenced solely by the tree of life and God's love, Satan's word very subtly fragments that. Love flows from the heart to the mind, just as thoughts from our mind can (if we allow it) also flow into our hearts, one influencing the other. Such an interplay of ideas and desires seems to also apply to the two trees, one which is primarily experienced or felt in the heart (1 Ne 11:22), and the other which represents what is conceived (imagined) in the mind. For good reason we are told that we will be judged by the desires we allow into our hearts (D&C 137:9), which seems to be the case in Eve's story. Ultimately, over time, we become what we desire.[66]

When we, (like Eve) allow our hearts to be led astray by false seeds planted in our minds, we are "born" of the ideas of the bogus tree. As explained by James earlier, Satan is the Father of lies who has begotten children. John 8:44 affirms this: "Ye are of your father the devil, and **the lusts** (desires) of your father ye will do. He was a murderer from the beginning, and abode not in the truth, because there is no truth in him. When he speaketh a lie, he speaketh of his own: for he is a liar, and the father of it." Col 2:18 adds that the devil's offspring possess a "fleshy mind," one that is sensual. "Let no one cheat (beguile) you of your reward, taking delight in false humility and worship of angels, intruding into those things which he has not seen, **vainly puffed up by his fleshly mind.**"

As this relates to our initial endowment\creation pattern, the telestial realm could be designated as a realm of the "fleshly" mind (natural man), and the celestial world as a realm of the heart. Consider for a moment our initial endowment\creation pattern, this time with these two designations:

Carnal Mind – natural man *Telestial*

   Spirit Rebirth (enlightenment) – taste God's love *Terrestrial*

Heart – grow in love through the Spirit *Celestial*

However, in Eden, under Satan's influence, the endowment process is reversed. If someone is born of the forbidden tree (of Satan) then they start in the celestial with God's love and conversely descend to the telestial – born (in the middle) of Satan's doctrine\word. The following shows this reversal:

At Tree of Life – Temple

   Pure Heart and Mind – God's love, truth *Celestial*

     Partake of false (mixture of good and bad) ideas *Terrestrial*

   Carnal Mind, Darkened Heart – Satan's error *Telestial*

Satan's tree – Spacious Building – Satan's temple

In this scenario a person does not return to the tree of life, but is diverted to the spacious building (1 Ne 8) where their mind and heart is clouded by sensual desire, pride, and error-filled thinking. Jacob, in 2 Ne 9:39, uses familiar language to remind us of the terrible consequences of reversing the endowment (an endowment of darkness), "O, my beloved brethren, remember the awfulness in transgressing against that Holy God, and also the awfulness of **yielding to the enticings** of that cunning one. Remember, **to be carnally-minded is death**, and to be spiritually-minded is life eternal." *See Appendix 6 for more information concerning events in Eden.

- **Opposition in all things**

Consequently, there is further insight to be gleaned from this line of thinking. Let's look at a list of significant "oppositions":

- A tree (good and evil) that is "in opposition" to the tree of life (2 Ne 2:15-16)
- The word of Satan which grows into a tree and bears fruit that "bringeth forth death"(James 1:15-19) in opposition to the word of God which is planted in the heart and grows into the tree of life (Alma 32)
- A birth unto death (James 1) in opposition to a birth unto life
- A reverse endowment unto death in opposition to the true and living endowment
- Satan as father (Jn 8:44) in opposition to God the Father
- Satan's begotten children in opposition to God's children
- A gospel of damnation in opposition to the gospel of salvation
  (In the temple we see Satan preaching, mixing in the philosophies of men)
- A church of the devil (1 Ne 14:9-10) in opposition to the church of
  Christ (3 Ne 26:21)
- A spacious building (Satan's temple) in opposition to God's holy temple
- Satan's priesthood in opposition to God's priesthood
- Satan's priesthood intermediating earth and hell, in opposition to
  God's priesthood which intermediates heaven and earth
- Satan's dark priesthood robes in opposition to the white robes of
  the holy priesthood
- Satan, can "seal you his" (Alma 34:35) in opposition to God who "may seal you his" (Mosiah 5:15).

In addition, the symbolism of the white robes which represent the inner righteousness of the saints (Rev 19:8) is opposed to the symbolic meaning of Satan's dark robes, which surely represents the inner corruption and filthiness of those who follow him; are born of him, belong to his church, bear his priesthood, and worship in his unholy temple.

- **Chastity at the Center – Terrestrial Marriage**

There are certain ordinances of the endowment that are not done sequentially during the endowment session. For instance, receiving the garment is actually an important step within the endowment, but is given at a time before the endowment when one is washed and anointed (which is out of sequence). During the endowment this is remembered and cited at the appropriate time. The other part of the endowment that is broken out is the marriage sealing. We do not stop the endowment and go to the sealing room to be sealed for time and eternity with our spouse, but if time permitted, we would. The Law of Chastity, given at the endowment's center, commemorates this sealing. In relation to God's plan, our marriage for time and eternity is simultaneously symbolic of Christ's marriage to his bride (Israel, you and me); sealed to Christ and to our spouse. All the other endowment covenants are exclusively between a man and God except the most center one – the law of chastity – which represents spiritual chastity (purity) to our Lord as much as it does to our spouse. There is a significant new name given at this time which is reminiscent of a bride (us) who take's a new name.

The implications here are myriad. Marriage suggests the ability to now create earthly children (seed), but it also implies that we are now betrothed to our beloved bridegroom (Christ), ready to enter the celestial world and produce (create) spiritual fruit through the sanctifying and sealing power of the Holy Ghost; procreation (bearing fruit) is a celestial event.

Interestingly, in Hebrew there is no word for chastity. Rather the word that is used is *kadash*, which is the same word that is used for consecrated or holy! Spiritually speaking, to be holy before the Lord is to be chaste, having no other "gods before him", wholly consecrated body and soul. This is reflected in the words on every temple "Holiness to the Lord," which has distinct marriage overtones. (In Hebrew the word for marriage is *kiddushin,* which comes from the verb *kadash*, meaning holy!) In Exodus 19:5-6 the Lord covenanted with Israel at Mt Sinai. Since that time, this event has been recognized as God's marriage covenant with Israel; "Now therefore, if ye will obey my voice indeed, and keep my covenant, then ye shall be a peculiar treasure unto me above all people: for all the earth *is* mine: And ye shall be unto me a kingdom of **priests,** and an **holy** (*qadash*) nation." Thus, God's bride (Israel) is covenanted to be holy and bear priesthood. Moses was also instructed to have this written on the mitre (hat) of the high priest (Holiness to the Lord). If we connect this imagery, the implication is that a priest in the temple (ancient or modern) is necessarily also betrothed – to his bridegroom and God.

- **Token, Name, Sign – Symbols of Progression**

Tokens, names, and signs are parallels. Each name reveals to us the meaning of the overall symbolism. Together they follow the progression of the plan of salvation (telestial, terrestrial, celestial); from less, to more, to most. For instance, temple signs begin by using one hand, then two hands, until finally the hands become dynamic (in motion) as our voices are also engaged. At this point as much of ourselves as possible is required to make the sign (a fitting expression of its accompanying covenant). The tokens also follow this same creation pattern, from less complicated to more intertwined, or from mortal to divine, as do the names.

From this we understand that tokens, names, and signs are not just words or outward hand gestures, but are symbols of what we are to become within (markers of our celestialization process). Therefore, the criteria for passing the angels which guard to way back into the presence of God is not so much being able to reproduce or pronounce them outwardly, but having internalized what they symbolize into the nature of our soul, who we truly are. (As Nibley would say, they are "mere forms" of what they represent.) [67] Our words and gestures will have little meaning if our hearts have not been beautifully created; at-one with God's divine nature. (See chapter 11 for more information on how the widow's hand is used as a divine sign; **simultaneously filled** yet **turned to release** its fullness; a sign which seals and unseals the heavens.)

- **Stunning Explanation of Center-most Signs**

However, the most concrete information that we have regarding these endowment signs has been right before our eyes, viewed in the first ordinances already performed by the priesthood. As you look at the pictures below, pay attention to the position of John the Baptist's arms and hands. As well, look at the arms and hands of Jesus. Imitate them and you discover that you are making signs familiar to all temple patrons.

68

The baptismal embrace of Christ and John represents an important transition. John the Baptist signifies the Aaronic priesthood after the order of Aaron, and Jesus represents the Melchizedek. John also represents the old covenant and the outward law, while Christ is the new covenant, after the order of God and his Son (Alma 13). Together they symbolize an event in every believer's journey, leaving the telestial and entering the terrestrial; when the greater light of the Holy Ghost appears (in the form of a dove) and the lesser life forms of creation (Genesis 1-2) are replaced by the greater; the earth about to become beautiful and fruitful; new birth and entering into the kingdom of God.

The fact that the two central endowment signs imitate the ordinance of baptism (and vise-versa) is supported by the understanding that baptism itself is a sign. Joseph Smith said that, "baptism is a <u>sign</u> and a commandment which God has set for man to enter into His kingdom. Those who seek to enter in any other way will seek in vain; for God will not receive them, neither will the angels acknowledge their works as accepted, for they have not obeyed the ordinances, nor <u>attended to the signs</u> which God ordained for the salvation of man, to prepare him for, and give him a title to, a celestial glory." (*History of the Church,* 4:554.) [69] Here we see that the sign of baptism is needed in order to pass the angels and enter into God's kingdom and celestial glory, just as the signs in the temple (also images of baptism it turns out) are needed for the same purpose. Truly, the temple endowment is iterating and celebrating anew the ordinances found in the fullness of the gospel – faith repentance, baptism, gift of the Holy Ghost. (See pgs 18 and 22 for the centrality of baptism in the creation pattern, which the 1st principles and ordinances represent.)

- **Praying with True Order – Spirit Filled**

We know that at Christ's baptism the Holy Ghost, and its greater light, descended from heaven in the form of a dove. The following picture of this event should also look familiar to temple patrons, an image of praise, thanksgiving, and prayer (anciently this is how Israel prayed, 1 Ki 8:54).

Such exultation is the joy that Nephi described as he experienced that which is "most delicious and joyous to the soul," the revealed knowledge God's love. (also the center of 1 Nephi – an image of the temple endowment, see chapter 9.) Most important, the true order of prayer refers to the ORDER of Melchizedek, the holy order of the Son of God (see Alma 13) – possessed by His spiritual sons and daughters as kings and queens of righteousness, a title (see JS quote above) needed to enter into his presence (Alma 13). This is because the Melchizedek priesthood is especially associated with the sanctifying power of the Holy Ghost (linked with the celestial world). A scripture which explains this is D&C 121, which states that the priesthood is inseparably connected to the powers of heaven, and that if we offend the Holy Ghost, amen to the priesthood. Notice how the "powers of heaven" is paralleled to, and substituted for, the "Holy Ghost." (In other words, the priesthood is inseparably connected to the Holy Ghost.)

As you read the following verses from Alma 13, consider how the "order of the Son of God" lists the sanctified characteristics of those in His order, ready to enter into the Lord's rest. Only those of a truly Melchizedek nature (connected to God through the Holy Ghost) can offer a prayer able to part the veil into His presence.

> 10 Now, as I said concerning the **holy order**, or this high priesthood, there were many who were ordained and became high priests of God; and it was on account of their exceeding faith and repentance, and their righteousness before God, they choosing to repent and work righteousness rather than to perish; 11 Therefore they were called after this **holy order**, and were sanctified, and their garments were

washed white through the blood of the Lamb. **12** Now they, after being sanctified by the Holy Ghost (celestialized), having their garments made white, being pure and spotless before God, could not look upon sin save it were with abhorrence; and there were many, exceedingly great many, who were made pure and entered into the rest of the Lord their God (his presence). **13** And now, my brethren, I would that ye should humble yourselves before God, and bring forth fruit meet for repentance, that ye may also enter into that rest. **14** Yea, humble yourselves even as the people in the days of Melchizedek, who was also a high priest after **this same order** which I have spoken, who also took upon him the high priesthood forever.

Finally, the name of the last token (given at the veil) is particularly mysterious for some people. Without revealing the specifics, I can give you some general information to ponder that might help you better understand its meaning. Elohim comes from El, which means *strength* in Hebrew, and is also the short form for the name of God. (In the Hebrew Old Testament they are sometimes used interchangeably.) Also, patriarchal is a word meaning "of the Father" or "rule of the father." You might want to consider why this word is reserved for use at this time.

*For more information on the true order of prayer see pgs. 243 and 244

9

Scripture Stories that Celebrate the Endowment Pattern

President Boyd K. Packer, of the Quorum of the Twelve Apostles, has said that the eternal plan of happiness "is worthy of repetition over and over again. Then the purposes of life, the reality of the Redeemer, and the reason for the commandments will stay with [you]."[70] Also, President Ezra Taft Benson declared that we should use "the messages and the method of teaching found in the [scriptures] to teach this great plan of the Eternal God."[71] The scriptures often teach the eternal plan through types and shadows, patterns and similitudes.[72] The next part of this book will examine several scriptures which are replete with the pattern of salvation; the temple endowment. Let's start with a few examples from the New Testament.

- **The Garden of Gethsemane – Endowment Pattern**

In Mathew and Mark's version of Gethsemane we are told that Jesus prayed *to* the Father *three* times with an identical prayer; "O my Father, if it be possible, let this cup pass from me: nevertheless not as I will, but as thou [wilt]." Luke, on the other hand, does not specify that there were three prayers, but instead he divides the Savior's praying into three stages; Christ begins to pray, then an angel appears to comfort him (divine event or promise), and finally, as Christ prays more earnestly, he sweats great drops of blood.

Christ begins to pray   *Telestial*

An Angel comes to comfort him   *Terrestrial*

Christ sweats great drops of blood   *Celestial*

Perhaps we could liken the third stage of Christ's prayer to the third period of all our lives, when sanctification and transformation is possible through strict obedience to the Spirit's voice. This 3rd period is when our faith and desire to obey is ultimately tried and refined. While some of the sins of mankind for which Christ atoned may have occurred in the first two prayers (or in Luke's account, earlier in the prayer), it seems obvious that the final period required increased faith, and was the most difficult and agonizing. Applying these verses to our fallen nature, in our lives we all have impure desires that are more difficult, even with the aid of the Holy Ghost, for us to overcome. Such impurities require the third or more agonizing part of Christ's prayer in Gethsemane when he shed great drops of blood. These tightly held sins surely represent the last of the embedded dross of wickedness that persistently remains in us, and are the most difficult to dislodge from the heart, and which would be impossible to eliminate without the deepest sufferings of the Atonement.

- **Eutychus – "Not a little" Fortunate**

In chapter 20 of Acts, Paul is wrapping up his 3rd missionary journey to the Jew and Gentile. He is returning to Jerusalem from Philippi where he was once beaten with stripes and fastened to the stock in the inner prison (as Christ is fastened to the tree), at which time there was also an earthquake (as when Christ was crucified) which opened all the doors of the prison at midnight. Now in Troas, Paul is involved in another typifying story.

> 7 And upon the first [day] of the week, when the disciples came together to break bread, Paul **preached** unto them, ready to depart on the morrow; and continued his speech until **midnight**. 8 And there were many **lights** in the **upper chamber**, where they were gathered together. 9 And there sat in a **window** a certain young man named **Eutychus**, being fallen into a deep **sleep**: and as Paul was long preaching, he sunk down with sleep, and fell **down** from the **third** loft, and was taken **up** dead.

If we look at the symbolism in this story, we might say that light represents life, whereas darkness (sleep) represents death. Also, the name of the young man, Eutychus, is significant and gives additional meaning to this story. In the Greek it means:

> Εὔτυχος [i. e. fortunate; on accent cf. W. 51; Chandler § 331 sq.], -ov, ὁ, *Eutychus*, a young man restored to life by Paul: Acts xx. 9.*

Eutychus, or fortunate, therefore represents mankind, who also must "sink down" and sleep. The window in this verse symbolizes the same as the doors of the prison in Philippi. Death is a portal that we all must pass through. Eutychus "falls down" from the third loft which represents Christ's three days "going down" into the tomb, or the three periods of mortality. However, as the gospel teaches, such a fall is fortunate. "Except the corn of wheat must fall to the ground and die, it abideth alone: **but if it die it bringeth forth much fruit**" (John 12:24). We read next:

> 10 And Paul went **down**, and fell on him, and **embracing** [him] said, Trouble not yourselves; for his life is in him.

Paul, as a type of Christ, also goes down (condescends) into the outer darkness of midnight and embraces him, affirming that life is in him. The word for "trouble not" in the Greek is *thorubeo,* which means to loudly wail, indicating that probably all the people have also descended into the dark and are incredibly sad about what has happened. As well, the Greek word here for "embrace" is only used once in the New Testament (*sumperilambano),* but is a powerful word meaning to embrace completely, or embrace together around. I am reminded of Hugh Nibley's remarks concerning the word Atonement, and that the concept of "embrace", from the Hebrew *kaphar,* best describes what the Atonement represents; the "close embrace of the prodigal son."[73] Acts 20 continues:

> 11 When he therefore was **come up again**, and had **broken bread**, and eaten, and talked a long while, even till break of day, so he departed.

They ascend up to the room that is well lit again, out of the darkness, where they renew\celebrate their covenant promises, breaking bread together.

12 And they brought the young man alive, and were **not a little comforted**.

The phrase in the Greek for "not a little" is *ou metriows*, which is best rendered, "without measure." The word for "comforted" is *parakaleos*, which is the root verb for the Holy Ghost, and implies that its (the Spirit's) working is evident. Indeed, having redeemed Eutychus (us) from his fall to death, the redeemed saints are comforted beyond what can be measured!

How fortunate, and how unlikely, is it that one person should fall three stories and live, not to mention that each one of us takes the same plunge. What are the odds that all of humanity should suffer that same fall and be so "fortunate"? Using the King James rendering, I'd say, "not a little" to none. If we were to outline this as an endowment pattern it would look like this:

In the light of upper room – Instructed
    Fall into darkness (death)
        1ˢᵗ story   *Telestial*
        2ⁿᵈ story   *Terrestrial*
        3ʳᵈ story – Embraced by Christ (Paul) *Celestial*
    Ascend through darkness (death)
In the upper room instructed until the light of day

Without this kind of insight this story in Acts 20 might merely be a funny story about how Paul's preaching puts this young man to sleep, causing him to fall to his death. However, against the endowment backdrop it becomes a moving testimony of the Savior, highlighting Christ's descent into death, bringing us to life through his resurrection.

- **Mark 8 – Men as Trees**

In another short story, only a few verses long, this saving pattern is again identifiable. Mark 8 contains the brief account of Christ and a blind man. When Christ heals him, he must put his hands on him twice for the miracle to be complete. Many have asked why it took two tries for Christ to perform this miracle, suggesting that his power had limits. However, it may well be that this miracle was fashioned as it was just to demonstrate the plan of salvation; the endowment. In Mark 8 we read:

> 22 And he cometh to Bethsaida; and they bring a blind man unto him, and besought him to touch him. 23 And he took the blind man by the hand, and led him out of the town; and when he had spit on his eyes, and put his hands upon him, he asked him if he saw ought. 24 And he looked up, and said, I see men as trees, walking. 25 After that he put *his* hands again upon his eyes, and made him look up: and he was restored, and saw every man clearly. 26 And he sent him away to his house, saying, Neither go into the town, nor tell *it* to any in the town.

Notice that the blind man has left his home and gone (fallen) into "the world" (represented by the town). He is on a journey seeking salvation (God's mercy) for his blindness. Upon meeting, we observe that Christ leads the blind man somewhere private, perhaps even sacred, to treat his illness. We are not told that he took him to a mountain (temple) to heal him, but that may have been the case. The man's blindness is a representation of his telestial state. When Christ blesses him the first time, however, he only begins to see (terrestrial). This, of course, is a foretaste or promise of the full light of day to come, and is symbolic of Christ's covenant promises to mankind. Jesus blesses him a second time, whereupon "he was restored, and saw every man clearly" (celestial). With clear vision, he is sent away and returns to his own house where he began. If we were to chart this circuit it might appear as follows:

Outside town – in his house
    Into town – falls
        Blind – cannot see   *Telestial*
            Blessed by Jesus – begins to see *Terrestrial*
        Healed – sees clearly *Celestial*
    Is sent away
Returns to his house

Though short, this story nevertheless preserves important central elements of the endowment. Like the two Melchizedek priesthoods in the temple, this man comparatively receives the first Melchizedek priesthood in the terrestrial and second in the celestial. It is also interesting that Jesus tells him afterwards not to "go into the town, nor tell *it* to any in the town." Though this has generated a lot of speculation, perhaps the best reason for this is that sacred sight of this kind is personally given, and each man must come by this knowledge through a special encounter with Christ, it cannot be borrowed from another; those in the telestial world cannot comprehend such knowledge. As evidence that this is possibly the case, in the very next verse (Mark 8:27) Christ asks his disciples, "Whom do men say that I am." Peter answers, "Thou art the Christ." And, though Mark's gospel does not include the following details, in Mat 16:17 we find, " And Jesus answered and said unto him, Blessed art thou, Simon Bar-jona (son of the dove): for flesh and blood hath not revealed *it* unto thee, but my Father which is in heaven." Then Jesus requests the same thing of his disciples, "that they should tell no man of him." The lesson to both the blind man and to the disciples is that what they know has been revealed to them by the Father, through the Holy Ghost (the dove), which is sacred, personally sanctifying those that have a revelatory knowledge of Christ. Sharing such information with the telestial realm often generates insincere sign-seekers and persecution, something Christ did not want his disciples to endure at this particular time.[74]

- **Three Locations – Shazer, Nahom, Bountiful**

In the Book of Mormon, Nephi documents three locations or camps while journeying with his family in the wilderness (1 Nephi 16). To be sure, Nephi could have documented more encampments during their wilderness travels, but the fact that he gives us only three is perhaps intentional and significant. If we chart these locations using the endowment pattern, we would have the following:

In land of inheritance
    Cross River Laman
        Shazer *(telestial)*
            Nahom *(terrestrial)*
        Bountiful *(celestial)*
    Cross great sea
In promised land

Hugh Nibley has written about the meaning of Shazer, the telestial component. He said:

> The first important stop after Lehi's party had left their base camp was at a place they called Shazer. The name is intriguing. The combination shajer is quite common in Palestinian place names; it is a collective meaning "trees," and many Arabs (especially in Egypt) pronounce it shazher. [75]

From another source (Joseph F. McConkie) we find that in scripture "trees are the symbol for man: Trees represent men: green trees are the righteous, dry trees the wicked (Luke 23:31; D&C 135:6)."[76] Coincidently, Moses' first official encampment with Israel was Elim, which in Hebrew also means trees.[77] Shazer, therefore, would be a good symbol to represent the telestial place of fallen man.

The middle encampment, Nahom, subsequently has a meaning in Hebrew which helps to designate it as the terrestrial part of Nephi's narration. The footnotes of the Book of Mormon tell us what Nahom in Hebrew probably means: "consolation," from the verb *naham,* "be sorry, console oneself" (often transliterated as *nacham*). For related scriptural context, *naham* is used in Psalms 23:4, "Yea, though I walk through the valley of the shadow of death, I will fear no evil: for thou [art] with me; thy rod and thy staff they **comfort** *(naham)* me." Speaking of the Messiah, Isaiah uses *naham* in 52:9-10, "Break forth into joy, sing together, ye waste places of Jerusalem: for the LORD hath **comforted** *(naham)* his people, he hath redeemed Jerusalem." The events at Nahom suggest the same sort of meaning; Ishmael dies and they grieve, are sorry for their rebellion, and afterward are comforted by the voice (words) of the Lord!

Consistent with the endowment pattern, Nahom is the second of three encampments, and is therefore the period in which the Lord should reveal himself and his promises (the light comes up). What happens in Nahom is consequently very similar to what happened to Nephi when he was grieved by his brothers on their second attempt to get the plates (discussed in the next segment). At that time an angel arrived with promises of deliverance and comfort (1 Ne 3). Correspondingly, 1 Nephi 17: 39 relates: "And it came to pass that the Lord was with us, yea, **even the voice of the Lord came and did speak many words (seed) unto them**, and did chasten them exceedingly; and after **they were chastened by the voice of the Lord** they did turn away their anger, and did repent of their sins, insomuch that the Lord did bless us again with food, that we did not perish."

As the last encampment, Bountiful, is perhaps the easiest to assign symbolic understanding. Its meaning in English connotes a place of fruitfulness, easily identified with the celestial period of our mortal journey. In Bountiful Nephi will receive divine communication (on the mount) concerning how to build a celestial vessel capable of taking his family across the great waters to their promised land.

- **Three Items – Bow, Ball, Boat**

Along with the three encampments, Nephi's account is also built around three objects – the steel bow, the liahona, and the ship of curious workmanship. These objects coincide with the three locations we just discussed. If we were to overlay these items on the three places to which they belong, we would have:

In land of inheritance
    Cross River Laman
        Shazer – Bow *(telestial)*
            Nahom – Ball *(terrestrial)*
        Bountiful – Boat *(celestial)*
    Cross great sea
In promised land

The bow is associated with carnal man and Shazer because it was used by Lehi's group to secure food (physical appetite). With it, Lehi's family did not need to rely upon the Lord. Only after the bow is broken do they humble themselves and seek the Lord for direction. (The people in the spacious building of Lehi's dream no doubt still have their steel bows.)

The Liahona is associated with the terrestrial because it represents the word of God (Alma 37:33-34) which the Lord provided to lead Lehi's family. It functioned based on their faith and diligence (as they yielded their hearts to its instruction). It is at the apex because by the power of the Holy Ghost that God's word speaks his love and promises to our hearts; the truth that Jesus is the Christ, our redeemer. It represents the greater light given to Lehi's family – coinciding with the Lord's actual voice also heard while at Nahom.

And finally, the vessel which Nephi is instructed to build in Bountiful was of a celestial nature, of curious workmanship, crafted by special instructions received upon the mount (temple). Significantly, in 1Nephi 17, Nephi wonderfully compares this vessel to the brass serpent of Numbers 21:6-9, which was a symbol of Jesus Christ (to which the Israelites looked and lived).[78] What Nephi wants us to understand, therefore, is that our vessels must also be crafted in the image of Jesus Christ; the only blueprint capable of taking us to the Promised Land. In some regard, the timbers of this vessel are crafted from the wood of the tree of life, which we personally nurture and grow in our hearts (Alma 32).

- **Nephi's Fall Into Jerusalem**

In 1 Nephi 3, Nephi is directed by his father to return to Jerusalem to get the brass plates. This short journey is once again a fractal image of the temple endowment. Nephi begins and ends in the tent of his father, and like the section we just studied, the word of God and its promises, is at the center. As we peel back its layers, this account also contains many figurative elements which deepen our understanding of the Atonement. Reminiscent of Abraham sacrificing Isaac, Nephi makes a difficult decision which has near and long-term covenant implications.

Returning *three* days back to Jerusalem, in verse 3:10 the brothers cast lots to see who will go to the house of Laban to ask for the plates of brass. If we apply the creation\endowment pattern to Nephi's story then we might predict that their first attempt will be unsuccessful, like Noah's first dove that returned with nothing. We might also predict that someone with little appreciation for his spiritual birthright will be chosen, and Laman is an obvious perfect choice. True to the pattern, Laman is unsuccessful; his attempt bears no fruit.

Afterwards Laman and Lemuel are disheartened, but Nephi resolutely declares that they need to be "faithful in keeping the commandments of the Lord" (1 Ne 3:16). When all the brothers return to petition Laban a second time they again fail, fleeing from Laban who steals their "gold, silver, and precious things and seeks to kill them (1 Ne 3:23-26). If we refer to the temple paradigm, and if Nephi and Laban's story is in fact such a presentation, then we might expect a revelatory event or divine promise to occur sometime during this second of three typifying periods. As if on queue, an angel of the Lord appears to the brothers as they are smiting Nephi and Sam (perhaps an allusion to Isaiah 53:1-5; Nephi is "despised and rejected" by his brothers; he is smitten, and bruised):

> 29 And it came to pass as they smote us with a rod, behold, an **angel of** the Lord **came and stood before them**, and he spake unto them, saying: Why do ye smite your younger brother with a rod? Know ye not that **the Lord hath chosen him to be a ruler over you**, and this

because of your iniquities? Behold ye shall go up to Jerusalem again, and **the Lord will deliver Laban into your hands.** 30 And after the angel had spoken unto us, he departed.

The angel repeats to Laman and Lemuel the promise made earlier to Nephi, that he will be a ruler over them (1 Ne 2:22). As we read this we might be reminded of Joseph in Egypt who was promised to be a ruler over his brethren (Gen 37:8). The angel's prediction might have also reminded them of the repeated patriarchal pattern where the younger brother received the covenant promise of birthright and seed; e.g., instead of Cain it was Abel, instead of Ishmael it was Isaac, instead of Esau it was Jacob, instead of Reuben or Simeon it was Joseph, and instead of Manasseh it was Ephraim. Though Laman and Lemuel are apparently oblivious to any of this, the promise from the angel suggests to us a lot about who Nephi represents in this story. Joseph and Moses (who was also told he would be a ruler over his brethren) were ones like unto the Lamb – is Nephi?

In addition, the angel promises them; "go up to Jerusalem again, and the Lord will deliver Laban into your hands." It is interesting that the angel doesn't promise that they will get the plates, which seem to be secondary at this point. Removing the obstacle of Laban has now become the key to securing the plates (the word). In chapter 4 we next read of Nephi's renewed hope and encouragement to his brothers:

> 1 AND it came to pass that I spake unto my brethren, saying: **Let us go up** again unto Jerusalem, and let us be

faithful in keeping the commandments of the Lord; for behold he is mightier than all the earth, then why not mightier than Laban and his fifty, yea, or even than his tens of thousands? 2 **Therefore let us go up**; let **us be strong like unto Moses**; for he truly spake unto the waters of the Red Sea and they divided hither and thither, and our fathers came through, out of captivity, on dry ground, and the armies of Pharaoh did follow and were drowned in the waters of the Red Sea. 3 Now behold ye know that this is true; and ye also know that an angel hath spoken unto you; wherefore can ye doubt? **Let us go up;** the Lord is able to deliver us, even as our fathers, **and to destroy Laban, even as the Egyptians.**

Nephi begins the narration of the *third* attempt to obtain the word of God (the brass plates) by *three* times using the phrase, "Let us go up". Here Nephi also bolsters his brothers' confidence by continuing to develop the angel's reference to Moses, recounting the story of Moses leading their fathers through the parted Red Sea and preserving them in miraculous fashion. Nephi concludes (vs 3) by drawing a fascinating and clear parallel, comparing Laban to Egypt, "the Lord is able to **deliver us, even as our fathers,** and to destroy **Laban, even as the Egyptians**." For Nephi's ancient fathers, Egypt represented captivity, bondage, and death, which symbolism Nephi now categorically equates\parallels to Laban!

In figurative terms, in Nephi's story Laban is a figure of death who is ultimately delivered to Nephi (a type of Christ) that he might in obedience slay him on the third attempt (*third day*), thereby delivering his people. Temporally and spiritually, his family's fruitfulness hangs in the balance. In 1Nephi 4:13 we read the reason why Nephi is divinely constrained to slay Laban, "13 Behold the Lord slayeth the wicked to bring forth his righteous purposes. It is better that **one** man **should perish** than that a nation (mankind) should dwindle and perish in unbelief." The "one man" here is also the "carnal man" in all of us.

During Nephi's third attempt, Nephi walks by faith, as do all who have experienced a revelation of Christ as the promised Savior (*terrestrial*), when a spiritual witness is received and the new man is formed\created. Nephi tells us in Nephi 4:6 – "And I was led by the Spirit not knowing beforehand the things which I should do. Nevertheless I went forth". We are all led in faith to the same place Nephi was led, which is to a confrontation with the Laban (sin,death) within us. If we were to outline this story as a seven-day creation endowment pattern it would appear as follows:

Nephi in tent of father
   Sent into spiritually dead Jerusalem
      Laman (natural man) attempts but fails   *Telestial*
         Angel appears and promises deliverance   *Terrestrial*
            Nephi succeeds, yields to Spirit, slays Laban (sin)   *Celestial*
   Leave Jerusalem
Return to tent of Father

Very much like Gethsemane, Nephi records, "And I shrunk and would that I might not slay him." Reminiscent of the Savior in the garden, Nephi shrinks because of the severity of God's command (much as we shrink to overcome the sin in our lives).

Referring to this event in Gethsemane, in D&C 19:18 we read: "Which suffering caused myself, even God, the greatest of all, to tremble because of pain, and to bleed at every pore, and to suffer both body and spirit—and would that I might not drink the bitter cup, and **shrink**." But just as Christ would do the Father's will and endure the Atonement for all his children, so Nephi faithfully follows the Spirit's constraint, slaying death's figure (Laban), which preserves his posterity. It is wondrous to ponder Nephi's apparent insight into Gethsemane, as well as his willingness (perhaps even eagerness) to also cast himself in the same role as his Savior in the midst of his personal challenge. From Jeffrey R. Holland we read how this also applies to us:

> "A bitter test? A desire to shrink? Sound familiar? We don't know why those plates could not have been obtained some other way—perhaps accidentally left at the plate polishers one night, or maybe falling off the back of Laban's chariot on a Sabbath afternoon drive. For that matter, why didn't Nephi just leave this story out of the book altogether?... It is not intended that either Nephi or we be spared the struggle of this account.

> "I believe that story was placed in the very opening verses of a 531-page book and then told in painfully specific detail in order to focus every reader of that record on the absolutely fundamental gospel issue of obedience and submission to the communicated will of the Lord. If Nephi cannot yield to this terribly painful command, if he cannot bring himself to obey, then it is entirely probable that he

can never succeed or survive in the tasks that lie just ahead.

"'I will go and do the things which the Lord hath commanded.' (1 Nephi 3:7.) I confess that I wince a little when I hear that promise quoted so casually among us. Jesus knew what that kind of commitment would entail and so now does Nephi. And so will a host of others before it is over. That vow took Christ to the cross on Calvary and it remains at the heart of every Christian covenant. 'I will go and do the things which the Lord hath commanded'? Well, we shall see."[79]

As Brother Holland so aptly attests, Nephi's struggle is like Christ's atoning struggle. The bitter choice that each of them must make will have far-reaching consequences; peoples will perish or prosper based upon their decision. And as Brother Holland affirms, their situation is one common to all of us. Will we be obedient and prosper, or will we heed to devil's lies, allow sin to continue in our lives, and perish?

10

Nephi's Temple Endowment

Nephi's first book (1 Nephi) is thought by many to be chiastic, with its center focused on 1 Ne 11, which is the vision of the tree of life.[80] Such an emphasis helps us to understand that the course of Nephi's entire life (both temporal and spiritual) was influenced by this experience. If he had never felt the love of God shed abroad in his heart it is unlikely that he would have endured the trials of leading his family through the wilderness to Bountiful. Without such an experience he would not have gone to the mount where he received divine instruction on how to build a ship (ark) to cross the great gulf. Similarly, we cannot reach the Promised Land or enter the Kingdom of God (Luke 17:20-21), without the same knowledge – we must taste that which is most desirable and joyous to the soul – the voice of His love in our hearts.

Whenever we speak of the tree of life, by association we are also talking about the temple; found in Eden just as it is found in John's end-time vision in Revelation, in God's heavenly temple. It might not be too surprising to find that when we examine Nephi's literary structure (with the tree of life at its center) we discover that it also follows the pattern of the temple endowment, that is, there is a telestial period when Nephi lacks knowledge, followed by the terrestrial when he the receives the divine promise or revelation, followed by the celestial when fruit (seed) of the Spirit is created within him. Below is 1 Nephi, outlined as the endowment:

A Lehi's account of God's throne room (*ch 1*)

    B Depart into wilderness, Nephi told that he will teach brothers (*ch 2*)

        C Death – Laban (prefigure of Christ's Atonement) (*ch 4*)

            D Lehi tells of Israel – centers on Bread (*ch 5*)

                Telestial

                E Ishmael's family – Physical seed (*ch 7*)

                    F Lehi tree of life – not understood (*ch 8*)

                      G Lehi's Olive tree – not understood (*ch 10*)

                          H Nephi's Revelation – Love, Christ (Ch *11-14*)

                              Terrestrial

                      G' Nephi explains Olive tree (*ch 15*)

                  F' Nephi explains tree of life (*ch 15*)

                E' Ishmael (natural man) dies, led by word (*ch 16*)

            D' Nephi tells of Israel – centers on Water (*ch 17*)   *Celestial*

        C' Try to kill Nephi when crossing chaos, water, death, bring down to grave (prefigure of Atonement) (*ch 18*)

    B' Arrive in new land, Nephi teaches brothers Isaiah 48-49 (*ch 19-21*)

A' Nephi's throne room vista (sees one fold and one shepherd, Israel gathered, dwell in righteousness, the Holy One of Israel reigneth)

In chapters 1-10 Nephi is primarily relating his father Lehi's experiences. However, after coming to the tree of life we find a transformed Nephi who is able to explain Lehi's visions; that he is now the leader, teaching and guiding his family. For instance, chapter 1 is an account of Lehi's vision at the throne of God where he is shown "many great and marvelous things," whereas chapter 22 is Nephi's vision of future events surrounding the coming of "one like unto Moses," given to him by the Spirit as he teaches from the brass plates. Nephi here is likely drawing from divine information already revealed to him during the second half of his vision of the tree of life (1 Ne 12-14), or information he received on the mount while in Bountiful. Let's discuss a few more of these telestial to celestial parallels.

B – B'

In 1 Ne 2:17-24, just after departing into the wilderness, Nephi tells us that he desired to know the truth of his father's words, and that the Lord visits him and tells him that if he keeps the commandments he will be a ruler and teacher over his brethren (vs 22). Later this is exactly what happens in 1 Ne 20-22 where Nephi, having just arrived in the new land, teaches Isaiah 48 and 49 to Laman and Lemuel from the brass plates.

C – C'

Here we find events that represent the two deaths that typically bookend the endowment\plan of salvation. If we examine Laban's story typologically, Laban (representing sin) is the one man who must perish so that a nation will prosper and not dwindle in unbelief. This is a type of what Christ's sacrifice did for mankind, and is a symbol of the natural man which must perish in each one of us so that we will prosper. Its parallel, chapter 18 (C') is also a story figurative of Christ's atonement. Like the Jews that bound Christ at the time of the crucifixion, Nephi's brethren bind him. And like the crucifixion the sky grows dark and the earth shakes, or in this case the sea, which churns into a "terrible tempest" and all are about to be perish; they were "about to be brought down to lie low in the dust;

yea even they were near to be cast with sorrow into a watery grave." When Nephi's rebellious brethren realize that they are "about to be swallowed up in the depths of the sea," they repent, loosen Nephi, and he intercedes for them; praying to the Lord he calms the storm. We then read that, "I Nephi did guide the ship, that we sailed again towards the promised land" (vs 23). Overcoming the chaotic sea is a type of overcoming death.

D – D'

In 1 Ne 5, Lehi reads from the just recovered brass plates, in particular about his ancestor Joseph who was, "sold into Egypt and who was preserved by the hand of the Lord, that he might preserve his father Jacob and all his household from perishing with **famine**" (vs 14). In 1 Ne 17 (D'), instead of Lehi, Nephi now gives an account of their ancestor Moses who led the children of Israel out of bondage, through the Red Sea and into the wilderness, where by his word he "smote the rock, and there came forth water, that the children of Israel might quench their **thirst.**" You might pause to ponder for a moment that in these two parallel accounts, one by Lehi (telestial) and one by Nephi (celestial), we have the tokens of the sacrament; Joseph's bread and Moses' water! Nephi in fact uses these terms only once in 1 Nephi, placed in exact parallel symmetry. (See book, And He Spake Unto Me, for more information of these fascinating parallels.)

E – E'

In chapter 7 Nephi returns to Jerusalem to get Ishmael's family; the physical seed (telestial) required to continue Lehi's family line, providing wives and husbands for his sons and daughters. Historically speaking, Ishmael in the bible is the son of Abraham who was not the covenant heir (but who was Isaac). In 1 Nephi, Ishmael is a type\figure of the same thing, the natural or telestial man which must be "put off" as man is celestialized. In Galations 4:22-30 Paul uses this precise imagery for Ishmael. He begins by speaking of creation, "19 My little children, of whom I travail in **birth** again until **Christ be formed in you**. 22 It is written, that Abraham had two sons, the one by a bondmaid, the other by a freewoman. 23 But he *who was* of the bondwoman (Ishmael) was born after the flesh; but he of the freewoman *was* by promise. 24 Which things are an allegory: for these are the two covenants; the one from the mount Sinai, which gendereth to bondage, which is Agar. 28 Now we, brethren, as Isaac was, are the children of promise. 29 But as then he that was born after the flesh (Ishmael) persecuted him that was born after the Spirit, even so it is now." Twice in these verses Paul tells us that Ishmael is allegorically a representation of the flesh. Where did Paul get this interpretation, and is it possible that Nephi came by it from the same ancient source as Paul? Regardless, in D' (chapter 16) Ishmael dies, just as the endowment pattern suggests he should. Indeed, the natural or carnal man is overcome through the Spirit when "Christ be formed" in us; a celestial process.

F – F'

In 1 Nephi 8, Lehi experiences his vision of the tree of life. He offers no explanation of its meaning. However, Nephi desires to see the same vision and understand its meaning. In 1 Nephi 15, after he personally tastes of its fruit, Nephi is able to explain to his brothers the significance of its various elements, something which he previously did not "know."

G – G'

In 1 Nephi 10, Lehi has finished relating his vision of the tree of life and continues to teach his sons; explaining that the Jews would go into captivity, that man was in a fallen state, that the Messiah would come and be baptized, slain, and rise from the dead. Then he tells them that the house of Israel is like an olive tree, "whose branches should be broken off and should be scattered," and that by the word of God Lehi's group also should be led to a land of promise and likewise scattered until the fullness of the Gospel was restored, at which time they would be grafted back into the olive tree and come to a full knowledge of their Redeemer. (We might even see the endowment pattern in this narration).

In chapter 15 (G'), Nephi returns from his own vision of God's love (filled with the knowledge of God), whereupon he finds his brothers still disputing over the meaning of Lehi's words, which he is now (like his father Lehi) able to explain.

H – The Tree of Life

Nephi is changed by the light he receives and the love he feels in his heart at the tree of life. Interestingly, chapter 11 of 1 Nephi is also a marvelous chiasmus. Below is the chiastic center of 1 Nephi 11, which is also the center focus of all 1 Nephi:

J 16 Knowest thou **the condescension of God**?

> K 17 And I said: I know that he loveth his children. 18 And he said unto me: Behold the virgin whom thou seest is the mother of the Son of God, after the manner of the flesh. 19 And it came to pass that I beheld that she was carried away in **the Spirit**; 20 And I looked and beheld the virgin again, bearing a child in her arms. 21 And the angel said to me, behold **the Lamb of God**, yea even the Son of the Eternal Father!

L 21 Knowest thou the **meaning of the tree**?

> > M 22 And I answered him: It is the **love of God** which **sheds abroad** in the hearts of **the children of men (seed).**
>
> > O 23 wherefore, it is **the most desirable** above all things
>
> > And he spake unto me saying
>
> > O' 23 yea, and **the most joyous** to the soul
>
> > M' 24 I beheld the **Son of God** (love) **going forth** among **the children of men (seed);** and I saw many fall down and worship him.
>
> L' 25 And I beheld that the rod of iron, which my father had seen, was the word of God, which led to the fountain of living waters, or to **the tree of life; which waters are a representation of the love of God**; and I also beheld that **the tree of life was a representation of the love of God.**

J' 26 Behold **the condescension of God!**

> K 27 And I looked and beheld the Redeemer of the world, and the prophet who should prepare the way before him. And **the Lamb of God** went forth and was baptized of him; and after he was baptized I beheld the heavens open, and **the Holy Ghost** come down out of heaven and abide upon him in the form of a dove.

J and J', on either side of Nephi's central thought, is perhaps the most stunning parallel in chapter 11. As told in the bible, Nephi sees in verse 18 that Jesus was of divine mortal birth, and in verse 27 (J'), that he was also "born of the water and the Spirit." These verses represent the two births of all our lives, the natural (18) and that of the Spirit (27)! Also note that the Holy Ghost is present in the form of a dove, which we know is *yonah* (Jonah) in Hebrew, the only sign that Jesus gives of his messiahship. Moreover, sandwiched between these two condescension's or births, Nephi relates the details of his own rebirth!

Nephi is asked to answer his own question, "Knowest thou the meaning of the tree?" Without hesitation he replies, "Yea, it is the Love of God, which sheddeth itself abroad in the hearts of the children of men, wherefore it is the most desirable above all things." We might ask, how does Nephi know this? Certainly there is no way that he could have intellectualized that the tree of life symbolizes the love of God. Rather, we must assume that he answers using only what has been "shed abroad" in his heart at that very moment – the beauty of God's love, revealed by the Spirit. (Rom 5:5 – "the love of God is shed abroad in our hearts by the Holy Ghost") Not only is Nephi able to correctly identify the tree's symbolism, but because of the joy which fills his heart, he also knows that it is the "most desirable of all things."

Nephi's vision thus climaxes, defined by what he feels in his soul. And wonderfully, if you are like me, it is hard to read his account and not feel what he is feeling – God's very love shed abroad in our hearts right along with Nephi and the angel! In this way, as our hearts stir, we also "see" the beautiful tree – a tree whose beauty is not experienced outwardly, but one which is felt within.

The tree of life is also spoken of by Alma, who also tasted the joy of its fruit and confirmed Nephi's experience: "I have labored without ceasing, that I might bring souls unto repentance; that I might **bring them to taste of the exceeding joy of which I did taste**; that they might also be **born of God**, and be **filled with the Holy Ghost**" (Alma 36:24) Clearly, tasting of the tree of life symbolizes rebirth – being born of the Spirit and coming to Christ. It is the gateway to the celestial kingdom and eternal life, where the fruit of love is multiplied unceasingly.

11

The Sealing Power of Elijah

The life of Elijah is another wondrous story with the temple endowment (i.e. the plan of salvation) woven into its pages. When we first encounter Elijah in the Old Testament, he is about to "seal" the heavens, which is a concept very much associated with the temple. In fact, in order to understand more fully what "sealing power" is, it makes sense to study Elijah's life. Although nothing is known about him before this event, based on the magnitude of divine power entrusted to him, the Lord seems sure that Elijah will act only according to His will. (This "surety" is an important aspect of sealing power.) Elijah's story begins in 1 Kings 17 and continues for a few chapters until he transfers his prophetic mantle to Elisha (2 Kings 1-2). He is briefly mentioned again in Malachi – "I will send you Elijah the prophet before the coming of the great and dreadful day of the LORD: And he shall turn the heart of the fathers to the children, and the heart of the children to their fathers, lest I come and smite the earth with a curse" (Mal 4:5-6). Malachi's use of "turning the hearts" is not only a reference to future events, but also an allusion to Elijah's mortal life when he returned the hearts of Israel to the Lord's covenant promises during his day (1 Kings 18:37). In 1836 a transfigured Elijah visited Joseph Smith and restored to the earth the same power to seal and unseal the heavens (D&C 110:13-16). However, his short narrative in 1 Kings 17-18 is an exposé which illuminates the fundamental nature of temple sealing power. Below is a review which outlines Elijah's journey, as chronicled in 1 Kings 17-18.

Elijah tells King Ahab the heavens will be sealed, stopping the rain. The word of the Lord tells him to go to the brook Cherith to be fed by ravens. The brook dries up and Elijah is then told to go to Zerephath and that a widow will sustain him. The widow has only a last handful of meal and a cruse of oil. Elijah asks her to give him **water** and to use the last of her meal to make **bread** for him. She does and is told by Elijah that the cruse of oil will not fail, nor the barrel of meal. Before leaving the widow's son dies. Elijah "stretches himself" upon the boy 3 times and his life returns to him. The widow declares to Elijah that the word of the Lord "in thy mouth "is true

Elijah is told in the third year to return to Samaria and that rain would be sent. Elijah returns and tells Ahab (the king) to gather the people to Mt Carmel. Elijah asks the people, "How long halt ye between two opinions," choose Baal or God. Elijah proposes that the priests prepare a sacrifice. He does as well. Both sacrifices are without fire. It is determined that the god who sends fire to consume the sacrifice will be "the God." Baal's 450 priests try all day, but fail. Elijah prepares his altar with 12 stones. Three times he covers it with 4 barrels of water. Fire consumes everything and the people declare – "The Lord, he is the God." They slay the priests at the river Kishon and Elijah ascends Mt. Carmel, "for there is a sound of abundance of rain". While cast on the earth, Elijah's servant goes to the top 7 times to look for rain. On the 7th time he sees a small cloud forming which looks like a hand. The rain returns as Elijah races king Ahab to Jezreel.

- **Descent and Ascension**

Elijah's journey begins and ends in Samaria, making it circular (chiastic) in nature. In between he spends *three* years divided into *three* separate locations, each location having spiritual significance. Below is Elijah's journey as it parallels our mortal journey (the endowment) that we have examined several times in this book, which is also the pattern of our life.

With king

    Heavens sealed – no rain

        Cherith – fed by unclean ravens   *telestial*

            Zarephath – widow's bread and water,   *terrestrial*
            a resurrected son

        Carmel – Baal defeated with fire   *celestial*

    Heavens unsealed – rain

With king

In a spiritual sense, the three years of no rain is analogous to the three days of Christ's death and resurrection to new life. Certainly, at the end of three years previously apostate Israel declares that the Lord is God (they are resurrected from a spiritually dead state). More precious than the return of rain is what it symbolizes, the spiritual "water of life" available again to believing Israel.

- **Cherith (telestial)**

Cherith from the lexicon means:

כְּרִית (" separation"), [*Cherith*], pr. n. of a stream to the east of Jordan, 1 Ki. 17:3, 5.

[81]

Having descended into mortality, like Elijah we are also in Cherith, "separated" from the presence of our Heavenly Father. And, also like Elijah, we are fed by the unclean ravens, which bring us flesh morning and evening, feeding our carnal condition. The spiritual water from the brook will eventually dry up in such a fleshy place, as it did for Elijah. In Hebrew the word for raven is *oreb*, which stems from its color, meaning darkness (a condition of the place Cherith).

- **Zarephath – refining light (terrestrial)**

The center or second stage of our mortal journey is a revelation of Christ, which in Elijah's story is expressed through the lowly widow of Zarephath. As a widow, she is the least in society with seemingly the least to give, only a small measure of meal. The tokens of Christ are revealed as the widow provides water and uses her last handful of meal to make bread for Elijah. Fittingly, for her sacrifice she is promised a barrel of meal and cruse of oil that <u>will not waste</u>, implying eternal provision (eternal life). Her selfless actions bring into focus Christ's life and teaching, which is why it is perhaps no coincidence that Christ begins his ministry referring to her exemple, standing to read on the Sabbath.

> Luke 4:24 And he said, Verily I say unto you, No prophet is accepted in his own country. 25 But I tell you of a truth, many widows were in Israel in the days of Elias (Elijah), when the heaven was **shut up** (sealed) three years and six months, when great famine was throughout all the land; 26 But unto none of them was Elias sent, save unto Sarepta, [a city] of Sidon, unto a woman [that was] a widow.

The proud Jews in Nazareth are angered by Jesus' suggestion that Elijah "unsealed" the heavens for an unclean widow (given endless provision), while they were "shut up" against Israel, for which they seek to kill him (just as Israel sought to kill Elijah in his day). Unfortunately, because their hearts are "shut up" they do not understand how the widow's selfless love prophetically anticipated the Savior's gift to all men. In rejecting the widow's example, they reject Christ's new covenant. The sealing (and unsealing) of heaven is truly connected to the "love of God shed abroad" in one's heart (1 Ne 11:22), prerequisite to divine power.

Zarephath's meaning in Hebrew also adds a wonderful dimension to this story:

> צָרְפַת (perh. "workshop for melting and refining metals," Schmelzhütte), with ה parag. צָרְפָתָה, [*Zarephath*], pr. n. of a town of the Phœnicians situated between Tyre and Sidon, 1 Ki. 17:9, 10; Obad. 20; Gr. Σάρεπτα, Lu. 4:26; now called صرفند.

We might be reminded of the verses from Malachi where we are told how a converted and redeemed Israel will be refined as precious metal, able to reflect the Refiner's image when its impurities are removed:

> Mal 3:2 But who may abide the day of his coming? And who shall stand when he appeareth? For **he [is] like a refiner's fire** *(tsaraph)*, and like fullers' soap: 3 And **he shall sit [as] a refiner** *(tsaraph)* **and purifier** of silver: and he shall purify the sons of Levi, and purge them as gold and silver, that they may offer unto the LORD an offering in righteousness.

The Hebrew root for Zarephath (*tsaraph*) is the same Hebrew word used in these Malachi verses. (This is also the verb used at the center of Psalm 105, where Joseph is "tried" by the word, which was also a hinge upon which Israel's history turned [see next chapter]) Wonderfully, the widow of Zarephath's loving actions reflect (like purified metal) the Savior's sacrifice. As the widow gives her last full measure for another, she reveals Christ, as well as the refining secret of God's sealing power, which is that those who are "sealed his" (Mosiah 5:15) must love (as He loved). In giving one's life to God and others, we are sealed unto life eternal (or as Elijah's story indicates – the heavens are unsealed).

In addition, in Zarephath there is another foreshadow of Christ. Before Elijah leaves, the widow's son dies, and Elijah brings him back to life. This example of rebirth is done by Elijah "stretching" himself on the boy, which is perhaps reminiscent of the mercy seat, which "covers" sin (death). Since Elijah does this *three* times, it is also a marker which prefigures Christ's resurrection after three days in the tomb. The son's resurrection foreshadows the Son of God's (Christ's) resurrection, as well as the many lives that are about to be raised from spiritual death (after three years) in Carmel. Sealing power, the power of life over death, which is demonstrated on a personal scale in Zarephath, will be amplified as Elijah unseals the heavens in Carmel, giving life to many.

- **Mt Carmel (celestial)**

As previously mentioned, the *third* phase of our mortality is a fruitful place where man walks in faith, reborn and capable of producing fruit of the Spirit. For instance, the third place recorded

135

on Lehi's patriarchal journey to the Promised Land was Bountiful, which Mt Carmel parallels. From the Lexicon we find:

> (1) *a garden, a place cultivated as a garden, planted with fruit trees, herbs, corn*, etc. (Kimchi, מקום אילנות פירות ושדות תבואה), sometimes used in opposition to a desert, sometimes to a forest ; Isaiah 29:17, "Lebanon is changed into a garden, and the garden shall be a forest;" Isa. 32:15, 16; Jer. 2:27, " I brought you forth אֶל־אֶרֶץ הַכַּרְמֶל into a land like a garden, that ye might eat the fruit thereof," Isai. 10:18; 16:10; Jer. 48:33; 2 Ch. 26:10; with suff. בַּרְמִלּוֹ 2 Ki. 19:23;

Spiritually armed with a revelation of Jesus Christ ("reflected" by the all-consuming sacrifice of the widow in Zarephath), Elijah is now prepared to overcome the worldly forces of darkness represented by the priests of Baal. To accomplish this, Elijah builds an altar (much like Nephi who faithfully builds a boat in Bountiful) and calls down sanctifying fire from heaven. The 450 priests of Baal, who represent the worldly system of false worship, attempt to do the same thing, but cannot. After God's fire from heaven is poured out and consumes the sacrifice (a symbol of the cleansing power of the Holy Ghost), they are taken down to the river and slain, which is reminiscent of Phinehas who obeyed God's word and also slew the worshippers of Baalpeor, a sacrifice which the Lord called "an atonement", and for which he was given an everlasting priesthood (Num 25:5-13). Likewise, by Elijah's actions, the evil of Baal (worldly sin) is destroyed; Israel is cleansed and prepared for the blessings of heaven to be sealed upon them.

- **Bread and Water – The widow's sign, Christ's sealing tokens**

Finally, like the endowment there is a sign given which relates to the celestial sign\token received in the temple. Elijah sends a servant to the top of Mt Carmel to look for a *sign* of the coming rain. The servant goes up 7 times (creation, completeness, perfection) before seeing the token of renewal and fruitfulness, a small cloud shaped like a hand. Poignantly, this image also portrays the elements of the sacrament – the cloud which brings **the water**, shaped as the hand of the widow which gave **the bread**! The sign which unseals the heavens plainly alludes to Elijah's request to the widow: "Fetch me, I pray thee, a little **water** in a vessel, that I may drink. And as she was going to fetch [it], he called to her, and said, Bring me, I pray thee, a morsel of **bread in thine hand**." (1 Ki 17:10-11) When the widow willingly releases what little (which is all) she holds in her hand to Elijah (God Jehovah) it is a revelation of Christ's future selfless sacrifice, assuring that there will be **bread** that never wastes and living **water** springing up into everlasting life (Jn 4:14). The tokens of Christ's sacrament revealed in the story of Elijah's widow remind us of Christ's atoning words, "not my will, but thine, be done". We might wonder if perhaps on the night of the last supper, as Jesus shared the bread and poured the wine, did he also think of the widow's extended hand and its last full measure? As he instructed his disciples (that by these tokens they should remember him) did he reflect upon Elijah's sign that unsealed the heavens, also a token of His obedience and love?

The "forerunner" (like Elijah) to releasing God's provision and fruitfulness is always charity – the pure love of Christ which never faileth. By it, the sealing power of the priesthood is operable – "Let thy bowels also be full of charity towards all men, and to the household of faith, and let virtue garnish thy thoughts unceasingly; then shall thy confidence wax strong in the presence of God; and the doctrine of the priesthood shall distil upon thy soul as the dews from heaven. The Holy Ghost shall be thy constant companion, and thy scepter an unchanging scepter of righteousness and truth; and thy dominion shall be an everlasting dominion, and without compulsory means it shall flow unto thee forever and ever." (D&C 121:45-46)

* Important Notes

- The word in Hebrew that is used to describe the widow's measure of seed is *melo,* which means "a fullness". In the verb form it is the word also used for "to consecrate". For instance, Aaron was consecrated (*malo*) and sanctified by Moses to be a priest. When the priests would bring a handful (*melo*) of flour, mixed with oil and spices to the altar before the veil in the temple, it would rise as a sweet-smelling savor unto the Lord (Lev 2:2). Gideon's consecrated (*malo*) 300 were chosen because they filled their hands (*melo*) with water to drink. Symbolically, their hearts were also a sweet-smelling savor before the Lord. (You might also recall that in the story of Gideon, there were also two emblems given by the Lord to assure them of victory – the **water** which determined the consecrated 300, and the barley **bread** which in vision rolled through the Midianite camp [Judges 7:14]!)

- We cannot be "halt between two opinions" (Elijah's words to the Israelites in 1 Ki 18:21) and be a priest in God's kingdom. Sealing power is all about heaven's surety that man will give all of himself\herself to God. That is power in the priesthood, upon which all eternal blessings hinge. As the widow gave all, so the covenant of consecration (the celestial covenant) made in the temple requires "all" – and that is also exactly how much of Elijah's sacrifice was consumed in Carmel – "all", even the rocks! The temple covenants that we keep in Carmel (the celestial kingdom) releases the blessings of fruitfulness sealed up to those who consecrate all they have, even their last handful of meal. In Carmel (celestial), reflecting Christ's selfless sacrifice and possessing sealing power of the Spirit, we can call down fire from heaven and defeat the worldly priesthood of Baal in our lives.

- When Malachi, in 4:5-6, speaks of Elijah's fiery return, he may be using Elijah's widow of Zeraphath (refining fire) as his source, a powerful example of how Malachi's prophecy of Elijah is fulfilled? The widow's loving example is the purest meaning of having your "heart turned" (by the fire of the Holy Ghost), and surely what she offered in her hands to Elijah was not just the last of her meal, but it was her heart; a fitting symbol of heavenly sealing power which rose in clouds over Carmel.

- The story of Elijah is a patterned story of our personal plan of salvation. Saving Israel was dependent on the widow and her sustaining portion of meal, given to Elijah because of her faith. If Elijah had gone to Zarephath and the widow had refused to die for him (which is pretty much what she agreed to), the implication is that he would have perished. And if he had perished, who would have released the rain after three years? Oh, you say, well the Lord would certainly have made other plans. The fact is that there is only one plan for man's salvation, and there is no other. Abraham didn't refuse to offer his only son, Judah didn't fail to offer his life for Benjamin, Jonathan interceded with his life for David, the widow's life and her son's for Elijah, and Christ his life for ours – all of whom preserved the covenant. Ultimately, all covenants are fulfilled in this way, or not at all. It is how we are true and faithful. God has no backup. Such devotion is the sealing power which binds heaven and earth. It is the power of priesthood – our selfless actions, doing the Father's will in service of others, a reflection of Christ's loving obedience. Not reserved for a special few, all who wish to enter God's presence must be possessed of it.

12

Song of Joseph and the Lamb

Surprisingly, the first psalm in the Bible is not found in the Book of Psalms, nor was it written by David. In fact, the first psalm is the Song (Psalm) of Moses found in Exodus 15, which was the inspiration for the "Song of Moses and the Lamb" heard by John at the throne of God in Revelation 15, and by Lehi in 1 Ne 1. Several of the later psalms pay tribute to this first. For instance, in Psalm 9:1-3 we read, "I will praise [thee], O LORD, with my whole heart; I will shew forth all thy **marvellous works**. I will be glad and rejoice in thee: I will **sing praise** to thy name, O thou most High. When mine enemies are turned back, they shall fall and **perish** at thy presence." These beautiful verses include many of the elements of the Song of Moses – e.g. singing and praise, marvelous works, the most High, and enemies who perish. It is easy to imagine this psalm as a short remembrance of the Song of Moses.

Psalm 105 is another such example — a stunning song of praise and also a chiasmus. Sections of this psalm are also recorded in 1 Chronicles 16, where we are told they were sung in celebration on the steps of the temple (before the throne of God – an image of Rev 15), and that only those who held the priesthood could participate (king and queens, priests and priestesses – as related in Rev 1:6).

In addition, at the center of this psalm there is an unexpected focus, which leads those who find it to investigate the life of the patriarch Joseph.

Psalm 105

A 1 **O give thanks unto the LORD**;
  B call upon his name: make known his deeds among **the people**.
    C 2 Sing unto him, sing psalms unto him: talk ye of **all his wondrous works**.
      D 3 **Glory ye in his holy name**: let the heart of **them rejoice** that seek the LORD. 4 Seek the LORD, and his strength: seek his face evermore.
        E 5 **Remember his *marvelous works*** that he hath done; *his wonders*, and the judgments of his mouth; 6 O ye seed of **Abraham his servant**, ye children of Jacob his chosen.
          F 7 He is the LORD our God: his *judgments are in all the earth.*
            G 8 He hath **remembered his covenant** for ever, the word which he commanded to a thousand generations. 9 Which covenant he made with **Abraham,** and his oath **unto Isaac**; 10 And confirmed the same unto **Jacob** for a law, and to Israel for an everlasting covenant:
              H 11 Saying, Unto thee **will I give** the land of Canaan, the lot of your inheritance:
                I 12 When they were **but a few men in number**; yea, very few, and strangers in it.
                  J 13 When they **went from one nation to another**, from one kingdom to another people;
                    K 14 He **suffered no man** to do them wrong: yea, **he reproved kings** for their sakes; 15 Saying, **Touch not mine anointed**, and do my prophets no harm.
                      L 16 Moreover he called for a famine upon the land: he brake the whole **staff of bread**.
                        M 17 He sent a man before them, even **Joseph**, who was sold for **a servant**:
                          N 18 Whose feet they hurt with fetters: he was **laid in iron:**
                            19 Until the time that his **word** came: the **word** of the LORD tried him.
                          N The king sent and **loosed him**; even the ruler of the people, and **let him go free**.
                        M 21 He made **him lord of his house**,
                      L and ruler of all **his substance**:
                  K 22 To **bind his princes** at **his pleasure**; and **teach his senators** wisdom.
                J 23 Israel also came into Egypt; and Jacob **sojourned in the land** of Ham.
              I 24 And **he increased his people greatly**; and made them stronger than their enemies.
            H 25 He turned their heart to hate his people, to **deal subtilly** with his servants.
          G 26 He sent **Moses** his servant; and **Aaron** whom he had chosen. 27 They **shewed his signs among them, and wonders** in the land of Ham.

> F 28 *He sent darkness, and made it dark; and they rebelled not against his word. ²⁹He turned their waters into blood, and slew their fish. ³⁰Their land brought forth frogs in abundance, in the chambers of their kings. ³¹He spake, and there came divers sorts of flies, and lice in all their coasts. ³²He gave them hail for rain, and flaming fire in their land. ³³He smote their vines also and their fig trees; and brake the trees of their coasts. ³⁴He spake, and the locusts came, and caterpillars, and that without number, ³⁵And did eat up all the herbs in their land, and devoured the fruit of their ground. ³⁶He smote also all the firstborn in their land, the chief of all their strength.*
>
> E *37 He brought them forth also with silver and gold: and there was not one feeble person among their tribes. ³⁸Egypt was glad when they departed: for the fear of them fell upon them. ³⁹He spread a cloud for a covering; and fire to give light in the night. ⁴⁰The people asked, and he brought quails, and satisfied them with the bread of heaven. ⁴¹He opened the rock, and the waters gushed out; they ran in the dry places like a river.* ⁴²For he **remembered his holy promise, and Abraham his servant**.
>
> D 43 And he brought forth his people **with joy**, and his chosen **with gladness**:
>
> C 44 And **gave them the lands of the heathen: and they inherited the labour**
>
> B of **the people**; 45 That they might observe his statutes, and keep his laws.
>
> A **Praise ye the LORD**.

In verse 19 the psalmist climaxes hundreds of years of Hebrew history, from Abraham to Moses, to a somewhat unexpected center; "the word came, and the word of the Lord tried him." As we are about to investigate, there is more to this than meets the eye. But first, just a couple of notes regarding some of these parallels:

> In verse 44 the Lord gives the land of Canaan (promised land) to Israel, which act is called a "wondrous work" in its parallel, verse 2. (C,C')

> Verse 5 admonishes the seed of Abraham to remember his "marvelous works" and "wonders", and verses 37-42

143

lists the miracles of Israel's sojourn in the wilderness. (E,E')

Verse 7 reminds us that his "judgments are in all the earth", and its parallel verses 28-36 list all of the judgments or plagues wrought upon Egypt. (F,F')

Verses 8-10 mention the patriarchs before Israel's fall into Egypt (Abraham, Isaac, Jacob), and its parallel verses 26-27 designate the prophets when leaving Egypt (Moses, Aaron). The everlasting covenant in verse 8 is perhaps also compared to "signs" and "wonders" in verse 27. (G,G')

In verse 11, whereas the Lord is "giving" Israel covenant land, in its parallel verse 25, Pharaoh is "dealing subtilly" with Israel to take away their inheritance. Obviously, this parallel is antithetical. (H,H')

In verses 14-15 the Lord "reproves kings", and "suffers" no man to touch his anointed prophets In its parallel verse 22, Joseph has the power comparable to the Lord's; to "bind princes" and "at his pleasure" to teach senators wisdom. Curiously, prophets are paralleled to senators. (K,K')

- **The Psalmist's word – Joseph's visions and dreams**

Like the Song of Moses in Exodus 15, Psalm 105 celebrates a familiar song of deliverance. But instead of Moses' crossing the Red Sea, the "marvelous work" centrally highlighted is a surprising allusion to the dreams and visions of Joseph, which is comparable since Joseph and Moses are saviors, deliverers, and types of the Lamb. Below is a reprint of the apex:

> 17 He sent a man before them, even **Joseph**, who was sold for **a servant:**
> 18 Whose feet they hurt with fetters: he was **laid in iron:**
> 19 Until the time that his **word** came:
> the **word** of the LORD tried him.
> 20 The king sent and loosed him; even the ruler of the people, and **let him go free**.
> 21 He made him **lord of his house**,

Before "the word" comes to Joseph he is sold for a servant and laid in iron (*telestial*), but after the word "tried him" (*terrestrial*) he is set free and becomes lord of the ruler's house (*celestial*); a surprising 180 degree reversal. You may ask, "What incident does verse 19 refer to, and how did the word try Joseph?" Clearly, the psalmist is pointing to a particular scriptural event as the focus of this entire psalm so that those who read it, if not familiar, will inquire. The answer is found in Gen 40, which is the story of the chief baker and the chief butler (*mashqeh* – a cupbearer, literally "one bringing drink"). There we find that Joseph's release from prison is linked to the divine words given in dreams to these two who are also in prison. In fact, only because he can correctly interpret the dreams, is he ultimately released. In order to better understand his prison experience, let's first look at some other important events in Joseph's life.

Joseph's life will be influenced by 3 sets of double dreams. As a matter of fact, many events of Joseph's life are doubled. For instance; Joseph goes to Dothan (which means two wells) to find his brothers; Joseph's brothers device two plans to get rid of him; they also propose two plans to later return to Egypt with Benjamin; the brothers take two trips to Egypt; in Joseph's personal dream there are 11 sheaves and 11 stars for a total of 22 – double 2; when the brothers come to Egypt they bow down twice; Joseph is in prison twice; he waits two years in prison after the butler is freed; Joseph's story involves two coats – one of many colors and the one that Potipher's wife took (both of which get him into trouble); Joseph has two sons – Ephraim and Manasseh; Ephraim means double fruitfulness; Joseph will be buried at Machpelah – which means "a doubling". Also, though Joseph is not the traditional firstborn, he is given a double portion inheritance from Jacob (1 Chron 5:2), presumably because he is the firstborn spiritually.

Though there are many more such occurrences, we should look at one in particular. When Rachel prophetically named Joseph, she derived it from two words *yasaph* (to add) and *asaph* (to gather away). Joseph's name, therefore, has a double meaning, and is a paradoxical expression – "by taking away, I am added to". If you remember, Rachel was barren before Joseph was miraculously born. In her joy Rachel pronounces the reason for Joseph's name – "And she conceived, and bare a son; and said, God hath **taken away (*asaph*) my reproach**: And she called his name Joseph; and said, The LORD shall **add to (*yasaph*) me** another son" (Gen 30:23-24). Joseph, like his mother, will experience remarkable and miraculous reversals of fortune in his life. Events that at first seem impossibly tragic become great blessings. In fact, the paradoxical heart of the gospel is embodied in Joseph's name, which is that "whosoever will save his life shall lose it: but whosoever will lose his life for my sake, the same shall save it."

Next, an important clue to understanding the butcher and the baker's dreams is found when Joseph later interprets Pharaoh's dreams. At that time Joseph tells pharaoh *twice* that his two dreams are really one dream.

> Gen 41:25 And Joseph said unto Pharaoh, **The dream of Pharaoh [is] one**: God hath shewed Pharaoh what he [is] about to do. 26 The seven good kine [are] seven years; and the seven good ears [are] seven years: **the dream [is] one**.

This follows the pattern of Joseph's name – two meanings that are one name. And, if we examine the earliest dreams in Joseph's story, they could also be interpreted as one dream (Gen 37:5-11) because they essentially repeat the same message twice; that he will rule over his brothers. If you recall, in his first dream his brother's sheaves bow to his sheave (perhaps representing the earthly or present fulfillment), and in the second dream the "stars" bow to his star (representing a celestial fulfillment to come later). Applying this same pattern, though the dreams in prison are given to two, the baker and cupbearer, they are really one dream. In a prophetic sense they foretell the "one" who offers both the bread and the cup of wine. Jesus Christ, as the provider of the bread of life, will be hung on a tree, but as the cupbearer of living water He will also resurrect and be restored to his position at the right hand of the Father (as Joseph is at the right hand of pharaoh). Indeed there is only one, the divine Son of God, who can do such seeming opposites – die yet live. In death's prison Jesus is the falsely accused cupbearer and baker, but as the first fruits of the resurrection he is the promise of redemption and life — "Though he were dead, yet shall he live (Jn 11:25)! **In a very significant and symbolic way, Joseph is saved by the wine of the cupbearer and the bread of the baker, and of course, so are we! Joseph's release from prison depended on these covenant emblems, as does ours! Only because he knew their proper interpretation was he set free, as we can also be!**

Each week as we partake of the sacrament emblems, our hearts are likewise tried by the word of God, which proclaims that there is one who can save us, who died yet lives. And so, our accurate interpretation of the bread and wine (water) is confirmed in how we live our lives, which pattern is attested in the life of Joseph – taken away I am added to. Truly, if we would save our life, we must lose it (Mk 8:35); that is His and our covenant (sacramental and temple) commitment.

O what a marvelous scriptural exodus we have taken! Our table has truly been set with a double portion. Pointing us toward the double patterns of Genesis 36-41, the psalmist has centered his unique song of Moses on the incomparable hinge of Joseph, "one" like unto the cupbearer and the baker, Christ! A scriptural and spiritual double portion! We may not have seen the Red Sea part, but like those who sang upon the shore celebrating such a marvelous wonder, I feel my heart swell to sing the same redeeming song of love! Like Alma, our soul is expanded and illuminated by the light of the everlasting word (Alma 5:7,9), and I feel perhaps as though I were an angel, singing with Lehi upon the sea of glass before the throne – great and marvelous are thy works, Lord God Almighty!

- **Joseph's double chiasmi**

Joseph's first dream (when his brothers' sheaves bowed down to his sheaves) depends upon and only becomes reality because of the second set of dreams. What at first appears unfortunate, that Joseph is put in prison, is quite the opposite, and in fact is the means for Joseph's ultimate rise to a powerful appointment in Egypt. This fortunate turn of events is what Joseph tells his brothers when later revealing his identity, which is that if he hadn't been sold into Egypt then there would have been no one to prepare the way for their salvation (Gen 45:5).

It shouldn't surprise us, then, if the life of Joseph has two primary patriarchal\endowment chiasmi! First, lets' look at the chiastic outline of the narrative that we have just examined, which is based on Joseph's *three* dreams:

Joseph's first dreams. The brothers reproach Joseph. *Telestial*
Joseph's dreams bear no fruit.

Joseph interprets the dreams of the cupbearer and baker. Tokens of a promised atoning sacrifice is revealed when dream is properly interpreted

Pharaoh's dream interpreted. As ruler over the bread *Celestial*
of Egypt Joseph is doubly fruitful – preparing in 7 years
what they will use for 14!

It should be noted that Joseph never offers an interpretation of his first double dream. It is as if at that point he is unable to interpret dreams. Only with the 2nd and pivotal dream do we know for sure that Joseph has divine understanding, which is consistent with the patriarchal pattern. The third phase is also very consistent with this pattern. Joseph, exercising faith, is fruitful, in fact **doubly so as he produces in seven years enough food for fourteen!**

The other key narrative of Joseph's life was presented by Stephen to the Sanhedrin (which we already looked at in chapter 6 of this book). We needn't be confused by a different center, and in fact should almost expect it because of Joseph's double portion. Below is from Acts 7:9-16.

Brothers first sent for wheat (seed), meet
but do not know Joseph, not fruitful   *Celestial*

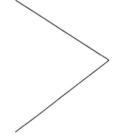

Brothers sent second time; Joseph is made known, (their redeemer, Christ). Explains that being sold into Egypt was good thing.   *Terrestrial*

All of the kindred (seed) called by Joseph
into Egypt, they multiply, and are given lands
and cattle (fruitfulness)   *Celestial*

I am led to ponder how much of this was Jesus aware of during his mortal ministry? Since he had received a fullness of the Spirit at his baptism, perhaps as he studied the life of Joseph he was illuminated to see these same ideas. Or, had his mortal father Joseph, named after the same Joseph of Egypt, taught him the lessons that we have just learned? At the Passover supper, as He broke the bread and passed the cup, did He reflect upon Joseph's story (as perhaps he also reflected on Elijah's widow), and how in that moment it was a fulfillment of ancient prophecy and dream? We can only imagine!

13

Moses 1 – Christ's Mission Prefigured in the Story of Moses

Moses 1:39 reveals the Lord's desire for mankind, "For behold, this is my work and my glory, to bring to pass the immortality and eternal life of man." From the council in the preexistence, Christ was chosen and designated as the instrumentality for how this would be accomplished. His atoning sacrifice is the center piece of the plan of salvation; an act of redemption ordained to break the bands of sin and death, both spiritual and physical.

To the degree that we understand Christ's mission we better understand our own life's purpose as we seek to follow him. For a moment let's turn to the *journey* of Moses in the Pearl of Great Price. In the Book of Moses, we read that Moses is taken up into a high mountain and there receives instruction from the Lord. We might remember that in scripture the mountain is a symbol for the temple where we also receive similar instruction concerning our life's purpose (the plan of salvation). In this setting Moses was told that his life would be a pattern (similitude) of the Savior's:

> 1:6 And I have a work for thee, Moses, my son; and **thou art in the similitude** of mine Only Begotten; and mine Only Begotten is and shall be the Savior, for he is full of grace and truth; but there is no God beside me, and all things are present with me, for I know them all.

As Moses, our lives are also a likeness of Christ's, and as Moses, the Lord also has an eternal work for us. However, God first qualifies and deepens Moses' faith, which is also a figure of our mortal test.

> 9 And the presence of God withdrew from Moses, that his glory was not upon Moses; and Moses was left unto himself. And as he was left unto himself, **he fell** unto the earth.

After Moses has "fallen", descending below all things, we learn that he begins to comprehend his carnal nature and lowly stature without God:

> 10 And it came to pass that it was for the space of many hours before Moses did again receive his **natural strength like unto man**; and he said unto himself: Now, for this cause I know that **man** is **nothing**, which thing **I never had supposed**.

As spirits in God's presence there were many lessons or "things" that we (like Moses) had "never supposed", all of which we experience by our own fall into mortality. In a fallen world, alienated from God, Moses next encounters the proud owner of Lehi's "great and spacious" building, the prince of this world:

> 12 And it came to pass that when Moses had said these words, behold, Satan came tempting him, saying: Moses, son of man, worship me.

13 And it came to pass that Moses looked upon Satan and said: Who art thou? For behold, I am a son of God, in the similitude of his Only Begotten; and where is thy glory, that I should worship thee?

14 For behold, I could not look upon God, except his glory should come upon me, and I were transfigured before him. But I can look upon thee in the natural man. Is it not so, surely?

15 Blessed be the name of my God, for his Spirit hath not altogether withdrawn from me, or else where is thy glory, for it is darkness unto me? And I can judge between thee and God; for God said unto me: Worship God, for him only shalt thou serve.

16 Get thee hence, Satan; deceive me not; for God said unto me: Thou art after the similitude of mine Only Begotten.

17 And he also gave me commandments when he called unto me out of the burning bush, saying: Call upon God in the name of mine Only Begotten, and worship me.

18 And again Moses said: **I will not cease to call upon God**, I have other things to inquire of him: for his glory has been upon me, wherefore I can judge between him and thee. Depart hence, Satan.

Though a fallen man (natural man, verse 14), Moses retains a divine spark, (the light of Christ which is given to all men, Jn 1:9), whereby he is able to discern darkness from light. When Satan demands to be worshipped, Moses also remembers the first commandment – to serve only God. Reflecting his telestial state and lack of knowledge, Moses states that as he has "other things to inquire" of God. Notice here that he twice commands Satan to depart, but he does not call upon God to do so.

In the next verses we see that Satan does not give up easily:

> 19 And now, when Moses had said these words, Satan cried with a loud voice, and ranted upon the earth, and commanded, saying: I am the Only Begotten, worship me.
>
> 20 And it came to pass that Moses began to fear exceedingly; and as he began to fear, he saw the bitterness of hell. Nevertheless, calling upon God, he received strength, and he commanded, saying: Depart from me, Satan, for this one God only will I worship, which is the God of glory.

Sowing seeds of confusion (mixing the fruit of the tree of life with that of the forbidden, calling evil good and good evil) Satan again tempts Moses to worship him, this time deceitfully proclaiming himself to be the Only Begotten (a false messiah with a counterfeit salvation). During this second encounter, however, Moses receives divine strength from God (i.e. a greater portion of the Spirit). He declares that he will be *true and faithful* in worshipping only "this one God" (takes God's name upon himself). Also, notice that unlike the first time, here Moses calls upon God when he demands that Satan depart.

Finally, we read of a third encounter where Moses is further strengthened and at last delivered:

> 21 And now Satan began to tremble, and the earth shook; and Moses received strength, and called upon God, saying: In the name of the Only Begotten, depart hence, Satan.
>
> 22 And it came to pass that Satan cried with a loud voice, with weeping, and wailing, and gnashing of teeth; and he departed hence, even from the presence of Moses, that he beheld him not.

Reminiscent of the temple endowment, in the "name of the Only Begotten," Satan is ultimately cast out. Notice that here, for the first time, Moses invokes this name to rebuke Satan.

Overcoming the world (natural man), Moses is then filled with the Spirit (fruitfulness\bountiful):

> 24 And it came to pass that when Satan had departed from the presence of Moses, that Moses lifted up his eyes unto heaven, being filled with the Holy Ghost, which beareth record of the Father and the Son;
>
> 25 And calling upon the name of God, he beheld his glory again, for it was upon him; and he heard a voice, saying: Blessed art thou, Moses, for I, the Almighty, have chosen thee, and thou shalt be made stronger than many waters; for **they shall obey thy command as if thou wert God.**

Moses, who has overcome the powers of hell through the name of the Only Begotten, is reborn and also chosen. He is given a promise

– a celestial covenant that his command will be obeyed, "as if thou wert God"! Because Moses has been faithful while journeying in the mists of darkness, God entrusts him with the sealing powers of heaven! (Notice that the Father is now mentioned in verse 24, approximating the same sequence as the endowment.) Moses is also promised:

> 26 And lo, I am with thee, even unto the end of thy days; for thou shalt deliver my people from bondage, even Israel my chosen.

Moses is a "similitude" of Christ and is given the same commission as Christ, to "deliver my people from bondage", which is perhaps our great work\purpose\mission as well. We descend into mortality to walk for a time in the darkness of this world, to be tempted by Satan, who offers a counterfeit plan of happiness (founded on the acquisition of things, titles, and pleasures). As we overcome his unending enticements to worship the world and instead obey God's command to serve him only, and as we take the name of the Only Begotten upon us, the Spirit can fill our hearts and minds, we are reborn and become divinely directed instruments to deliver God's "chosen" (those around us – our friends and families, even those who have passed on) from the world's bondage; to partake of the tree of life. As we love and serve others, we worship and serve our God (Mosiah 2:17).

There is nothing in Moses' experience that we can expect to avoid. Like him, we will "fear" and doubt, and become acquainted with the bitterness of sin and hell, as if passing through a refiner's fire. However, if we are to return to God's presence, if our command is to be as if it "wert" from God, then the sealing power that binds all of God's covenant promises to us must be matched by the equal "surety" of our abiding faithfulness, which surety is that we will always do the Father's will, not our own. Such trials in a fallen world reveal and shape our true character.

In fact, for a moment, consider the story of Peter in the New Testament, who was also told that his command would be "as if thou wert God." In Mathew 16 Christ asks Peter who He, the Son of Man, is. The Spirit reveals to Peter that Jesus is the Christ, and Peter is given the keys of the kingdom of heaven being told: "and whatsoever thou shalt bind on earth shall be bound in heaven, and whatsoever thou shalt loose on earth shall be loosed in heaven." However, within just a few verses we read words of another sort. Christ tells Peter, "get thee behind me Satan, for thou savorest not the things that be of God, but those that be of men." Obviously, Peter is still being prepared and taught, as Moses was, how the power to seal heaven and earth works. We might wonder, how has Peter exhibited the mind of Satan instead of Christ's? When Christ explained that he would suffer many things, die, and rise on the *third* day, we are told that Peter – "took him, and began to rebuke him, saying, Be it far from thee, Lord: this shall not be unto thee." Like many of us, Peter has momentarily forgotten (perhaps like Eve) how the plan of salvation works. Jesus poetically explains his and our mission within this great plan:

> Mat 16:23 And he said to [them] all, If any [man] will come after me, let him deny himself, and take up his cross daily, and follow me. 24 For whosoever will save his life shall lose it: but whosoever will lose his life for my sake,

the same shall save it. 25 For what is a man advantaged, if he gain the whole world, and lose himself, or be cast away?

Christ savored the cross and the weight of the Atonement for others, selflessly serving those he loved. By comparing his cross to ours (to be taken up daily), the Savior clearly illustrates that our purpose\mission is to be a "similitude of the Only Begotten" (Moses 1:6). If you are like me you hear these words and have a longing to follow Him, to put off the natural man, to lose your life serving God. Why, then, is it so difficult to remember and act accordingly? Undoubtedly, it is meant to be a struggle, just as it was for Moses. (Christ, in "similitude" is also tempted three times by Satan in Mat 4.) As Satan demands that we worship him, using the invasive and subtle avenues of the media, pop culture, the internet, peer pressure, and so on, we must not cease to call upon God in the name of the Only Begotten. By ourselves we cannot prevail. To save our life we must lose it first to the only true and living God.

We have been called to do a mighty work, like unto Moses, and like unto the Savior himself. New names, white raiment, heavenly powers, divine son-ship, and the tree of life are all reserved for the overcomer (Rev 2:7-3:21), those who have been born again, are filled with the Spirit and have given to God the only thing that they truly have power to give – their hearts filled with his love. All covenant blessings and promises (baptismal and temple) that we would have sealed by the Holy Spirit of Promise hinge on this "surety" (see the story of Judah's surety in Gen. 44:32).

- **Chiastic Outline of Moses' Creation Story**

As we have done previously, Moses' fall from the light to darkness and re-ascension could be presented in nearly the same chiastic\endowment pattern of seven:

Moses is in presence of God. Beholds his glory and creations (vs 1-8)

  God withdraws from Moses, he falls to earth, loses spiritual eyesight (vs 9-11)

    Satan tempts Moses, wants to be worshipped. Unable to cast out Satan (vs 12-18)

      Satan tempts Moses again; Moses receives strength (Spirit) as he calls on God in name of Only Begotten (vs 19-21)

    Satan departs and Moses is filled with the Holy Ghost. He begins to behold God's glory, given promises (vs 22-26)

  Discerns earth with spiritual eyes (vs 27-29)

God's full glory upon Moses, stands in presence of God, is instructed concerning creation (vs 30-42)

Interestingly, the debated question throughout the entirety of this story concerns the identity of the Only Begotten. For instance, early on Moses is told that he is in the similitude of the Only Begotten (vs 6). After he falls, Satan comes the first time and asks to be worshipped, at which time Moses' defense is that he is in the similitude of the Only Begotten and was told to call upon God in the name of the Only Begotten (vs 17). When Satan returns the second time he falsely declares that he is the Only Begotten and demands to be worshipped (vs 19). Only when Moses actually invokes the name of the Only Begotten (because he is strengthened by the power of the Holy Ghost) does Satan permanently depart (on the third command). As Moses returns to God's presence (vs 25) he is promised that his command will be "as if thou wert God", which is another way of stating that Moses is now truly a similitude of the Only Begotten. In verses 26-41 Moses then "discerns by the Spirit" all the inhabitants of the earth (even as he did when he first fell to earth [vs 8]). Finally, the glory of God is upon Moses fully as he talks with Him "face to face" (vs 31). Moses is shown God's glorious creation and told, "by the power of my word have I created them, which is mine Only Begotten Son, who is full of grace and truth" (vs 33).

The pattern of Moses' fall and ascension is seven steps, as are the days of creation, a parallel which indeed Moses is next shown. Though we see the physical creation first in the modern temple, it is nonetheless significant that Moses is also shown it, albeit in second position. Consider the days of creation as outlined in Moses 2:

Earth without form, Light shines (divided) out of darkness
    Water divided above (heaven) and below (earth)
        Dry land divided from water, lower life appears, grass and herbs yield fruit
            Lights in firmament appear, Sun divided from lesser lights
        Waters told to bring forth abundantly, birds in firmament (above) appear
    Man created (above) and given dominion over (divided from) the beasts (below)
The Lord God sees that his creation is good, sanctifies (divides from others) 7th day.

The pattern of temporal creation is remarkably similar to the pattern of Moses' spiritual creation. For instance, proceeding in an orderly fashion, only enough light is initially given to bring forth the lower forms of life (telestial), while greater forms (celestial), including man, appear after the light of the Sun appears (terrestrial) at the apex – one side antithetical to the other.

You'll also notice that something is divided on each day, a trademark of how creation works (especially in the natural world). As mentioned earlier, the Hebrew word used in Genesis 1:1 for create is *bara*, which means to divide.[82] If you think about it, starting at the cellular level, life begins with division, and fruitfulness is a process of greater division. Also worthy of consideration is the fact that the Hebrew word for covenant, *berith*, is formed from this verb *bara*, which means to create\divide a covenant, and covenants play a role in how we are created spiritually. Nested in ordinances, covenants sift and divide us from the world; as tools to prove if we are "true and faithful." On the seventh day (to which all creation leads) the word "sanctify" is used, which in Hebrew is *qadash*, meaning to be consecrated or set apart,[83] which signifies being divided from all wickedness and corruption. To wit, this is what the Lord is saying in D&C 84:20-22 in the Oath and Covenant of the Priesthood. "Therefore, in the ordinances thereof (with their covenants), the power of godliness is manifest. And without the ordinances thereof, and the authority of the priesthood, the power of godliness is not manifest unto men in the flesh; For without this no man can see the face of God, even the Father, and live." In other words, by obedience\faithfulness to covenant promises (provided in ordinances) we grow (are created) spiritually. Only to such a righteous, godly, and sanctified (divided) people will God eternally manifest himself. Accordingly, the Lord later says in verse 33 of section 84, "For whosoever is faithful unto the obtaining of these two priesthoods of which I have spoken (and their covenant promises), and the magnifying their calling, are sanctified by the Spirit unto the renewing of their bodies." Though the sentence order here might cause us to think that we are sanctified by the Spirit AFTER we are faithful and magnify our calling, in fact the Spirit is the catalyst to spiritual creation and is the power which enables us to magnify our covenant calling – not something that we are rewarded with after we have, by our own efforts, attempted to magnify them.

Finally, covenants are designed as tools to bring us into closer relationship with our covenant partner, who is God. In love he upholds his promises, and in turn we move closer to him as we express our love for him by doing what he has asked of us (Jn 15:10-14). As in any relationship, we do for those we care for. Doing nothing indicates a lack of relationship. The amount of commitment in any relationship or covenant is readily measured by the amount of doing by either party. God daily gives us his Spirit to be our constant companion. For our part, we move closer to God as we yield to its enticings.

14

King Benjamin at the Temple – Son of the Right Hand

A book about the temple wouldn't be complete without including King Benjamin's speech. In Mosiah 2-5 King Benjamin calls his people to the temple to put them under covenant and to give them a new name, which are elements that we associate with our modern temple endowment. In order to prepare them to enter into a covenant, King Benjamin will first teach them the plan of salvation, which is also what happens in (and is a primary purpose of) the modern temple endowment (see quote from Gordon Hinckley on Pg 9). Touching upon consecration several times, the general theme throughout his discourse is selfless service – Christ-like sacrifice for others.

Which raises an interesting question: from dispensation to dispensation, when the endowment is upon the earth, must the presentation of the temple drama be word-for-word the same, or is a general sense of the same thing (the plan of salvation) adequate? King Benjamin's speech, regardless of how it varies from the modern endowment, is still a gift of saving knowledge sealed with covenant promises. As well, there is also anecdotal evidence that other temple related things were said which were not necessarily recorded. For instance, in his speech there are echoes of the creation account from Genesis, which was available on the brass plates. If we do a word analysis on the use of the phrase "creation" or "create," we find that Mosiah 2-5 has the highest usage of these words in the Book of Mormon, suggesting that a fuller creation account may have been discussed at or near the time of King Benjamin's temple discourse. (See Mosiah 2:20, 21, 23, 25, 4:2, 9, 12, 21.) Below is a graph with this analysis.

Creation, Create

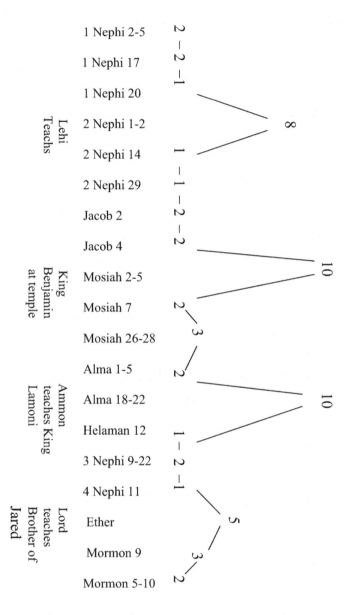

From the preceding chart we see that the other incident with high usage is Alma 18-22, where Ammon and Amulek are also teaching the plan of salvation (the endowment paradigm), just as our missionaries do today (see pgs 15-20).

- **King Benjamin's Endowment Outline**

King Benjamin has called his people to the temple, and they arrange themselves as families around its perimeter. Mosiah then records King Benjamin's instructions. Chapter 2 contains his words, whereas chapter 3 is the words given to him by an angel. For this reason, we might deduce that chapter 2 represents the telestial, whereas chapter 3 is the terrestrial. Of course, when we get to chapter 4, we would expect to find instruction relating to celestial things.

Telestial – Chapter 2 has several parts; verses 1-9 they gather to temple; verses 10-19 King Benjamin reports on **his service** as king; he tells them that he has lived a life of service. Verses 20- 25 are about creation; also that man is as dust of the earth. In verses 26-31 he announces his coming death and Mosiah as the new king, and in verses 32-40 he warns them of their mortal condition and the efforts of the devil to lead them astray (the telestial condition)

Terrestrial – Chapter 3 is a revelation of the promised Christ. Verses 1-10 read very much like Nephi's vision concerning **Christ** (1 Ne 11); celebrating his future birth, ministry (**service**), atoning sacrifice, death and resurrection. Verses 10-20 are about Christ's atoning blood. The word "atone" or "atonement" is used several times. In verse 19 we read how we become "saints through the atonement", which is to put off the natural (telestial) man by yielding to the enticings of the Spirit. (According to John Welch this is the exact center of King Benjamin's speech; see pg. 174-175.) The term "put off" means to take off a garment, in preparation to "putting on" or being endowed with Christ through the Holy Ghost. Verses 24-27 repeat the warning of remaining in a fallen sinful condition.

Celestial – Chapter 4 is about sanctification through the Spirit by those who have received King Benjamin's message of salvation through Christ. The people fall to the earth, recognize their carnal condition and cry out for mercy and to be purified. The Spirit of the Lord comes upon them. King Benjamin speaks of growing in the "knowledge" of Christ, and that since they have tasted of God's love (come to the tree of life), and since he has poured his Spirit out upon them, they should love and **serve one another, consecrating** their substance to "feed the hungry, clothing the naked, and visiting the sick."

Chapter 4 affirms the truth that knowledge of God is evidenced by loving others. Dedicating one's "substance" (consecration) is subsequently a main course of discussion in Mosiah 4:15-26, which we are told is the means whereby we can "remain guiltless," and "retain a remission of your sins from day to day" – a celestial recipe. If we outline these three chapters based on service, the temple pattern is easily observed:

>Ch 2 People receive king's service   *telestial*
>   Ch 3 Christ's service and sacrifice   *terrestrial*
>Ch 4 People give loving service   *celestial*

It is important to note that service alone cannot sanctify, but rather, service is a result (a fruit) of spiritual rebirth. Serving without this important component is like Adam's telestial obedience, not capable of saving or transforming him (see pg 8).

- **Chapter 5 – At the Veil, Prepared to enter the Father's Presence**

In Mosiah chapter 5 King Benjamin pauses and asks his people if they have understood and agree with his message concerning God's saving plan. We read, "And they all cried with one voice, saying: Yea, we believe all the words which thou hast spoken unto us; and also, **we know** of their surety and truth, because of the Spirit of the Lord Omnipotent, which has wrought a mighty change in us, or in our hearts, that we have no more disposition to do evil, but to do good continually." In the modern temple endowment something similar occurs – just before we enter into the Father's presence we go to the veil to repeat all that we have learned (names, signs, tokens). It is a time to recommit to each covenant that we have made, and a time to "cry with one voice," as King Benjamin's people, that we also "believe all the words which have been spoken unto us," that "**we know** of their surety and truth, because the Spirit of the Lord Omnipotent has wrought a mighty change in our hearts; and that we have no more disposition to do evil, but to do good continually." Certainly, in order to be "true and faithful" in all things (keeping our covenants), such a spiritual change\transformation must occur.

King Benjamin's people are also put under an all-encompassing covenant. In verse 5 they say that they "are willing to enter into a covenant with our God to do his will, and to be obedient to his commandments **in all things** that he shall command us, all the remainder of our days" (vs 5). While we make more covenants in the modern endowment, the covenant to be "obedient in all things" evokes our highest covenant – consecration of all that we are and possess, superceding all other covenants. Again we might ask – if the endowment's purpose is accomplished (the participants are empowered and enlightened) when the plan of salvation is taught, regardless of exact wording (liturgy), can the number of covenants also vary as long as the those placed under covenant commit all they possess (substance, heart, mind, soul) to build God's kingdom of love?

At this time, King Benjamin's people mention something else about the celestial state they are in. In verse 3 they say, "And we, ourselves, also, through the infinite goodness of God, and the **manifestations** of his Spirit, **have great views of that which is to come;** and were it expedient, we could prophesy of all things." This wonderfully alludes to the heavenly temple scene in Revelation 15, where John writes about a heavenly people dressed in white before the throne of God. "2 And I saw as it were a sea of glass mingled with fire: and **them that had gotten the victory** over the beast, and over his image, and over his mark, and over the number of his name, **stand on the sea of glass,** having the harps of God. 3 And they sing the song of Moses the servant of God, and the song of the Lamb, saying, Great and marvellous are thy works, Lord God Almighty; just and true are thy ways, thou King of saints.4 Who shall not fear thee, O Lord, and glorify thy name? for thou only art holy: for all nations shall come and worship before thee; for thy judgments **are made manifest**." This is the same song that Lehi hears when he visits God's temple in 1 Nephi 1. Originally, the Song of Moses was sung by the Israelites in Exodus 15 after they had miraculously crossed the Red Sea; a saved, redeemed, and newly created people – an image remembered and celebrated in heaven forever.

Similarly, in the modern endowment, when we assemble before the veil, prepared to enter God's presence, we are a reflection of the celestial group in Revelation 15. Assembled in a circle before the veil of God's temple, we are "them that have gotten the victory of the beast;" we are those dressed in white who sing the Song of Moses and the Lamb (who is Jesus Christ), the song of salvation; we are those who glorify his holy name in the true order of worship. We are told in modern-day scripture that the sea of glass is a Urim and Thummin, which allows those before God's throne to "**have great views of that which is to come,**" so that it would be possible to "prophesy of all things." Concerning the Urim and Thumin and the sea of glass, in D&C 130 we read, "7 But they reside in the presence of God, on a globe like a sea of glass and fire, **where all things for their glory are manifest, past, present, and future,** and are continually before the Lord. 8 The place where God resides is a great Urim and Thummim. 9 This earth, in its sanctified and immortal state, will be made like unto crystal and will be a Urim and Thummim to the inhabitants who dwell thereon, whereby **all things** pertaining to an inferior kingdom, or all kingdoms of a lower order, **will be manifest to those who dwell on it**;"

Finally, King Benjamin gives the people a new name and tells them, "for behold, this day he hath spiritually begotten you (created by the Spirit); for ye say that your hearts are changed through faith on his name; therefore, ye are born of him and have become his sons and his daughters." (Mosiah 5:7) In other words, King Benjamin's people have "become" newly created; are spiritual creations in Christ. There is intertextual help available concerning the significance of the "new name" given at this time. In Revelation 3:5

(also part of a temple pattern; see pg 269) we read about those who have received the new name: "He that overcometh, the same shall be **clothed in white** raiment; and **I will not blot out his name** out of the book of life, but **I will confess his name before my Father**, and before his angels." Notice that the goal of the endowment, modern or ancient, is to bring us to the Father, which is done only through Christ (who confesses our name, telling the Father of our worthiness). To that end, King Benjamin's final remarks celebrate the "new name" by which they have been created, which will allow them/us into the Father's kingdom. Notice, that like Rev 3:5, King Benjamin also speaks of "blotting out" a name; in this case Christ's name from our hearts, which effectively blots our name out of "the book of life." These verses are also chiastic:

9 And it shall come to pass that whosoever doeth this (**serve**) shall be found at the right hand of God, for he **shall know the nam**e by which he is called; for he shall be called by the name of Christ (**the master**).

    A – whosoever shall not take upon him the name of Christ

        B – must be called by some other name

            C – therefore, he findeth himself on the left hand of God

                D – And I would that ye should remember also, that this is the name that I said I should give unto you

                    E – that never should be blotted out, except it be through transgression

                    E' – therefore, take heed that ye do not transgress, that the name be not blotted out of your hearts

                D' – I say unto you, I would that ye should remember to retain the name written always in your hearts

            C' – that ye are not found on the left hand of God,

        B' – but that ye hear and know the voice by which ye shall be called,

    A' – and also, the name by which he shall call you

13 For how **knoweth a man the master** whom he has not **served**, and who is a stranger unto him, and is far from the thoughts and intents of his heart?

If we cast our minds to Eden, we might remember that although Adam and Eve had been "created" in the image of God, because of their transgression their names were "blotted out" of Eden. These words compare (are a type of) our probation to theirs, admonishing us to remain at the tree of life where God's love abounds, because those found at the left (at the other tree) are "far from the thoughts and intents" of God's heart, not "retaining the name written always in their hearts." To some degree this describes Eve's state as she saw (and imagined) that the other tree was "good for food, pleasant to the eyes, and desired to make one wise" (Gen 3:6). Indeed, such a spiritual course, if yielded to, is destruction and the opposite of creation; a reason for the fall and a need for restoration.

- **King Benjamin – Son of the Right Hand**

There are other considerations which make the preceding chiasmus astounding. In verse 9 we read that the righteous will be found on the "right hand" of God, which is a wordplay in Hebrew because Benjamin in Hebrew means **son of the "right hand"**! Being on the right hand is linked in verses 13 (and its parallel verse 9) to the idea of "knowing" the master and serving him. This harkens back to Mosiah 2:17 where King Benjamin said of service, "When ye are in the service of your fellow beings ye are only in the service of your God." To be sure, we know God as we love and care for others.

The connection of "right hand" and "knowing God" has an extra-fascinating biblical connection. In Matthew 25 we read *three* parables about **knowing** God, which are also Christ's last parables (see pg 211). The first is about the ten virgins, which ends when the 5 foolish virgins are told by the bridegroom that they never **knew** him (for if they had their lamps would have been full of the oil of the Spirit and God's love). The next parable in Matthew 25 is about the talents. In its climax the unfaithful servant, who buried his talent of love and service, in error insists that he **knew** his master, saying that, "he was a hard man, and reaped where he did not sow," which of course is not true, because those who know the Lord **know** that he is kind and merciful, always reaping where he sows. Last is the story of the sheep which go to the **right hand**, and the goats which go to the left. Again, this parable pivots on "knowing God." We are told that the sheep of the right hand are those that saw their brethren naked and clothed them, hungry and fed them, in prison and visited them. When they are told that they had actually done this to the Lord, the **right hand** sheep say that they have not met the Lord (do not know him), to which the Lord replies, "Inasmuch as ye have done it unto one of the least of these my brethren, ye have done it unto me." (Mat 25:40) The surprise here is that it had to be explained to them that they in fact **knew** God! (Christ's words concerning service here in Mathew 25:40 are almost exactly King Benjamins' found in Mosiah 2:17, which we read on the last page.) In both cases, personal care for others brings intimacy with God, i.e. knowledge of God depends on one's love for others.

As well, both Christ (in Mat 25) and King Benjamin (in Mosiah 5) finish with the same conclusion. Matthew 25:45-46 tells us, "Then shall the King say unto them on his right hand, Come, ye blessed of my Father, inherit the kingdom prepared for you from the foundation (*creation*) of the world: And these (of the left hand) shall go away into everlasting punishment: but the **righteous into life** eternal." Similarly, in Mosiah 5:15 we read, "Therefore, I would that ye should be steadfast and immovable, always abounding in good works, that Christ, the Lord God Omnipotent, may seal you his, that **you may be brought to heaven**, that ye may have **everlasting salvation** and **eternal life**, through the wisdom, and power, and justice, and mercy of him who *created* all things, in heaven and in earth, who is God above all."

King Benjamin's utilization of the Hebrew meaning of his name (son of the right hand) is fascinating, but as remarkable is his parallel equating service to knowledge of God, which aligns so perfectly with Christ's explanation of what it is to "know" him. Moreover, consider again a few seminal verses which tie together this idea of knowing God, love of fellow man, and rebirth. John 17:3 tells us that life eternal is to know God, and 1 John 4:7-8 defines what it is to know God, "Beloved, let us love one another: for love is of God; and every one that loveth is born of God, and knoweth God. He that loveth not knoweth not God; for God is love."

- **King Benjamin's Over-arching Chiasmus**

We owe a great debt of gratitude to John W. Welch for his work on chiasmus in the Book of Mormon. One of his most interesting studies is an examination of the overarching chiastic structure of King Benjamin's speech. This study is available online at the BYU Maxwell Institute web site. I highly recommend that you read the entirety of his study which charts the astounding complexity and precision of King Benjamin's chiastic thought. For our purposes, however, I will include only his summation which outlines the *seven* parts of King Benjamin's speech-wide chiasmus:[84]

Section 1 (2:9–28) Physical creation

    Section 2 (2:31–41) Accountability, warning against rebellion

        Section 3 (3:2–3:10) Angel Proclaims Christ

            Section 4 (3:11–27) Saint through the Atonement

        Section 5 (4:4–12) Knowledge and power of God

    Section 6 (4:13–30) Curse for not repenting, need to share substance

Section 7 (5:6–15) Spiritually begotten (created) this day

Of course, the reason that I include this information is because it corroborates that King Benjamin is in sync with the creation pattern (symphony) of seven, and the modern temple endowment, which further validates the consistent truth of the Book of Mormon as well as the antiquity of the ceremony practiced in the modern endowment. Though these divisions are not precisely the seven periods advanced in my book, they nonetheless follow the general creation paradigm of telestial (temporal) sections 1-2, terrestrial (revelation of Christ) sections 3-4, and celestial (spiritual) sections 5-7.

At the very center of King Benjamin's speech, Welch identifies the verse upon which this discourse, the inner temple, as well as the plan of salvation, swings. It is same one that has been mentioned several times in this book but is worth repeating – Mosiah 3:19 (Section 4).

> "For the natural man is an enemy to God, and has been from the fall of Adam, and will be, forever and ever, unless he yields to the enticings of the Holy Spirit, and putteth off the natural man and becometh a saint through the atonement of Christ the Lord, and becometh (creation) as a child, submissive, meek, humble, patient, full of love, willing to submit to all things which the Lord seeth fit to inflict upon him, even as a child doth submit to his father."

Viewed chiastically, this verse shows us exactly how\where the fall is reversed within the parameters of the Atonement (c); when the natural man is put off and Christ is put on. It is the intersection of the worldly and the divine (heaven and earth), illustrating to us how the endowment works on a daily basis in our lives. God's desires are made manifest (given dimensionality) into this world when we act upon his impressions, which are like packets of potentiality, releasing the power within us to become the celestial being we truly are.

    (a) They humble themselves
       (b) and become as little children
          (c) believing that salvation is in the atoning blood of Christ;
             (d) for the natural man
                (e) is an enemy to God
                   (f) and has been from
                      (g) the fall of Adam
                   (f) and will be forever and ever
                (e) unless he yieldeth to the Holy Spirit
             (d) and putteth off the natural man
          (c) and becometh a saint through the atonement of Christ
       (b) and becometh as a child
    (a) submissive, meek and humble

Nephi describes this event (God speaking to us through his Spirit) as tasting that which is most desirable and joyful to the soul – His love. It is nested centrally within a speech on service, because it is the driving force of service; a snapshot of the sufficiency of grace and a picture of the Atonement's enabling power; a portrait of God's love around which service orbits – held by its gravity, outside of which our service and good works are vain.

15

Mosiah 15 – Abinadi's Tree of Life

Like 1 Nephi or King Benjamin's discourse, all of Mosiah (30 chapters) can also be expressed chiastically with Mosiah 15 as its nexus:

A King Benjamin exhorts his sons (1:1-8)
 B Mosiah chosen to succeed his father (1:10)
  C Mosiah receives the records (1:16)
   D Benjamin's speech and the words of the angel (2:9-5:15)
    E People enter into a covenant (6:1)
     F Priests consecrated (6:13)
      G Ammon leaves Zarahemla for the land of Lehi-Nephi (7:1-6)
       H People in bondage, Ammon put in prison (7:15)
        I The 24 gold plates (8:9)
         J The record of Zeniff begins as he leaves Zarahemla (9:1)
          K Defense against the Lamanites (9:14-10:20)
           L Noah and his priests (11:1-15)
            M Abinadi persecuted and thrown in prison (11-12)
             N Abinadi reads the old law and old Messianic prophecies to the priests that are about Christ (13-14)
              O How beautiful upon the mountains (15)
             N'Abinadi makes new prophecies about Jesus Christ (16)
            M' Abinadi persecuted and killed (17:5-20)
           L' Noah and his priests (18:32-20:5)
          K' Lamanites threaten the people of Limhi (20:6-6-26)
         J' Record of Zeniff ends as he leaves the land of Lehi-Nephi
        I' The 24 gold plates (21:27, 22:14)
       H' People of Alma in bondage (23)
      G' Alma leaves the land of Lehi-Nephi for Zarahemla (24)
     F' The Church organized by Alma (25:14-24)
    E' Unbelievers refuse to enter covenant (26: 1-4)
   D' The words of Alma and the words of the angel of the Lord (26-27)
  C' Alma the Younger receives the records (28:20)
 B' Judges chosen instead of a king (29:5-32)
A' Mosiah exhorts his people (29:5-32)

[85]

In chapter 10 of this book we examined 1 Nephi as a chapter-wide chiasmus whose pattern demonstrates characteristics of the endowment. Nephi's center-most thought was the tree of life, where he came to **know** God's love as he beheld the "condescension of God" – Christ's birth, baptism, ministry, and sacrificial death. Perhaps we can find something similar at the apex of Mosiah, maybe even another tree of life. Mosiah 15 is Abinadi's discourse about Christ's "seed", those who have tasted of the tree of life, his spiritually begotten sons and daughters who have heard the gospel and are now declaring the "desirable" and "joyous" tidings of God's word. And like Nephi's vision of the tree of life, there are two condescensions which frame or bookend Aninadi's remarks.

As background – in Mosiah 12 Noah's priests try to ensnare Abinadi in his words, whereupon one of them (Alma?) asks him the meaning of Isaiah 52:7, "How beautiful upon the mountains are the feet of him that bringeth good tidings, that publisheth peace; that bringeth good tidings of good, that publisheth salvation; that saith unto Zion, Thy God reigneth!" Abinadi's explanation forever changes one man – Alma, who believes Abinadi's words concerning Christ and who later preserves for us a tribute to Abinadi; the very words which softened his heart and altered the course of his life.

You may recall that the first discussion in the temple prep class is – The Temple Presents the Plan of Salvation, i.e. the plan of redemption. Here in Mosiah 15 we find the highest usage of the word "redeem" in the Book of Mormon – 11 times, denoting a heightened focus on this very subject. Subsequently, whether we realize it or not, since God's plan to redeem\save us is discussed here, so is the temple – a presentation of the same thing. In fact, the center of this chapter is the revelation of a new and saving name.

The following is Abinadi's chiasmus, which is the entirety of Mosiah 15. However, because it requires two pages to view its full length, go to Appendix 9 to see all the detail (along with some additional notes). Still, this abbreviated version is surprisingly accurate:

AA 1 **God himself shall come down,** 2 **dwell in the flesh,** being **the Father and the Son,** 3 The Father because he was conceived by power of God, the Son because of the flesh, 4 They are one God, 5 Suffers temptation, mocked scourged, but yields not.

BB 6 After working mighty miracles, he shall be led, yea, even **as Isaiah said,** as a sheep before the shearer is dumb, so he opened not his mouth. **(Isaiah 53:7)**

                He breaketh bands of death
                   Power to intercede
                      For children of men
a vs 7-9   **Mercy and Compassion**
                    Towards children of men
                 Betwixt them and justice
             Broken the bands of death

                          Who shall be his seed?
                          They shall be his seed
                          Are they not his seed?
                          Holy prophets are his seed
b vs 10-18   They have published **Salvation (Jesus),**
                          And said unto Zion: **Thy God reigneth**
                          How beautiful were there feet
                          How beautiful are their feet
                          How beautiful will be their feet
                          How beautiful are His feet

                      Bands of death broken, Son has power over death
                      Commeth a resurrection
                          Those **who** have been, **who** are, **who** shall be
b' vs 20-23   **Christ (Messiah)** – so **he** shall be called
                          All the prophets, **all** believers, **all** obedient
                      Shall come forth in resurrection
                    Bands of death broken, though Christ they have
                    eternal life

       They that died not having salvation declared
           Have part in resurrection
              Being redeemed of the Lord,
                  Ought to fear and tremble
a' vs 24-28   **None redeemed that rebel against God**
                  Ought ye not to tremble?
              Neither can the Lord redeem such and deny justice
           They have no part in resurrection
       Salvation to be declared to all people

BB '28-30 Yea Lord, thy watchmen shall **lift their voice, shall they sing,** they shall see eye to eye when the Lord shall bring forth Zion. Break forth into joy, **sing** together; for the Lord had comforted his people. **(Isa 52:9)**

AA' 31 The Lord has made **bare his holy arm in the eyes of all** the nations; and **all shall see the salvation** (Yeshua – Jesus) **of our God.** (Isaiah 52:10)

Here we can easily identify four fully developed chiasmi. Further, the two middle chiasmi (b,b') are parallel, as are the outer chiasmi (a,a') – creating beauty and symmetry. Notice that the outside two chiasmi are antithetical, the first (a) centering on the Son's mercy and compassion, and the second (a') telling of His justice, that it lays claim on those who willfully rebel. The two inner chiasmi share a common focus intended to reveal the two names of the Son of God who shall dwell in the flesh – "Salvation" which is the meaning of Jesus' name (b), and "Christ – so he shall be called" (b'), which means Messiah (anointed one). Let's take a look at the greater detail in this chiasmus (b).

Vs 10-18

A 10 And now I say unto you, who shall declare his generation? Behold, I say unto you, that when his soul has been made an offering for sin he shall see his seed. And now what say ye? And **who shall be his seed**?

   B 11 Behold I say unto you, that whosoever has heard the words of the prophets, yea, all the holy prophets who have prophesied concerning the coming of the Lord—I say unto you, that all those who have hearkened unto their words, and believed that the Lord would redeem his people, and have looked forward to that day for a remission of their sins, I say unto you, that **these are his seed**, or they are the heirs of the kingdom of God.

      C 12 For these are they whose sins he has borne; these are they for whom he has died, to redeem them from their transgressions. And now, **are they not his seed**?

         D 13 Yea, and are not the prophets, every one that has opened his mouth to prophesy, that has not fallen into transgression, I mean all the holy prophets ever since the world began? I say unto you that **they are his seed.**

            E 14 And these are they who have **published peace**,
              F who have brought good tidings of good,   Isa 52:7
            E' who have **published salvation**;
              F' and said unto Zion: Thy God reigneth!

         D' 15 And O **how beautiful upon the mountains were their feet!**
      C' 16 And again, **how beautiful upon the mountains are the feet** of those that are still publishing peace!

   B' 17 And again, **how beautiful upon the mountains are the feet** of those who shall hereafter publish peace, yea, from this time henceforth and forever!

A' 18 And behold, I say unto you, this is not all. For O **how beautiful upon the mountains are the feet of him** that bringeth good tidings, that is the founder of peace, yea, even the Lord, who has redeemed his people; yea, him who has granted salvation unto his people;

179

Just as the tree of life was described as beautiful in 1 Nephi 11, Abinadi here describes as beautiful all those who publish his message of salvation. You may recall from chapter 8 of this book (pg 77-79) a discussion of beauty's role in the temple; that our spiritual beautification and creation is the purpose of the covenants we make there; that Aaron's sons were endowed with beautified garments (bonnets, aprons, robes) to serve in the temple, which represented their purity and righteousness. Here in this chapter we encounter again beauty's ever-present role in creation and the gospel plan.

Notice how the four uses of "his seed" in verses 10,11,12, and 13 match the four uses of "beautiful upon the mountain" in verses 15,16,17, and 18! The parallel verses 10 and 18 are particularly interesting. In fact, they are reminiscent of a parallel in Nephi's vision of the tree of life; the beautiful and precious tree parallel to the cross upon which the Son of God was "lifted up for the sins of the world". Here in Mosiah we have the similar parallel, "**his** soul has been made as offering for sin" (vs 10), which reflects "how beautiful upon the mountain are the feet of **Him**" (vs 18).

The center-most thought of the entire book of Mosiah, the inspiration of Abinadi's discourse, is Isaiah 52:7. It is also a wonderful parallelism. Referring to his seed (spiritual offspring) which have been, are, and will be, we read:

> 14 And these are they who have **published peace**,
>   have brought good tidings,
>   who have **published salvation** (Yeshua – Jesus);
>   and said unto Zion: Thy God reigneth!

Though the wicked priests don't understand, here at the center Abinadi prophesies for them the very name of the Messiah – Jesus. Wonderfully, the name Jesus comes from the Hebrew *Yeshua*, which means salvation! (See Mat 1:21) Jesus is the "good tidings" (gospel), is the Prince of Peace, and is the "God that reigneth"! God here is *Elohim*, the Father, which reaffirms Abinadi's opening declaration, that the Father and the Son are one. This is so because when we are born of the Son, we become his spiritual offspring, "heirs of the kingdom of God," (vs 11) and he becomes our Father.

- **A Parallel Center, Revelation of a Another Name**

In the first chiasmus we found a unique series of past, present, and future statements – the beautiful feet of those that were, are, and shall hereafter publish peace. In the second center chiasmus this distinct parallel sequence is repeated. Here Abinadi affirms that those who *have been*, who *are*, and *who shall* believe and keep the commandments, will come forth in the first resurrection. In other words, those with beautiful feet (b) are those who will come forth in the first resurrection (b'), i.e. the same group – both spiritually begotten of Christ. Below is the detail for vs 20-23 (b').

```
A 20 But behold, the bands of death shall be broken
   B and the Son reigneth,
      C and hath power over the dead;
         D therefore, he bringeth to pass the resurrection of the dead.
         21 And there cometh a resurrection,
            E even a first resurrection; yea, even a resurrection
               F of those that have been,
                  G and who are,
                     H and who shall be,
                        I even until the resurrection
                           J of Christ — for so shall he be called.
                        I' 22 And now, the resurrection
                     H' of all the prophets,
                  G' and all those that have believed in their words,
               F' or all those that have kept the commandments of God,
            E' shall come forth in the first resurrection; therefore,
         D' they are the first resurrection.
      C' 23 They are raised to dwell with God who has redeemed them; thus
         they have eternal life
   B' through Christ,
A' who has broken the bands of death.
```

Like the first central chiasmus (b), at the apex of this second a saving name is revealed, that of "Christ – for he shall be called." As previously mentioned, Christ is the Greek for messiah, which in Hebrew means "anointed one." This companion name is important because it identifies Jesus as the prophesied Messiah; his name followed by his title. When Christ begins his ministry, he announces to the Jews in Capernaum this title of Messiah, reading to them Isaiah 61, that "the Spirit of the Lord is upon me, he has anointed me to preach **good tidings**." Wonderfully, "good tidings" is the exact phrase found here in Isa 52:7, spoken of those who have beautiful feet, that they bring "good tidings" of salvation. Noticeably, only those anointed, who the Spirit of the Lord is upon, are "his seed."

Isaiah 61 tells us more about this anointed group, many elements of which are also temple related. In verse 61:9 we read that His spiritual "seed" has been placed under covenant. "8 and I will direct their work in truth, and **I will make an everlasting covenant with them**. 9 And **their seed** shall be known among the Gentiles, and their offspring among the people: all that see them shall acknowledge them, that **they are the seed which the Lord hath blessed**." Further, of this anointed group we read of their beauty, "3 To appoint unto them that mourn in Zion, **to give unto them beauty** for ashes, the oil of joy for mourning, **the garment** of praise for the spirit of heaviness; that **they might be called trees of righteousness, the planting of the Lord**, that he might be glorified." Once beautified we notice that his seed are given a special garment signifying that they are trees of life (Alma 32) and righteousness. Also alluding to the temple, we are told in verse 6 that, "**ye shall be named the Priests** of the Lord: men shall call you the Ministers of our God." Finally, in 61:10 Isaiah speaks again of garments and robes with special significance, "I will greatly rejoice in the Lord, my soul shall be joyful in my God; for he hath clothed me with the **garments of salvation**, he hath covered me with the **robe of righteousness**, as a **bridegroom** decketh himself with ornaments, and as a **bride** adorneth herself with her jewels." The bride\bridegroom relationship again reminds us of covenant ceremony, vows, and taking upon us the Beloved's new name (parallel to the temple).

- **Two Condescensions – Like the Tree of Life**

Mosiah 15's entire structure (pg 178) is marvelously buttressed at both end with quotes from Isaiah 53 and 52. When we look at these book-end Isaiah passages we find that they present a very fascinating antithetical. The first (BB), in verse 6, is from Isaiah 53:7 – "he shall be led, yea, even as Isaiah said, as a sheep before the shearer is **dumb,** so he opened not his mouth." It's parallel (BB'), verses 29-30, comes from Isaiah 52:9 – "with the **voice together shall they sing**; for they shall see eye to eye, when the Lord shall bring again Zion. Break forth into joy, **sing together**; for he the Lord hath comforted his people, he hath redeemed Jerusalem." Silently shorn as a sheep (symbol of shame, loss of covering) Jesus Christ brings our comfort and redemption, for which all nations break forth into joy, given a voice to sing! Whether these were actually the ordered words of inspired Abinadi, or whether we can attribute their artistic arrangement to Alma, these interwoven antitheticals are truly "beautiful", stirring and lifting our minds and hearts.

Finally, also notice that the first five verses of Mosiah 15 are about God's condescension (AA), "God himself will come down among the children of men" in the form of the Son. The parallel to this, verse 31 (AA') is fascinating – Isa 52:10, "The LORD hath made bare his holy arm in the eyes of all the nations; and all the ends of the earth shall see the salvation of our God." Below is a detailed comparison of these two condesensions, and though not previously indicated, both pericopes are chiastic:

A I would that ye should understand that **God** himself
   B shall come down among the children of men,
and shall **redeem his people.**
      C 2 And because he dwelleth in flesh he shall be called
the **Son of God,**
         D and having **subjected the flesh** to the **will of the Father,**
            E being the Father and the Son—
              a 3 The Father,
                 b because he was conceived by the power of God;
              a' and the Son,
                 b' because of the flesh;
            E thus becoming the Father and Son—

            E' 4 And they are **one God,** yea,
            E' the **very Eternal Father** of heaven and of earth.

         D' 5 And thus **the flesh becoming subject** to **the Spirit,**
      C' or **the Son to the Father,**
A being **one God,**
   B' suffereth temptation, and yieldeth not to the temptation, but suffereth himself to be mocked, and scourged, and cast out, and **disowned by his people.**

Next is its parallel, the end of Abinadi's thoughts, which is another version of God's condescension through his Son:

A The Lord
   B hath made bare his holy arm
      C in the eyes of
         D all the nations; and
            D' all the ends of the earth
      C' shall see
   B' the salvation (*Jesus, Yeshua*) of
A' our God.

Let's look at the upper chiasmus first (AA) where Abinadi rehearses the mystery of the condescension or incarnation of God into mortality, providing us with some instructive parallels. For instance, D and D' equate the "will of the Father" to "the Spirit"; i.e. Christ subjected himself to the will of his Father by yielding to the Spirit. This reminds us that we cannot do the Father's will unless we also follow the Spirit's voice. In fact, the role of the Spirit is again emphasized in E,E the center parallel where Abinadi informs us that Jesus was the Son because of the flesh, but that he was also the Father because "he was conceived by the power of God," which power is the Spirit (see 1 Ne 11:19-21, Luke 1:35). The implication for us here is that despite fleshly temptations we must also be conceived of the Spirit (spiritually created or reborn) in order to be his sons and daughters, whereby he becomes our Father. Like the temple, physical creation is also highlighted in the center (E',E') which tells us that Jesus (the Son) is the Father of heaven and earth, its material creator. Further, all of these are miracles – a man who is God, a son who is father, spiritual rebirth, and physical creation. Likewise, B-B' is also enlightening because it discloses the irony of Christ "redeeming his people," which he did even as he was "mocked, and scourged, and cast out, and disowned," by the very people he came down to save.

The second chiasmus here is Isa 52:10 (AA'), which again describes God's incarnation, paralleling "the Lord hath made bare his holy arm" to his dwelling "in the flesh" (AA). This takes on deeper meaning because again we find "salvation," which dually signifies the name of the Son, who is Jesus (*Yeshua*-salvation). The phrase "shall see the salvation of our God" literally refers to seeing the incarnate God, Jesus. Remarkably, the word salvation is used six times in Mosiah 15, the most in the Book of Mormon, supporting the notion that Alma (or Abinadi) is emphasizing its use in order to draw attention to the meaning of Jesus' name. Also, notice the parallel here of "the Lord" to "our God", one being Jehovah and the other Elohim, once again celebrating that the Son is the Father.

- **Abinadi and Mosiah – Significant Names**

In addition to Hebrew poetry and wordplay which emphasize the name of Jesus as the Christ, the Hebrew meanings of Mosiah and Abinadi names are tightly connected with the theme of Mosiah 15 in a wondrous way. Mosiah almost certainly comes from the Hebrew verb *yasha,* meaning "to save". It is the same verb that salvation *yeshua* comes from! From the BYU online omnasticon we find; "The name can be understood as the hiphil participle of the Hebrew root *yš'*, "to save, deliver," with the theophoric element *yāhū*, as shortened form of "Jehovah/Lord."[86] It is a moving analogue to the centerpiece of the book of Mosiah, chapter 15, and a celebration of the plan of salvation through Jesus (*yeshua*) Christ.

Abinadi also has an intense correlation to the theme of his discourse. It is posited that the meaning of his name comes from the Hebrew *abi,* meaning "my father", and the Akkadian *nadi*, which means "is present." Again from the BYU online omnasticon we read: "The suggestion that Abinadi could mean in Hebrew "my (divine) father is present" is made on the basis of the Akkadian nadû, "to throw," which, according to Stamm, is used to indicate presence. . . This meaning would indeed fit the prophet's message, which is that God himself—whom Abinadi calls "Father"—shall come down and be present among men"[87]

- **Beautiful Upon the Mount is Nauvoo**

Before we finish it would be fun to discuss how the name for the modern temple city Nauvoo comes from Isaiah 52:7; and that each time Abinadi says "how beautiful", in Hebrew he would be using *nauvoo*.

It has been noted that Joseph Smith most likely became acquainted with the meaning of the Hebrew word Nauvoo from Dr. Joshua Seixas, a Hebrew instructor who taught the prophet and several others Hebrew at the school of the prophets in Kirtland for several weeks before its dedication in 1836.[88] However, very little has been speculated as to why Joseph might have retained this particular Hebrew word from that instruction. The following is from a Hebrew primer used by Joseph Smith at the school of the prophets in Kirtland, which is perhaps the source of Joseph's introduction to Nauvoo's meaning.

VERBS לָה and לֹא.

§ 53. These verbs sometimes change their ה into י before ו *ye* or *they*, and also in the participle (*Kal*) Act. and passive; as חָסָיוּ *they trusted* for חָסוּ, אָתָיוּ *come ye;* גּוֹלָיָה fem., כָּסוּי (כָּסוּי) *covered,* בְּזוּי (בְּזוּי) *despised.* וּבְזוּי עָם *and despised (of) by people.* See § 80.

The verbs מַחֲוֵי (Gen. 21: 16), רָאוּי, נָאוּי (*nau-voo*) for נָאווּ, are from טָחָה, רָאָה and נָאָה. Verbs לֹא occasionally lose their א; as מָצָתִי from מָצָא, מְלָתִי מְלוּ from מָלֵא, etc.; א is sometimes changed into י; as נְשׂוּי (נְשׂוּי) *forgiven* from נָשָׂא. See § 80.

89

While many of the surrounding Hebrew words shown in the above illustration have definitions, you will notice that there is no definition for "nau-voo". As a beginning Hebrew student, Joseph could have never determined its meaning without assistance, which

187

likely came from Dr. Seixas. Because there is no scriptural reference for nau-voo, Joseph would have never known where to look in scripture for its use, especially since it is conjugated in this exact form only twice in the Old Testament (Psalms 93:5 and Isaiah 52:7). However, there is likely a much better explanation which has nothing to do with this primer. It could be that Joseph was fascinated by the prolific use of Isaiah 52:7 in the Book of Mormon, was inspired by Abinadi's sermon, and that he specifically sought from Dr. Seixas a translation of that exact verse. Or, Joseph, after finishing his training with Dr. Seixas, looked up the Hebrew verses in Isaiah himself at a much later date. It is recorded that during the time of the school of the prophets in Kirtland that Joseph had acquired enough fluency to translate Genesis 17 (March 7, 1836) and Genesis 22 (March 8, 1836) from Hebrew to English.[90] This indicates that he certainly had the ability to at least transliterate the words of Isaiah 52:7, which he could have done at any time up to the migration to Nauvoo.

Regardless, it is easy to believe that when Joseph used Nauvoo to name his temple city in Illinois he knew exactly its scriptural source in the Old Testament, its use by Abinadi in Mosiah 15, and its use by Christ in 3 Nephi. From Dialogue: A Journal of Mormon Thought, Louis Zucker wrote the following:

> "In April, 1839, Joseph Smith, surveying from a hill the wild prospect around Commerce, imagining what he could do with it, thought, "It is a beautiful site, and it shall be called Nauvoo, which means in Hebrew a beautiful plantation." B. H. Roberts comments: "The word Nauvoo comes from the Hebrew, and signified beautiful location:

"carrying with it also," says Joseph Smith, 'the idea of rest.'"[91]

Though Nauvoo is relatively flat, it is fitting that Joseph is "surveying from a hill" when he envisions the name for his city – Nauvoo. The word for mountain in Isa 52:7 in the Hebrew is *har*, which is also the word used for hill. Once it was built, local folk reported that, "the Temple's glistening stone walls could be seen from twenty-miles down river."[92]

When Joseph states that the word Nauvoo has an idea of rest, he is correct. In fact, in the lexicon, rest is listed as the primary meaning for *naah*, the verb from which nauvoo is formed:

> נָאָה not used in Kal, i. q. נָוָה TO SIT, TO DWELL. (Kindred is the Greek ναίω, ναός.) The primitive meaning appears to me to be that of *quiescence*, see Hab. 2:5; Æth. ኀደፈ: to respire, to rest, and it even approaches in meaning to נוּחַ.) Hence נָאָה plural constr. נְאוֹת habitations.

[93]

Notice that Joseph uses the word beautiful "plantation" to describe Nauvoo, which is very similar to "habitations" circled above. More importantly, notice the Greek word *vaos* (pronounced naos) which is also circled, and which we are told is its "kindred." If we look up this Greek word in the lexicon we find:

> ναός, -οῦ, ὁ, (ναίω to dwell), Sept. for הֵיכָל, used of the temple at Jerusalem, but only of the sacred edifice (or sanctuary) itself, consisting of the Holy place and the Holy of holies

[94]

Indeed, Nauvoo refers to not just any beautiful dwelling place, but is connected in meaning to the holy sanctuary of the Lord, the temple! In the Song of Moses (Exodus 15), sung before the throne of God, it begins with the phrase, "The LORD *is* my strength and song, and **he is become my salvation**: he *is* my God, and I will prepare him **an habitation** (*nauvah*)", and ends with its parallel, "thou **hast redeemed:** thou hast guided *them* in thy strength unto **thy holy habitation** (*nauveh*)." In both these verses Moses compares being saved out of Egypt (into a promised land) to being redeemed and brought to the temple of God, his holy habitation. Abinadi affirms these sentiments in his multiple uses of "beautiful" in Mosiah 15, and in particular verse 18, "And behold, for **how beautiful** (*nauvoo*) **upon the mountains** are the feet of **him** that bringeth the good tidings, that is the founder of peace, yea even the Lord, who **has redeemed** his people; has **granted salvation** (*yeshua* – Jesus)"

Isaiah's use of temple imagery also has allusions to the story of Moses on Mount Sinai (Ex 3:5). Moses must remove his shoes when his "feet are upon" the Lord's mountain, for it is holy ground. When Moses removes his dirty shoes (soiled by the world) and touches the ground of God's sanctuary (Naos or Nauvoo), he is made holy. [95] Because God's sanctuary (naos or Nauvoo) is beautiful, that virtue is also transmitted to Moses. Moses then receives instruction, the good tidings of God's plan for redemption and salvation, which he publishes to Israel (as Abinadi chiasmus outlines). How beautiful upon the mountain are the feet of Moses!

In the final analysis, Nauvoo's purpose matches the meaning of its name. Joseph Smith may not have known it initially, but it seems clear in retrospect that Nauvoo was beautiful not only because it was where the living saints (His seed) were being gathered and instructed in righteousness, but because the dead were also about to be gathered. A temple was needed in which to properly perform the work for the dead, and the Lord was clear it had to be done in the temple (naos\nauvoo) and nowhere else (D&C 124:37-44). Completing the temple and beginning the work for the dead would be the last great labor accomplished by the prophet Joseph before his martyrdom, and one of his most important. In that regard, how beautiful are the feet of Joseph Smith, the temple prophet through whom the Lord re-established his holy mountain in the latter days, where men both living and dead can receive divine instruction and worship "in the beauty of holiness" (1 Chron. 16:19) before His throne.

- **Breaking the Bands of Death**

Thus, Nauvoo represents a place where the good tidings are published, to the living and to the dead. Consider the following list of places and people in scripture that are beautiful, where sacred work for the dead was performed – the bands of death were broken:

Name	Meaning	Work for the dead
Shiphrah	beauty	Midwife who saved male babies when Pharaoh ordered them to be put to death (Exo 1)
Nauveh	beautiful habitation	Israel "resurrected" from Egypt, brought out from bondage (Exo 15)
Shunem	double rest (ancient Nain) beauty	Elisha – raises widows son from dead
Nain	beautiful, rest, pasture	Christ – raises widows son from dead

Naaman	pleasant, beautiful	Elisha – restores leper ("the living dead')
Joppa	beautiful	Peter – raises Tabitha from dead
Gate Beautiful	beautiful	Peter – raises man with lame feet at temple. The lame in ancient times could not enter the temple, limiting their access to its saving blessings
Joppa	beautiful	Jonah – his journey begins in Joppa, buried in sea, after 3 days rises to save Nineveh. In a fashion resurrects spiritually dead Nineveh
Naomi, Ruth	beautiful	Boaz – kinsman redeemer who restores Ruth's dead husband's inheritance and family line
Nephi	beautiful	Nephi – raises brother from the dead (3 Ne 7)
Nauvoo	beautiful	Joseph – begins modern work for dead. The Gospel's fullness is again restored.

16

Matthew 11 – Christ's Yoke

In chapter 19 of this book we will examine Moroni's invitation to come unto Christ and be perfected in Him. Matthew 11:28-29, however, is also an invitation to come unto Christ (and take his yoke upon us). Let's explore these verses further to deepen our understanding. To begin, we should first consider the meaning of the verses which precede it, and which reveal its context. Each section in Matthew 11 seems to develop a common theme – spiritual rebirth (creation), transformation from telestial to celestial.

- **The poor are made rich**

When Matthew 11 begins we find John the Baptist in prison wanting to know if Jesus is the Messiah. Christ sends two disciples to John and instructs them to say:

> 5 The blind receive their sight, and the lame walk, the lepers are cleansed, and the deaf hear, the dead are raised up, and the poor have the gospel preached to them.

It is a message of restoration and transformation wherein each miraculous statement is a parallel to the one which precedes it, leading up to the last and perhaps most important wonder.

The blind	→	receive their sight,
and the lame	→	walk,
the lepers are	→	cleansed,
and the deaf	→	hear,
the dead are	→	raised up,
and **the poor**	→	**have the gospel preached to them (they have become rich)**.

193

In the rhythm and logic of the first 5 parallels, which are opposites, the 6th statement (also opposite) in this series infers that the poor have become rich through the gospel! Whereas the first 5 are physical miracles, the last is the great spiritual equivalent, akin to the dead being restored to life, or the blind seeing. D&C 11:7 explains, "Seek not for riches but for wisdom; and, behold, the mysteries of God shall be unfolded unto you, and then shall you be made rich. **Behold, he that hath eternal life is rich**."

- **None greater born of woman – but least in kingdom is greater**

Christ then tells the multitude that John is also more than meets the eye; that he is more than just a prophet which one "goes out into the wilderness "**to see**"; that he is the messenger prophesied to prepare the way of the Lord. However, evidence of this fact is something that one cannot necessarily *see* with the eyes. (Christ uses the phrase "what went ye out to see" three times in verses 7-9 in order to make this point.) Then Christ says something that many have a difficult time understanding:

> 11 Verily I say unto you, Among them that are born of women there hath not risen a greater than John the Baptist: notwithstanding he that is least in the kingdom of heaven is greater than he.

Many wonder, if John is so great, how can I be greater than him? However, this is so because all those in the kingdom of heaven have been born again (of the Spirit), which is a far greater thing than physical birth (being born of women)! Like the preceding section, Christ is again showing his disciples the importance of the spiritual, as opposed to the physical (telestial vs celestial).

- **He that has ears to hear – let him be constrained**

Christ further develops the argument concerning what happens when the gospel is preached. He tells the multitude:

> 13 For all the prophets and the law prophesied until John. 14 And if ye will receive [it or him], this is Elias, which was for to come. 15 He that hath ears to hear, let him hear. 16 But whereunto shall I liken this generation? It is like unto children sitting in the markets, and calling unto their fellows, 17 And saying, We have piped unto you, and ye have not danced; we have mourned unto you, and ye have not lamented.

Those in the market place, which signifies the world (telestial), have heard the gospel message in the law (the first 5 books of the O.T.) and the prophets (Isaiah-Malachi) up until John, but they have not been earnestly seeking, and, because it is spiritual (experienced in the heart), they have not "felt" to dance or mourn. Christ chooses imagery of dancing and mourning because these are things which are heart felt, not necessarily of the logical mind. Christ also likens the gospel to music, saying that it has been piped unto them. It reminds me of Alma's words concerning the song of redeeming love, and how he questions whether those in the church (kingdom of God) have experienced a mighty change of heart (rebirth) and "**felt to sing (pipe) the song of redeeming love**" (Alma 5:26).

In General Conference of April 2015, Elder Wolford W. Anderson gave a wonderful talk on the "Music of the Gospel." He said, "We learn the dance steps with our minds, but we hear the music with our hearts. The dance steps of the gospel are the things we do; the music of the gospel is the joyful spiritual feeling that comes from the Holy Ghost. It brings a change of heart and is the source of righteous desires. The dance steps require discipline, but the joy of the dance will be experienced only when we come to hear the music."[96]

- **They would have repented**

Christ then condemns Chorazin, Bethsaida, and Capernaum for hearing, but not repenting:

> 20 Then began he to upbraid the cities wherein most of his mighty works were done, because they repented not: 21 Woe unto thee, Chorazin! Woe unto thee, Bethsaida! For if the mighty works, which were done in you, had been done in Tyre and Sidon, they would have repented long ago in sackcloth and ashes. 22 But I say unto you, It shall be more tolerable for Tyre and Sidon at the day of judgment, than for you. 23 And thou, Capernaum, which art exalted unto heaven, shalt be brought down to hell: for if the mighty works, which have been done in thee, had been done in Sodom, it would have remained until this day.

As Christ points out, these Israelite cities wherein Christ did his mightiest works (things seen) had not experienced a mighty change of heart (Alma 5:26); they had not been spiritually reborn. Or per

John the Baptist, they have not "brought forth fruit meet for repentance" (Mat 3:8). Christ, John, the prophets, and the law have piped, but they (these cities) have failed to **feel** the gospel in their hearts.

- **Revealed only to babes (the spiritual newborns)**

Next, Christ tells us that those who enter the kingdom of heaven are not the wise and prudent of the world, but the babes (newly born!).

> 25 At that time Jesus answered and said, I thank thee, O Father, Lord of heaven and earth, because thou hast hid these things from the wise and prudent, and hast revealed them unto babes. 26 Even so, Father: for so it seemed good in thy sight. 27 All things are delivered unto me of my Father: and no man knoweth the Son, but the Father; neither knoweth any man the Father, save the Son, and [he] to whomsoever the Son will reveal [him].

Notice that the words "reveal" and "know" are each used twice for emphasis. Through Christ, those that have been born of the Spirit (babe-newborns) can "learn" of the Father (who is love). Spiritual knowledge is "hid" from the wise (telestial) and prudent who need to physically "see" to believe.

- **His yoke is easy**

These last verses in Matthew 11 are not independent of, but a culmination of all the verses which have preceded them, all of which are about entrance into God's heavenly (spiritual) kingdom.

28 Come unto me, all [ye] that labour and are heavy laden, and I will give you rest. 29 Take my yoke upon you, and learn of me; for I am meek and lowly in heart: and ye shall find rest unto your souls. 30 For my yoke [is] easy, and my burden is light.

A key word in these famous verses is "learn," which gets its context from the previous verses which talked about revealed knowledge (to babes). In fact, Christ is confirming that we can only learn concerning spiritual things by being yoked to him through the Spirit. If we look at these verses chiastically we discover who He is and how we become like him:

28 Come unto me, all [ye] that **labour** and are **heavy** laden,
    and I will give you **rest.**
        29 Take my yoke upon you, and **learn of me;**
        for **I am meek and lowly in heart**:
    and ye shall find **rest** unto your souls.
30 For my yoke [is] **easy**, and my burden is **light**.

It seems that the primary knowledge revealed to babes (those spiritually born) is that He is meek and lowly in heart. Into such a heart God can pour his love. Indeed, meekness is a fruit of the Spirit (Gal 5:23), which we all must produce in order to inherit the kingdom of God (Gal 5:21). "Meek and lowly of heart" also reminds us of the" broken heart and contrite Spirit" which is the spiritual offering of the new covenant (putting off the natural man and yielding to the Spirit). By this offering ("doing not my will but the will of him that send me" [Jn 6:38]), Christ grew grace for grace until he received a fullness of the Father, which celestial fullness we are also promised – "all power in both heaven and earth." Below is this promise from D&C 93:12-18. Notice how everything depends upon the revelation of the Holy Ghost (dove*yonah*). You may also notice how these verses are a model of the telestial (no fullness), terrestrial (baptism), and celestial (fullness of power).

A 12 And I, **John**, saw that he **received NOT of the fulness** at the first, but received grace for grace;

> B 13 And he **received NOT of the fullness** at first, but continued from grace to grace, until he received **a fullness**;

>> C 14 And thus he was called the ªthe **Son of God**, because he received **NOT of the fullness** at the first.

Telestial

>>> D 15 And I, John, bear record, and lo, the **heavens** were opened, and

>>>> E the **Holy Ghost** descended **upon him**

Terrestrial

>>>> E in the form of a **dove**, and sat **upon him**,

>>> D and there came a voice out of **heaven** saying:

Celestial

>> C This is my **beloved Son**. 16 And I, John, bear record that he received a **fullness of the glory** of the Father;

> B 17 And he **received all power**, both in heaven and on earth, and **the glory** of the Father was with him, for he dwelt in him.

A 18 And it shall come to pass, that if you are faithful you shall **receive the fulness** of the record of **John**.

- **The tree of life – a yoke**

The yoke, therefore, deals metaphorically with the Spirit. It connects us to Him and to the revealed knowledge of the Father (vs 27). In modern scripture, D&C 19:23, the Lord recapitulates these verses, clarifying their meaning: "**Learn of me**, and listen to my

words; walk in the meekness **of my Spirit**, and you shall have peace in me." And in the Book of Mormon, Alma 33:23 also tells us that our burdens are light when we come to the tree of life (which represents the love of God shed abroad in our hearts by the Holy Ghost). "And now, my brethren, I desire that ye shall plant this **word** in your hearts, and as it beginneth to swell even so nourish it by your faith. And behold, it will become a tree, springing up in you unto everlasting life. And then may God grant unto you **that your burdens may be light,** through the joy of his Son. And even all this can ye do if ye will." Notice the similar parallel sequence of Mat 11 and Alma 33:

Mat 11:29-30   Take my yoke and learn of me → my burden is light

Alma 33:23   Grow the tree of life → that your burdens may be light

Consequently, "take my yoke and learn of me" is comparable to "grow the tree of life." Both are metaphors of the same thing; the Spirit driven process of coming unto Christ and experiencing the "joy of his Son." Whether it's the Bible, the D&C, or the Book of Mormon, all three indicate that we are yoked (covered in his love) by the Spirit, we learn by the Spirit (to be meek as he is meek), and it is the power of the Spirit which lightens the burdens of those born of the Spirit.

- **Odes of Solomon – Ode 42, 6, 2**

The following are some stunning verses from an apocryphal book called the Odes of Solomon which enhance our understanding of the Savior's yoke. From Ode 42 we read:

> 6. Then I arose and am with them, and will speak by their mouths. 7. For they have rejected those who persecute them; and I threw over them the **yoke of my love**. 8. Like the arm of the bridegroom over the bride, so is **my yoke** over those **who know me**. 9. And as the bridal chamber is spread out by the bridal pair's home, so is my love by those who believe in me.

The author wonderfully uses the yoke as a symbol of Christ's love, which reminds us again of the tree of life and the warmth of the Spirit. As well, notice the marriage imagery; that this yoke of love is reserved for only those who intimately "know" him (as a bride does her bridegroom) – an allusion to 1 Jn 4:7-8 (God is love). Also, love spoken of here is "spread out" over the bridal home, reminding us of the "covering" (*kaphar*) of the Atonement.

Another Ode of Solomon (number 6) compares the Spirit to music and the wind, and how its fruit is the love which consequently flows through us and out of our lips. As well, it (the Spirit) "destroys whatever is alien," meaning that it sanctifies us:

> 1. As the wind glides through the harp and the strings speak, 2. So the Spirit of the Lord speaks through my members, and I speak through **His love**. 3. For He destroys whatever is alien, and everything is of the Lord. 4. For thus it was from the beginning, and will be until the end.

Also, consider the spectacular poetry of Ode 2 and its wonderful celestial imagery:

1. My heart was pruned and its flower appeared, then grace sprang up in it, and my heart produced fruits for the Lord.

2. For the Most High circumcised me by His Holy Spirit, then He uncovered my inward being towards Him, and filled me with His love.

16. And He took me to His Paradise, wherein is the wealth of the Lord's pleasure.

I beheld blooming and fruit-bearing trees,

And self-grown was their crown.

Their branches were sprouting and their fruits were shining.

From an immortal land were their roots.

And a river of gladness was irrigating them,

And round about them in the land of eternal life.

17. Then I worshipped the Lord because of His magnificence.

18. And I said, Blessed, O Lord, are they who are planted in Your land, and who have a place in Your Paradise;

19. And who grow in the growth of Your trees, and have passed from darkness into light

Not found in the bible, these glorious verses nonetheless describe the celestializing of our hearts, pruned and circumcised by the Spirit, and bearing the fruit of His love (the "self-grown" tree of life). For historical perspective on the Odes of Solomon, see the footnotes section.[97]

17

Greater Than the Temple
Mat 12:1-8

Certainly, whenever Christ expresses his personal views concerning the temple it is worth our time to explore his comments. Matthew 12 is one of those fortunate times; verses filled with temple significance. Here, Christ declares 3 aspects of his ministry – that he is prophet, priest, and king.

In verse 42 Jesus proclaims: "One greater than Solomon is here" – Christ is the great King.

In verse 41 he proclaims: "Behold a greater than Jonas is here." – Christ is the great prophet.

In verse 6 he proclaims: "In this place is one greater than the temple" – Christ is the great temple high priest!

It is not surprising that three witness statements are selected by Matthew as a "sign" of his messiahship; reminiscent of the three days Christ would spend in the tomb before being newly created unto life; a connection to the sign of Jonah (dove\Spirit) – the only sign he gives (Mat 12:38-40).

Here, in Matthew 12, Jesus and his disciples are accused of violating the Sabbath, whereupon he largely appeals to the temple for his defense. Below is each verse in Matthew 12:1-8 with a commentary. Jesus alludes to creation and the temple, and at the same time, through Old Testament scripture declares his Messiahship:

12:1 *At that time Jesus went on the sabbath day through the **corn**; and his disciples were an hungered, and began to pluck the ears of corn, and to eat.*

> Christ and his disciples are enjoying the fruitfulness of creation. "Corn" is the word used for grain, from which bread is made, a symbol for life. The disciples are poignantly pictured with both temporal bread and the very "bread of life come down from heaven" (Jn 6:51), Christ.

3 *But he said unto them, Have ye not read what **David** did, when he was an hungered, and they that were with him;*

> Jesus compares his situation to King David, through whose branch the Messiah was anticipated. Like David the King, Christ will lead and save his people.

4 *How he entered into the house of God, and did eat the shewbread, which was not **lawful** for him to eat, neither for them which were with him, but only for the priests?*

> Fleeing Saul, David had entered the temple for nourishment (1 Sam 21). By law David could not eat the showbread, however, the high priest mercifully set the law aside so that David might live. The high priest (Ahimelech) would later be slain for his act of mercy\kindness (1 Sam 22:16); a type of Christ the high priest who would also be slain to satisfy the law for mercy's sake. Likewise, the shewbread that renewed David and assured his victory was a symbol of Christ's

merciful and atoning act (just as the sacrament). Our victory today also depends on our partaking of His emblems and taking His name upon us. David would not have been successful without this bread, nor can we. Because Jesus is about to proclaim his temple preeminence, his phrase "only for priests" is apropos for it includes him – the Great High Priest and therefore one having legal access to the Holy Place.

5 Or have ye not read in the law, how that on the sabbath days the priests in the temple profane the sabbath, and are blameless?

In the LDS scriptures footnote this event is tied to Num 28:8-9 wherein the priests were allowed to sacrifice and then eat the sacrifice on the Sabbath, something no one else could do. Moreover, priests were ordained to unite heaven and earth (Levite in Hebrew means to join); their purpose was to bring man closer to God through sacrifice, a symbol of Christ's atoning sacrifice which would satisfy the law, replacing it with mercy. Poignantly, they personally relied on mercy and sacrifice for survival. This is because they received no lawful inheritance in the land, but instead were given priesthood. In a sense, what the law materially provided to others was not provided to them. In order to live, they needed the people's offerings, portions of which they were mercifully allowed to partake. Instead of land for inheritance, the priesthood received a divine idea – that of service, sacrifice, and love.

*6 But I say unto you, That in this place is **[one] greater than the temple**.*

> For this statement to be true, Jesus would need to be the creator of all physical creation (the cosmic temple). And indeed, here stands the "One" who predates the temple, its designer and also the very reason for temple sacrifice. The tabernacle\temple, which was patterned after heavenly things and given to Moses on the mount (Heb 8-10), was in every way intended to prefigure Christ and his sacrifice. By "greater than the temple" Jesus speaks of new creation, intimating that his new covenant of compassion and spiritual sacrifice is greater than the old covenant of blood sacrifice (i.e. the old temple system).

*7 But if ye had known what [this] meaneth, I will have **mercy, and not sacrifice**, ye would not have condemned the guiltless.*

> As the *One* who created the temple, Jesus is well qualified to tell the Pharisees of its meaning and sacrifices, which he does in this verse. Significantly, our LDS footnotes point us to the scriptural source of Christ's words, found in Hosea 6 (parenthesis mine).
>
> 5 Therefore have I hewed [them] by the prophets; I have slain them by the words of my mouth: and thy judgments [are as] the light [that] goeth forth. 6 **For I desired mercy, and not sacrifice**; and the **knowledge of God more than burnt offerings.** 7 But they like men (Adam [singular], in the Hebrew) have transgressed the covenant: there have they dealt

treacherously (covered\clothed themselves – in Hebrew) against me.

There are some fascinating concepts here. A better rendering of Hosea 6:7 has Adam rather than "man" (most Bible translations have Adam here). Hosea likely compares Israel's broken covenant to Adam's in Eden, where he also attempted to "cover up" his transgression with fig leaves.[98] In both instances (Israel's and Adam's), the Lord contends that a lack of the "knowledge of God" is the cause of the problem. (Mercy, by the way, in Hebrew is *chesed,* which is often rendered as loving kindness.)[99] Burnt offerings and sacrifices represent the Old Covenant law, while mercy and knowledge of God are the New Covenant.

If we examine the poetry of Hosea 6:6 we find this profound truth developed in parallelism:

For I desired **mercy** (chesed- loving kindness),
> and not sacrifice;

and the **knowledge of God**
> more than burnt offerings.

The parallel here is that "knowledge of God" is related to "mercy" or loving kindness. We need look no further than 1 John 4:7-8 to corroborate this: "Beloved, let us love one another: for love is of God; and every one that loveth is born of God, and **knoweth God**. 8 He that loveth not knoweth not God; for God is love." Further, if we take this definition of what it is to "know God", then John 17:3 also takes on new meaning, which says, "And this is **life eternal**, that they might **know thee** the only true God, and Jesus Christ, whom thou hast sent." Truly then, life eternal is knowing God – which is to love, which is a fruit of the Spirit (Gal 5:22), which is the celestializing process talked about in this book, the third part of our mortal journey as portrayed in the endowment. Also, Hosea 6:6 helps to clarify verses such as D&C 84:19-22, which talk about the priesthood:

> 19 And this greater priesthood administereth the gospel and holdeth the key of the mysteries of the kingdom, even the **key of the knowledge of God.**
> 20 Therefore, in the ordinances thereof, the power of godliness is manifest.
> 21 And without the ordinances thereof, and the authority of the priesthood, the power of godliness is not manifest unto men in the flesh;
> 22 For without this no man can see the face of God, even the Father, and live.

The "key of the knowledge of God" could therefore be rephrased as the key to "life eternal," which is to know God (Jn 17:3), which is manifest in love for others and God. Without it (love) "no man can see the face of God" (who is love). Also, the greater priesthood mentioned here is the priesthood given to those in the celestial phase of the temple endowment, which is representative of those in whom the gift of the Holy Ghost (by ordinance) is shedding abroad the love of God. These are those who are partaking of the tree of life and who covenant to consecrate\sacrifice themselves completely to God's kingdom. They "know" this fruit as the most desirable and joyous to the soul (1 Ne 11). This group is being sanctified, purified, and perfected in Christ as they "deny themselves ungodliness" and "deny not the power of God" (Moro 10:32-33), which is His Spirit working in their hearts and minds. This is the royal priesthood spoken of in 1 Peter, making "spiritual sacrifices" (2:5-9), whose souls are "purified in obeying the truth through the Spirit unto unfeigned love" (1:22). Of this group Paul said in 1 Cor 2:11-19, "the things of God **knoweth** no man, but the Spirit of God. Now we have received, not the spirit of the world, but the Spirit which is of God; that we might know the things that are freely given to us of God. Which things also we speak, not in the words which man's wisdom teacheth, but which **the Holy Ghost teacheth**; comparing spiritual things with spiritual. But the natural man receiveth not the things of the Spirit of God: for they are foolishness unto him: neither can he know them, because they are spiritually discerned. But he that is spiritual judgeth all things, yet he himself is judged of no man. For who hath **known the mind** of the Lord, that he may instruct him? But we have the mind of Christ" (1 Cor. 2:11-16). And what is the mind of Christ – love (mercy, knowledge of God).

In addition, the power of godliness mentioned in D&C 84:20-21 is the purity and holiness acquired as we are true and faithful ("through the Spirit") to the covenants we have made within the ordinances of the Gospel. As previously mentioned, by keeping these covenants we are spiritually created and beautified in righteousness. Defining the "power of godliness"

J. Todd Christofferson said, "In all the ordinances, especially those of the temple, we are endowed with power from on high. This "power of godliness" comes in the person and by the influence of the Holy Ghost. The gift of the Holy Ghost is part of the new and everlasting covenant. It is an essential part of our baptism, the baptism of the Spirit. It is the messenger of grace by which the blood of Christ is applied to take away our sins and sanctify us (see 2 Nephi 31:17)."[100]

8 *For the Son of man is Lord even of the sabbath day.*

Leaving nothing to doubt, Jesus fully proclaims that he (the Son of Man) is the creator and Lord of the seventh day, and therefore the maker of the very law that they accuse him of violating. We can only imagine what these Pharisees might have thought. Could it be possible that the God of Abraham and Moses stood before them? Oh, that their hearts had been merciful, loving, and pure, that they might have "seen" Him (Mat 5:7-8).

18

Matthew 25 – Three Parables in One

Let's continue to examine the importance of what it is to know God. In Matthew 25 Jesus gives his final *three* parables. In a few days he will atone for mankind, performing the ultimate act of mercy and love on our behalf. It is easy to imagine that they contain a culmination of Christ's teaching. Remarkably, all of these parables teach the same lesson, which means that you can use elements and pieces of one to better understand the others. In the end, their collective focus is underscored in the final parable of the sheep and goats.

There are contextual considerations which will assist us. For example, Matthew 24, the Olivet discourse, which precedes these parables, is about events and signs that occur at the end of the world. These parables in Mat 25 are a continuation of that theme, and together relate information about how we will be judged when the Son of Man returns. Also, even earlier, Matthew 21-23 contains multiple stories and parables, narrated by Christ, which emphasize how the fruitless Levite priesthood would be left desolate; i.e. the fruitless fig tree withers, the vineyard is taken away and given to another husbandman able to produce fruit, along with seven statements of "woe ye hypocrites" (a reverse endowment). Matthew 25 is consequently about producing fruit, characterized by the requirement of extra oil, multiplying of talents, and various acts of mercy. Below is an organizational matrix of Mat 25. Notice how the three items under each heading, in every column, express related ideas:

Christ	Item Multiplied	Saved	Reward	Unsaved	Trait	Judgment	Know the Lord?
Bridegroom	oil-light	5 wise virgins	wedding supper	5 foolish virgins	unprepared	left in darkness	**do not know**
Man in far country	talents	2 talents 5 talents	ruler, and joy of Lord	1 talent	faithless fearful	outer darkness	**thinks he knows**
Son of Man, King	love & mercy	sheep	eternal life	goats	no mercy	everlasting punishment	**not sure he knows**

Each story wonderfully follows the same blueprint, every meaning broadened by the parallel elements found in the other parables. Some elements need little amplification. For instance, we readily see that Christ is typified in the Bridegroom, the man in a far country, and the King or Son of Man (1st row). Also, it is apparent that the judgments of darkness, outer darkness, and everlasting punishment are the same thing. But have you ever wondered about the fullest sense of the oil in the parable of the 10 virgins? Most have observed that oil in scripture is a symbol of the Spirit, but how do talents and acts of mercy relate and give this deeper meaning? Curiously, once we identify that these parallels exist, we realize that there is really no other way to fully appreciate the elements of one parable WITHOUT the others. The key to complete understanding is found in the parallels.

Most importantly, each story ends with a profound question, located in the last column of the above matrix, which is, "do you know the Lord", or what does it mean to "know the Lord"? The way in which we answer this question has a direct bearing on verses such as John 17:3, "**this is life eternal**, that they might **know thee** the only true God, and Jesus Christ, whom thou hast sent." Since our eternal life depends on how we answer this question, let's take a moment to examine these parables and what they have to say about knowing God.

- **10 virgins and their oil**

In the parable of the ten virgins, the olive oil symbolizes purity and the anointing of the Spirit (Luke 4:18).[101] We are told that all ten virgins are members of the church (Spencer Kimball).[102] The wedding feast is a fulfillment of Rev 19:7-9 and the supper of the Lamb, when Christ marries his church (his bride) upon his return. All ten virgins (brides to be) have some oil in their lamps, but only five wise virgins bring enough oil to keep their light shining long into the night. Mat 5:14-16 explains why light is so important: "Ye are the light of the world. Let your **light** so shine before men, that they may see your good **works**, and glorify your Father which is in heaven." However, we should remember that the light of the Holy Ghost within us is what "shines before men". Good works are the evidence of the Spirit's light within, and an indication that one is bearing fruit of the Spirit.

Becoming a member of the church is only the first step in preparing for the bridegroom. Sanctification (becoming a saint) is the ongoing process performed by the Holy Ghost in the lives of those who strive to live the gospel precepts – loving God and man. In D&C 45:56-57 the Lord has more to say about the wise virgins: "And at that day, when I shall come in my glory, shall the parable be fulfilled which I spake concerning the **ten virgins**. For they that are wise and have received the truth, and have **taken the Holy Spirit for their guide**, and have not been deceived—verily I say unto you, they shall not be hewn down and cast into the fire, but shall abide the day." This process of refinement under the tutelage of the Holy Ghost (light) produces the reserve of oil carried by the five wise virgins. The fruits of the Spirit – love, joy, peace, longsuffering, gentleness, goodness, faith, meekness, self-control (Gal 5), have changed their lives and those of others.[103]

- **Talents**

Once we understand that oil, talents, and acts of love are like-kind things, then we better appreciate in what way the faithful servants multiplied the talents which have been given to them (it wasn't shrewd business acumen). Talents, like the oil in the virgins' lamps, also represent the light of the Spirit or "gifts of the Spirit," and the acts of kindness and love which are a product of that light. By burying his talent, the faithless servant sins because he has extinguished the Spirit's warmth within his heart; emanating God's love no longer into the world. Certainly there is also significance in the fact that a talent anciently was a form of currency which could use to purchase a variety of things to better or maintain one's life. If not hidden away, a talent can move (circulate) from person to person, be invested over and over again as valuable goods and services are bought and sold. In this way an economy is strengthened and people's lives improved. Similarly, this is also how love and the light of the Spirit works, invested in one person and then another, it travels throughout the marketplace, exchanging hearts (not hands) many time, improving and changing each person's life. Love is heaven's currency.

- **Knowing God**

As mentioned, the critical moment in each parable is represented by the last column in the chart above. Each parable climaxes with an assessment of the person's knowledge of God, which, in the final analysis, is also the result of their behavior and the measure of how they will be judged. If that is so, what is it to know God? As just discussed in the last chapter, Christ explained this to the Pharisees who accuse him of breaking the Sabbath in Matthew 12. Hoping to show them how the Law of Christ (Gal 6:2) has replaced the Law of Moses, Christ quotes Hosea 6:6, For I desired **mercy,** and not sacrifice; and the **knowledge of God** more than burnt offerings.

To know God is to reflect his mercy and love. Sacrifice ("burnt offerings") without this element, is empty. In 1 John 4:7,8,11 we find an even clearer explanation of this idea: "he that **loveth,** is born of God and **knoweth** God", and he that 'loveth not knoweth not God." With this idea in mind, consider how the condemned in each parable fail to "know God". In the parable of the 10 virgins, the "door" is shut to the five foolish virgins, and the bridegroom tells them, "**I know you not**". Apparently, in the process of waiting their oil and "light" has run out, as have the fruits of that light (the Spirit) – love, kindness, and good works. In Mat 7:20 Christ reinforces this same idea, "Wherefore by their fruits **ye shall know** them." We are **known to** God by the fruit of our lives. Those who have "taken the Holy Spirit for their guide" (D&C 45:57) will be led to love and care for others, as Christ (who was anointed with a fullness of the Spirit) did for all of us.

In the parable of the talents, the faithless servant that hid his talent (light) tells the Lord, "**I knew thee** that thou art an hard man, reaping where thou hast not sown, and gathering where thou hast not strawed: And I was afraid, and went and hid thy talent in the earth:" Despite his claim, he obviously doesn't know God. In fact, God is not hard, but "so loved the world, that he gave his only begotten Son" (Jn 3:16). Likewise, He also sows in order to reap. In Galatians

6:8-10 we can read the law of the harvest, "For he that soweth to his flesh shall of the flesh reap corruption; but he that soweth to the Spirit shall of the Spirit reap **life everlasting**. And let us not be weary in well doing: for in due season we shall reap, if we faint not. As we have therefore opportunity, let us do good unto all [men]." Notice again that "well doing" and "doing good to all men" comes from "sowing to the Spirit". They go hand in hand and should remind us of the verse in Matthew (5:26) that we read earlier concerning the light\oil Spirit of the 10 virgins – "Let your light so shine before men that they may see your good works." If we map this sequence (a spiritual law of the harvest) we would have:

Soweth in the Spirit ⇨ fruit of doing good to all men ⇨ reap life everlasting

- **Sheep and the Goats**

Last of all, the parable of the sheep and the goats is fascinating because both groups seem puzzled by the idea that they had (or had not) performed acts of mercy to the Savior personally. The Lord has to point out to the sheep that they in fact **did know him**, because they had showed kindness to their fellow man. To them he declares, "When ye are in the service of your fellow beings, ye are only in the service of your God." On the other hand, the goats seem puzzled that they are accused of not knowing God – "when saw we thee an hungred, or athirst, or a stranger, or naked, or sick, or in prison, and did not minister unto thee?" – suggesting that had they known it was God they would have had compassion. In failing to love others they failed to love God. For this lack of compassion and knowledge they are promised everlasting punishment. The sheep, on the other hand, those who **know him**, are promised **eternal life** (Mat25:46)!

Finally: without "knowing God' there is no eternal life, which as we have seen, is an established process wherein mortal man, by the Spirit's light within, shows forth "well doing", "good works", and ongoing love towards others. In this regard, eternal life starts now as we abide in this process; "Herein is our love made perfect", and "as he is, so are we" (1 Jn 4:17). As we freely partake of the fruit of the tree of life, which is the love of God shed abroad in our hearts, our knowledge of God deepens and grows. In fact, the vision of the tree of life communicates all of these ideas through the life of the Savior, a pattern for us to follow. In vision Nephi sees the mortal birth of Christ, his baptism (or rebirth), the Spirit descending upon him, Christ going forth among the children of men (shining the light of the Spirit into their lives), healing the sick and afflicted ("doing good to all men"). Nephi also sees that Christ is "slain for the sins of the world" – the ultimate act of kindness, mercy, and love. By this pattern, Christ continues to bring eternal life to all men. We know him as we do what he did – love. This is the mystery of Godliness – "That Christ may dwell in your hearts by faith; that ye, being rooted and grounded in love, May be able to comprehend with all saints what [is] the breadth, and length, and depth, and height; And to know the love of Christ, which passeth knowledge, that ye might be filled with all the fullness of God" (Eph 3:17-19).

19

Perfected in Christ
The Marriage Imagery of Moroni 10:30-33

At the center of his vision of the tree of life, which is the center of his endowment pattern, Nephi comes to "know" the love of God. However, as was mentioned in chapter 8 of this book (pg 96), the center of the temple endowment (the terrestrial), also coincides with the law of chastity, which alludes to the marriage covenant with our spouse as well as our Lord – when the name of the bridegroom is taken. What I would like to do now is examine how Moroni uses this imagery of supreme love for one's beloved when he invites us to come unto Christ (the tree of life) and be perfected in him.

In order to better understand Moroni's invitation we have to start with an examination of God's covenant marriage to Israel as spoken of in various passages of the Old Testament.[104] For instance, we find: "For I am married unto you" (*Jer.* 3:14); "I was an husband unto them" (*Jer.* 31:32); "And I will betroth thee unto Me for ever; Yea, I will betroth thee unto Me in righteousness, and in justice, and in loving-kindness, and in compassion. And I will betroth thee unto Me in faithfulness; and thou shalt know the Lord." (*Hoshea* 2:21-22); As a young man marries a maiden, so will your sons marry you; as a bridegroom rejoices over his bride, so will your God rejoice over you (*Isa.* 62:3-5). This marriage metaphor helps us to comprehend the great love that the Savior has for Israel; compared to the love that a bride and bridegroom have for one another. Because anciently marriage was made with covenants and oaths,[105] God's covenant with Israel at Mt Sinai has long been viewed in terms of a marriage covenant.[106] In Exodus 24:7-8 we can read about how Israel covenanted at Sinai: "And he (Moses) took the book of the covenant, and read in the audience of the people: and they said, All that the Lord hath said will we do, and be obedient. And Moses took the blood, and sprinkled it on the people, and said, Behold the blood of the covenant, which the Lord hath made with you concerning all these words."[107] When Israel later disobeyed, her faithlessness was spoken of as breaking her marital vows with God (Exe 16:14-63, Hos 1:2).

It shouldn't be too surprising, then, if we also find this same imagery in the Book of Mormon, which in fact is the case in Moroni 10:30-33. In these final verses in the Book of Mormon, Moroni talks about how God's covenant with Israel will be fulfilled, and there he uses Hebrew word-play to connect the idea of perfection in Christ to the great love shared in a covenant marital relationship. Below are Moroni's final instructions (parenthesis are mine and indicate Moroni's source scripture).

> 30 And again I would exhort you that ye would come unto Christ, and lay hold upon every good gift, and touch not the evil gift, nor the unclean thing. (Isa 52:11) 31 And awake, and arise from the dust, O Jerusalem; yea, and put on thy beautiful garments (Isa 52:1), O daughter of Zion; and strengthen thy stakes and enlarge thy borders (Isa 54:2) forever, that thou mayest no more be confounded (Isa 54:4), that the covenants of the Eternal Father which he hath made unto thee, O house of Israel, may be fulfilled. 32 Yea, come unto Christ, and be perfected in him, and deny yourselves of all ungodliness; and if ye shall deny yourselves of all ungodliness, and love God with all your might, mind and strength, then is his grace

sufficient for you, that by his grace ye may be perfect in Christ; and if by the grace of God ye are perfect in Christ, ye can in nowise deny the power of God. 33 And again, if ye by the grace of God are perfect in Christ, and deny not his power, then are ye sanctified in Christ by the grace of God, through the shedding of the blood of Christ, which is in the covenant of the Father unto the remission of your sins, that ye become holy, without spot.

In particular, the last two verses (32-33) are best understood in light of Moroni's introductory verses, 30-31, which upon examination are a series of scriptures from Isaiah which allude to Israel as God's covenant bride. This is significant because in Hebrew the word for bride is *kallah*,[108] which comes from the Hebrew verb *kallal*, and means to be complete or perfect![109] This provides us the context needed to better understand Moroni's ensuing instruction, which is an invitation for Israel (the bride) to be perfect (*kallal*) in her bridegroom (Christ)! The word *kallah* suggests that a girl is incomplete until she becomes a bride, and is perfected by her union to her bridegroom. 1 Cor 11:11 tells us, "Neither is the man without the woman, neither the woman without the man, in the Lord. For as the woman *is* of the man, even so *is* the man also by the woman; but all things in God." According to the Talmud, "Adam and Eve were initially created as one, and then split. Therefore, the Jewish wedding is the reunion of **one whole soul**. This is also the reason why it is customary for the bride and the groom to fast on their wedding day: This day is in a way a private **"Yom Kippur"** (Day of At-one-ment), for both souls must be forgiven for all their mistakes (holy, without spot) before merging **into a new complete** soul."[110]

- **Moroni uses Isaiah 52 and 54**

Let's look a little closer at these Isaiah verses which Moroni uses to allude to Israel's marriage covenant. One of the first excerpts that Moroni uses (vs 31) is the image of Jerusalem putting on a "beautiful garment" which is spoken of in Isa 52:1. This verse is described by Gill Exposition Bible as a reference to Revelation 19:8-9, "when the saints will put on their beautiful garments, as on holy days, and times of rejoicing; their mourning will be over, and all signs of it shall be laid aside; the witnesses will no more prophesy in sackcloth; **the marriage of the Lamb will be come; the bride made ready**, being clothed with fine linen, clean and white, the righteousness of the saints, the garments of Christ's salvation, and the robe of his righteousness; which are the beautiful garments here meant."[111] In addition, Revelation 19:8-9 (referenced here) tells us that the bride is "clean and white", which is also how Moroni starts this pericope, citing Isa 52:11, "touch not the evil gift, nor the unclean thing." In ancient Israel, a bride was expected to be clean and virtuous.[112]

Even more important, Moroni also quotes verses from Isa 54:2, "O daughter of Zion; strengthen thy stakes and enlarge thy borders forever," and from Isa 54:4, "that thou mayest no more be confounded." These passages are a preamble to Isa 54:5, "For thy Maker *is* **thine husband**; the LORD of hosts *is* his name; and thy Redeemer the Holy One of Israel; The God of the whole earth shall he be called." In these same Isaiah verses we also read that this relationship between Israel (bride) and her Maker (bridegroom) is an eternal covenant. Isa 54:10 tells us, "For the mountains shall depart, and the hills be removed; but my kindness shall not depart from thee, neither shall **the covenant** of my peace be removed, saith the

LORD that hath mercy on thee." Like Isaiah, Moroni also explains how it is exclusively through the "covenants of the Eternal Father" (vs 31,32) that we are able to be perfected and sanctified in Christ.

- **Parallel structure in Moroni 10:30-33**

Having said all of that, Moroni's instruction can most easily be understood when viewing his parallels. Below is a general assessment of Moroni's parallelistic and chiastic thinking:

A 30 And again I would exhort you that ye would come unto Christ, and lay hold upon every good gift, and **touch not the evil gift, nor the unclean thing**. (Isa 52:11)
   B And awake, and arise from the dust, O Jerusalem; 31 yea, and **put on** thy *beautiful garments* (Isa 52:1), O daughter of Zion;
      C and strengthen thy stakes and enlarge thy borders forever, that thou mayest *no more be confounded* (Isa 54:4-5), that the **covenants of the Eternal Father** which he hath made unto thee, O house of Israel, may be fulfilled.
         D Yea, come unto **Christ,** and be **perfected in** him,
            E and **deny** yourselves of all un**god**liness; and **if ye** shall **deny** yourselves of all un**god**liness,
              F and love **God** with all your might, mind and strength,
                  G then is his **grace** sufficient for you,
                    G' that by his **grace** ye may be perfect in Christ;
              F' and if by the grace of **God** (his love) ye are perfect in Christ,
            E' ye can in nowise **deny** the power of **God**. And again, **if ye** by the grace of **God** are perfect in **Christ,** and **deny** not his power,
         D' then are ye **sanctified in Christ** by the grace of God,
   B' through the **shedding of** the *blood of Christ*,
      C' which is in **the covenant of the Father** unto the *remission of your sins*,
A' that ye **become holy, without spot.**

A – A'

Notice how A' parallels being holy and without spot, to not touching evil or the unclean thing (A). As mentioned, this is also a reference to the bride (*kallah*), who was to be pure and undefiled for her bridegroom. "Arise from the dust", which follows, is also a reference to new life or rebirth (when one is pure and unspotted).[113]

B – B'

Notice here the antithetical ideas, "putting on" in B as opposed to "shedding" in B'. The "beautiful garment" in B becomes so, washed in the "blood of the lamb" (B'). This parallel has clear implications to the temple garment, "gifted" by God in the slaying of the lamb (shedding its blood) to provide a covering for Adam and Eve. (Isa 1:18 – though your sins be as scarlet they shall as white as snow).

C – C'

C and C' then tells us the framework or means by which purity is attained – through the "covenant of the Father". In C, the "covenants of the Eternal Father" perhaps represent the covenants of the Old Testament, and the "covenant of the Father" in C' represent the new. Also, notice how the phrase "no more be confounded," is parallel to phrase "unto the remission of your sins" (C')

D – D'

D and D' suggest that "perfected in Christ" is synonymous to being "sanctified in Christ" – both accomplished through grace, power (Holy Ghost), and covenant blood. There is, in fact, no other way for us to be sanctified other than by the power of the Holy Ghost. That is its role (Alma 13:11-12).[114] For instance, when Christ says in Jn 17 that he has "sanctified them by his word" he is referring to how the Spirit brings the word alive in our minds and carries it to our hearts. As D&C 84:45 explains, "The word of the Lord is truth, and whatsoever is truth is light, and whatsoever is light is Spirit, even the Spirit of Jesus Christ."

E – E'

E highlights the use of our agency (our willingness to **deny** ourselves of ungodliness), and parallels it to (E') allowing (**not denying**) his "power" to work in our lives. For context of what Moroni means by "his power", examine verses 4-18 (also 25) of this chapter, wherein "power" is used synonymously to mean the Holy Ghost. Indeed, it is by this power that the covenant blood of Christ works to cleanse us "unto the remission of your sins" (verse 32).

F – F'

If you examine these parallels at the center of this structure you will also discover the heart of what empowers a marriage relationship (with your spouse and with God), which is to love with all your might mind and strength. There is a promise given that, "**if**" you do this you will receive His grace, and "that by his grace you may be perfect in Christ" (G'). We might recognize that this dependent clause suggests a covenant (i.e. if you do this, then I promise you that), patterned after the covenant made between God and Israel at Sinai. Indeed, the if/then statement (or condition) of God's covenant with Israel at Sinai is found in Ex 19:5 "Now therefore, **if ye will obey** my voice indeed, and keep my covenant, **then** ye shall be a peculiar treasure unto me above all people: for all the earth *is* mine.

And ye shall be unto me a kingdom of priests, and an **holy** nation."[115] Holiness is again the promised result of their covenant obedience to the Lord's voice, just as it is in Moroni's exhortation – "that ye become holy without spot." (A')

G – G'

The center of Moroni's instruction is that God's grace is sufficient, and that by it we can be perfected in Christ. The following sections will discuss grace – its various definitions and how it relates to the other interrelated elements (power, covenant, sanctification) of Moroni's admonition to come unto Christ.

- **Operation of grace, King Benjamin, Creation**

According to Moroni, grace is reserved for those within the covenant of the Father, inferring that those outside of his covenant conditions cannot receive the "fullness" of his grace. For a moment, then, let's consider covenants. As mentioned previously, in Hebrew the word for covenant is berith, which came from the Hebrew verb bara, which means to create. Covenants, therefore, are used by God to spiritually create us. Indeed, physical creation (*bara*) is a type or figure of our spiritual creation (*berith*) – the earth begins as void and without form and is progressively *endowed* with light and life until it is very fruitful. And so that we might become spiritually fruitful, covenants provide the parameters which test our will/agency (e.g. if you do this then I will bless you with that) to be *true and faithful*. However, God knows that we cannot be *true and faithful* to his covenant without help, promising us his "power" to assist us, which is the Holy Ghost (Moroni 10:7,8). Let's look at these concepts using Moroni's reasoning and compare it to King Benjamin's famous teaching in Mosiah 3:19.

Moroni 10:30-32	Mosiah 3:19
deny yourselves ungodliness	put off the natural man
and deny not his power	yield to the Holy Ghost
then are ye *sanctified* in Christ by the grace of God through the shedding of the blood of Christ which is in the covenant of the Father unto the remission of your sins, that ye become holy, without spot	and becometh a *saint* through the atonement of Christ the Lord, and becometh as a child, submissive, meek humble, patient, full of love

If you recall, this duplication of Moroni's doctrine is presented by King Benjamin at the temple, where his people are placed under covenant. Listen as this happens, and notice how the covenant they accept "creates" them spiritually. Mosiah 5:7-8, "And now, because of the *covenant* which ye have made ye shall be called the children of Christ, his sons, and his daughters; for behold, this day he hath spiritually *begotten* (created) you; for ye say that your hearts are changed through faith on his name; therefore, ye are *born of* him (created) and have become his sons and his daughters. 8 And under this head ye are made free, and there is no other head whereby ye can be made free. There is no other name given whereby salvation cometh; therefore, I would that ye should take upon you the name of Christ, all you that have entered into the *covenant* with God that ye should be obedient unto the end of your lives." What we

see here is a group of people who have agreed to put off the natural man and to yield to the enticing of the Spirit "unto the end of their lives." They are promised a new name (like a bride that takes her husband's name in marriage), and that their "salvation cometh" within this covenant framework. In terms of Moroni's apex and "his sufficient grace" this IS the grace (gift, power) that is sufficient to perfect us spiritually. To it we can add nothing. All that is asked of us is to walk in the Spirit each day, following its direction (obeying) to love and serve others. What grace is not, though widely believed by members of our church, is something we get after our life is over and we have tried our best – by our own efforts – to manufacture good works. To the contrary, grace is a present-tense living empowerment (the enabling power of the Atonement) to bless our lives as we operate within the parameters of the New Covenant, which is to follow the Spirit, who will write God's laws and expectations upon our hearts (Jer 31:32, Heb 10:16), the seat of love.
116

In the sacrament covenant which we renew each week, clearly we are in God's sufficient grace when we "remember him", "keep his commandments", and "have his Spirit to be with us". However, we should also remember that though the order is – keep the commandments to have his Spirit – the reverse is equally true, that we have his Spirit to help us keep the commandments. You might note that this is also the sentiment of Mosiah 3:19 and Moroni 10:30-32 (charted above). We are likewise promised that the tokens (bread and water) will sanctify the soul of all who eat and drink (are spiritually nourished). A sanctified soul is *holy, clean* and *without spot* (just like what the Lord promised in covenant to Israel in Exo 19 [a holy nation], or what Moroni explains in 10:32 [holy, without spot]). As this relates to Moroni's chiasmus above, "sanctified" and "perfected" are parallel terms, which indicates that we are perfected (sanctified) in Christ by keeping our sacrament covenant (having his Spirit to enable and empower us, yielding to its enticings). [117]

- **Grace – a definition**

Unavoidably, the preceding conversation leads us to a broader discussion of grace and its meaning. In the Webster dictionary we find a pretty good primary definition of biblical grace:

a : unmerited divine assistance given humans for their regeneration or sanctification
b : a virtue coming from God
c : a state of sanctification enjoyed through divine grace [118]

However, depending upon context, in the scriptures grace has several other nuances. Let's look at some commentaries on grace, and begin with what may seem an unlikely source, a respected non-LDS Bible commentator – John MacArthur. Surprisingly, he represents a view which agrees with Moroni's characterization of grace.

Writes John MacArthur, "Many professing Christians today utterly ignore the biblical truth that grace "instruct[s] us to **deny ungodliness** and worldly desires and to live sensibly, righteously, and godly in the present age" (Titus 2:12). Instead, they live as if grace were a supernatural "Get Out of Jail FREE" ticket-a no-strings-attached, open-ended package of amnesty, beneficence, indulgence, forbearance, charity, leniency, immunity, approval, tolerance, and self-awarded privilege divorced from any moral demands. Sadly, the rank-and-file Christian is further cemented in an unbiblical view of grace by what comes out of some seminaries. They advocate a "grace" that alters a believer's *standing* without affecting his *state*. Grace is not a dormant or abstract quality, but a dynamic, active, working principle: "The grace of God has appeared, bringing salvation...and instructing us" (Titus 2:11-12). It is not some kind of ethereal blessing that lies idle until we appropriate it. Grace is God's sovereign initiative to sinners (Ephesians 1:5-6). It is not a one-time event in the Christian experience. We stand in grace (Romans 5:2). The entire Christian life is driven and empowered by grace: "It is good for the heart to be strengthened by grace, not by foods" (Hebrews 13:9). Peter said we should "grow in the grace and knowledge of our Lord and Savior Jesus Christ" (2 Peter 3:18)."[119]

In addition, consider definitions of grace from several other non-LDS sources:

> "We have to be on our guard against the supposition that *grace* is an abstract quality; it is an active personal principle, showing itself in our dealings with those by whom we are surrounded. ... In the great proportion of passages in which the word grace is found in the New Testament, it signifies the unmerited operation of God in the heart of man, effected through the agency of the Holy Spirit. We have gradually come to speak of grace as an inherent quality in man, just as we talk of gifts; whereas it is in reality the communication of Divine goodness by the **inworking of the Spirit**, and through the medium of Him who is 'full of grace and truth.'" — Robert Girdlestone, *Synonyms of the Old Testament* (London: Longmans, Green and Co., 1871), p. 179.

"In Paul ... χαρις is never merely an attitude or disposition of God (God's character as gracious); consistently it denotes something much more dynamic—the wholly generous *act* of God. Like '**Spirit**,' with which it overlaps in meaning (cf., e.g., [Rom] 6:14 and Gal 5:18), it denotes effective divine power in the experience of men." —James D.G. Dunn, *Romans 1-8* (Dallas: Word Books, 1988), p. 17.

"Between "God's favor" and "God's favors" there exists a relation of active power, and as *charis* denoted both the favor and the favors, it was the natural word for the power that connected them. This use is very clear in 1 Corinthians 15:10, where Paul says, "not I, but the grace of God which was with me" labored more abundantly than they all: grace is something that *labors*. So in 2 Corinthians 12:9, "My grace is sufficient for thee: for my power is made perfect in weakness"; compare 2 Timothy 2:1, "strengthened in the grace," and 1 Peter 4:10, "stewards of the manifold grace." Evidently in this sense "grace" is almost **a synonym for the Spirit**, and there is little real difference between "full of the Holy Spirit" and "full of grace and power" in Acts 6:5,8, while there is a very striking parallel between Ephesians 4:7-13 and 1 Corinthians 12:4-11, with "gifts of grace" in the one passage, and "gifts of the Spirit" in the other. And this connection between grace and the Spirit is found definitely in the formula "**Spirit of grace**" in Hebrews 10:29 (compare Zechariah 12:10)." Burton Scott Easton, "Grace," in *The International Standard Bible*

Encyclopaedia, vol. 2 (Chicago: Howard-Severance Co., 1930), pp. 1290-92

And from the Dictionary in our LDS scriptures (pg 697) we read: "It is likewise through the grace of the Lord that individuals, through faith in the Atonement of Jesus Christ and repentance of their sins, receive *strength and assistance* to do good works that they otherwise would not be able to maintain if left to their own means. This grace is an enabling power that allows men and women to lay hold of eternal life." Consistent with the definitions from the previous pages, the "strength and assistance" or "enabling power" spoken of here likewise refers to the Holy Ghost; at least that makes sense in light of Moroni's teaching on grace in Moroni 10:30-32 (as well as 2 Cor 12:9-10 and Titus 2:11-14, which we are about to examine).

- **After all we can do**

What are we to make, then, of the instruction in 2 Ne 25:23 that, "It is by grace that we are saved, after all we can do." Does the "all we can do" somehow imply that there is any acceptable work outside of the Spirit's influence (outside of being in Christ)? Fortunately, Moroni also provides us with a scripture explaining this concept. In Moroni 10:24-25 we read, "24 And now I speak unto all the ends of the earth—that if the day cometh that the **power and gifts of God** shall be done away among you, it shall be because of unbelief. 25 And wo be unto the children of men if this be the case; for there shall be none that doeth good among you, no not one. For if there be one among you that **doeth good**, he shall **work** by the **power and gifts of God**." I have emboldened the phrase "power and gifts" of God because Moroni gives us a very clear context for the meaning of this phrase. As mentioned earlier, verses 4-18 of this chapter clearly define what the *power and gifts of God* are:

> 5 And by the **power of the Holy Ghost** ye may know the truth of all things.
>
> 6 And whatsoever thing is good is just and true; wherefore, nothing that is good denieth the Christ, but acknowledgeth that he is.
>
> 7 And ye may know that he is, by the **power of the Holy Ghost**; wherefore I would exhort you that ye **deny not the power of God**; for he **worketh** by power, according to the faith of the children of men, the same today and tomorrow, and forever.
>
> 8 And again, I exhort you, my brethren, that ye deny not **the gifts of God**, for they are many; and they come from the same God. And there are different ways that these **gifts are administered; but it is the same God who worketh all in all; and they** (the gifts of God) **are given by the manifestations of the Spirit of God** unto men, to profit them.

Moroni tells us in verse 7 to "deny not the power of God," which he then clearly parallels to the power of the Holy Ghost. Moreover, when we understand the phrase "power of God" to be synonymous with the Holy Ghost, then we can understand why Moroni tells us that "no not one" can DO good without these gifts of the Spirit (vs 25). Indeed, as he stipulates, "if there be one among you that doeth good, he shall **work by the power and gifts of God**." According to Moroni, there is no other acceptable way to "do all that you can do"; to be satisfactory it must be done within the boundaries set by the Spirit, using its gifts, producing its fruit, which, as we have discovered, is also sufficient grace.

- **Titus 2:11-14**

For a moment let's also consider the only other occurrence of "denying ungodliness" in scripture, which is found in Titus 2:11-14 (cited by John MacArthur earlier). Curiously, "grace" is also central in these verses, along with an allusion to God's covenant bride Israel!

> For the **grace** of God that bringeth salvation hath appeared to all men, Teaching us that, **denying ungodliness** and worldly lusts, we should live soberly, righteously, and godly, in this present world; Looking for that blessed hope, and the glorious appearing of the great God and our Saviour Jesus Christ; Who gave himself for us, that he might redeem us from all iniquity, and purify unto himself a **peculiar people**, zealous of **good works**.

Paul's use of grace in these verses refers to Jesus Christ, who brings salvation, and has appeared in flesh. (Yeshua or Jesus in Hebrew means salvation, hinting that Paul here is word-playing.) Like Moroni, Paul exhorts us to deny ungodliness so that we might be redeemed and purified unto a "peculiar people". This last phrase is significant because it is again an allusion to Exodus 19:5! – "if ye will obey my voice indeed, and keep my covenant, then ye shall be a **peculiar treasure** (*periousia*) unto me above all people." As mentioned, this is traditionally considered to be God's covenant promise to his bride Israel. The Greek word used here in Titus 2 is *periousias*, which is also the same word used in the Greek Old Testament (in Exo 19:5) for *peculiar treasure*. Thus, like Moroni, Paul is also alluding to the ideal of a purified bride to describe how one is purified (perfected, sanctified) in her bridegroom – Christ. However, whereas Moroni references verses from Isaiah to accomplish this effect, Paul alludes directly to Exodus 19! Notice how *grace* begins this thought and how it concludes (is completed, finished, perfected) with *good works*, implying that good works are its fruit.

- **2 Cor 12:9-10, Meaning of "made perfect in weakness"**

There is another well-known and similar sounding scripture which directly underscores grace's "sufficiency". In 2 Corinthians 12:9-10 we read:

And he said unto me, My grace is sufficient for thee: for my strength (*dunamis*) is made perfect in weakness. Most gladly therefore will I rather glory in my infirmities, that the power (*dunamis*) of Christ may rest upon me. Therefore I take pleasure in infirmities, in reproaches, in necessities, in persecutions, in distresses for Christ's sake: for when I am weak, then am I strong.

You will notice that the word "strength" and "power" in these verses is the same Greek word *dunamis*. Like Moroni's use in

10:32, the word "power" (and or strength) here also refers to the power of the Holy Ghost. Observe the sequence: The first sentence is the Lord telling Paul that his grace is sufficient because its power (*dunamis*) is allowed to more fully operate (is perfected) in the life of one who has a weakness. Paul then responds that since this is the case, he wants to have weaknesses so that this promised "power of Christ" (the Spirit), may rest on him. This idea of Christ's power (in the form of the Spirit) resting upon us is in fact the focus of these verses.

My grace is sufficient for thee: – A chiastic explanation

    A for my **strength**

        B is made perfect in **weakness.**

            C Most gladly therefore **will I rather glory**

                D in my **infirmities,**

                    E that the **power of Christ** may rest upon me.

            C Therefore **I take pleasure**

                D in **infirmities,** in reproaches, in necessities, in persecutions, in distresses for Christ's sake:

        B for when I am **weak,**

    A then am I **strong.**

From the lexicon we find the Greek word for "rest upon" is *episkenow*, which means – "of the power of Christ descending upon one, **working within him** and giving him help."[120] Elsewhere, in Ephesians 3:16 Paul reiterates how we are made strong by the power of Christ; "That he would grant you, according to the riches of his glory, to be *strengthened* with might by **his Spirit in the inner man**. That Christ may dwell in your hearts by faith; that ye, being rooted and grounded in love, may be able to comprehend with all saints what *is* the breadth, and length, and depth, and height; And to know the love of Christ, which passeth knowledge, that ye might be filled with all the fullness of God." Note that to feel his strength is to also comprehend his love – both done through the power of the Spirit (1 Ne 11). [121]

- **Temple Marriage – Learning Perfection**

As discussed in chapter 16 of this book, there is one other place in scripture where we read of "coming unto Christ." In Mat 11:28 Christ personally extends the invitation, "**Come unto me**, all *ye* that labour and are heavy laden, and I will give you rest. Take my yoke upon you, and learn of me; for I am meek and lowly in heart: and ye shall find rest unto your souls. For my yoke *is* easy, and my burden is light." Though we may not see the word grace used here, the implication is the same – that the process of learning of him, resting in him, and being yoked to him – is sufficient. Naturally, learning of Christ is only done through the Spirit. In fact, the yoke here represents the power of God or the Spirit, which tethers us to Christ (like the team of yoked oxen which move in unison, we move at-one with Him). Learning of Him through the Spirit, which allows us to "comprehend the length, depth, breadth and height" of His love (Eph 3:16-19), is the process of being perfected in Christ. And, as we trust in Christ alone, in the power of his Spirit (yielding to the

Holy Ghost which entices us to put off the natural man), ours souls find rest in that grace and power.[122]

It is also possible to envision the sufficiency of God's grace portrayed in Nephi's vision of the tree of life. Nephi describes the taste of its fruit as the most desirable and joyous to the soul. Curiously, in Greek the word for grace is *charis*, which comes from the verb *chairo*, meaning to be joyful! When we feel God's gracious love it consequently fills our hearts with joy. For this reason, in the Book of Mormon whenever the power of Holy Ghost is described, usually in the same verse we also find a mention of the joy, which accompanies its presence (see Mos 4:2, Mos 4:11, Mos 4:20, Alma 19:6, Alma 22:15, Alma 31:36-38).

Lastly, let's return to the beginning of this chapter and the marital context utilized by Moroni to introduce the idea of perfection in Christ; that a bride and bridegroom are perfected or completed in covenant marriage. This is especially significant because we believe that we can only be exalted to the highest degree of God's kingdom with an equally perfected (sanctified) husband or wife (D&C 132). Within the new and everlasting covenant of marriage, perfection is therefore a shared process; one undertaken individually, but not independently. In fact, the natural consequence of being individually perfected in Christ is that it simultaneously transforms all of our relationships. 1 Jn 4:12 tells us that us that as we love others we are "perfected in love." Therefore, our relationship with Christ is most immediately reflected in how we treat the person with whom we are most intimate. When each spouse (the bride and her groom) are bearing the fruit of God's love in their lives (fruit of the Spirit), then they are patient, kind, loving, and joyful; sharing a celestial heart and mind. God's grace is consequently sufficient (is the only way) for perfecting our marriages.

The term "temple marriage" still echoes the purpose of the original temple, to which ancient people (with broken and contrite spirits) brought a sacrifice. Today *temple* marriage carries on a likeness of this tradition – it is an altar where we bring the sacrifice (putting off) of our pride and selfishness (the animal within). To be sure, the hallmark of celestial marriage is when we think of our partner first; allow the Spirit to fill us with God's love and guide what we say and do. As God's love dwells in each spouse, Christ dwells in and seals that marriage – it is celestial because they are.

Conclusion

"O then, is not this real?"

In Alma 32, Alma gives us instruction about planting the word in our hearts, he explains that – "the word hath swelled your souls, and ye also know that it hath sprouted up, that your understanding doth begin to be enlightened, and your mind doth begin to expand." At this point he asks a decisive question – "O then, is not this real." Nephi might have asked the same question as he tasted of the tree of life (God's love). Indeed, his response to the gentle stirrings of the Spirit as he saw the condescension of the Savior (his birth, baptism, ministry, and death) changed forever the course of his life, just as knowing God's love in our hearts changes ours. And though it is spiritually perceived, is it not real?

Later, Alma gives a very specific definition of "the word" that swells our souls. In Alma 33:22-23 we read: "cast about your eyes and **begin to believe** in the Son of God, that he will come to redeem his people, and that he shall suffer and die to atone for their sins; and that he shall rise again from the dead, which shall bring to pass the resurrection, that all men shall stand before him, to be judged at the last and judgment day, according to their works. And now, my brethren, **I desire that ye shall plant this word in your hearts**, and as it beginneth to swell even so nourish it by your faith. And behold, it will become a tree, springing up in you unto everlasting life." Christ's mission portrayed here by Alma is another version of the condescension of God that Nephi saw in 1 Nephi 11, when "the word" of God's love was planted in his heart and he tasted of its fruit. To be sure, it has been planted in the hearts of countless others.

For instance, in John 3:1-2 Nicodemus also pondered "the word" of Jesus Christ – or as Alma might say, he "cast his eyes about" and had "began to **believe** in the Son of God." And, just as Alma explains that our mind needs to be enlightened, our hearts swollen, and our mind expanded by the Spirit, Jesus tells Nicodemus that he must be reborn (Jn 3:3). Christ also tells Nicodemus of his saving mission; that He must be "lifted up" to atone for sin (Jn 3:14). And then, just as Alma, Jesus reviews the promises of "everlasting life" reserved for those who plant and nurture this word by faith. In John 3:16 we read, "God so loved the world that he sent his only begotten Son. That whosoever **believeth** in him might have eternal life." At this point, as we consider the entirety of John's and Alma's context, we subsequently realize that the phrase "whosoever believeth" has very specific parameters; we understand that it refers only to those hearts that have been reborn and enlightened by God's love, that are growing the tree of life. Exclusively to this true "believer" is the promise of eternal life – those that can answer, "Oh yes, this is this real."

Alma's preaching in Alma 32 also follows the endowment pattern. He explains to the Zoramites how their lack of belief (telestial) can be changed by a heart that is enlivened\reborn by the word (terrestrial), and how it grows into a tree bearing the fruit of eternal life (celestial).

> Dormant belief or faith
> Word is planted with particle of faith   *Telestial*
>
>   Beginneth to swell, sprout, enlighten   *Terrestrial*
>
> Word takes root, nurtured w/ faith   *Celestial*
> bears fruit, eternal life

- **Terrestrial – the kingdom of transcendence**

You may have noticed that the terrestrial kingdom is more of a transition than a lengthy phase (it is the pivot "point" in the chiasmus). This is because it represents our rebirth, something that happens in the heart, an experience seemingly outside of linear time. The terrestrial moment is the reason for Alma's sentiment – "is not this real" – when divine knowledge (love) is felt (moves). Alma describes rebirth as the instant when the new sprout leaves the darkness of the husk and sees the light for the first time. It is the "blink of the eye" that we hear of in scripture, when man is translated, i.e. moves from one plane of existence to another, from the material to the spiritual world.

This is also the case in most of the examples we have looked at in this book. For instance, Moses was in Midian 40 years, but transcends in an extraordinary pivotal vision on Sinai. As well, Nephi's transformative vision of the tree of life could not have taken very long because when he returns his brothers are still talking about the same thing as when he left. Baptism itself is also illustrative of this. We are living in the telestial state until we descend into the water, die with Christ, and then emerge (resurrected) unto new life – clean and celestial.

Another example is the story of the blind man in Mark 8. The man's blindness to the world around him did not negate its existence; he was simply unable to see it. When Christ anoints him he suddenly, in a moment that "surpasses all understanding," begins to see, and at first his vision is not clear, he can see "men as though they were trees." This is exactly what Alma describes, that something in their heart has begun to stir – a new vision of the world seen through spiritual eyes, though not yet perfect. When Christ anoints the man a second time the veil is completely taken away and he sees Christ clearly before him (enters the celestial). So it is with us, we are children of God, have always been, and his love is all around us. We need this same anointing of the Spirit to remove the telestial scales from our eyes, and its continued presence (celestial) to bring Christ clearly into focus.

- **True order of prayer is a review of all covenants**

For this reason – to bring Christ into focus – we repeat everything that we have learned in the endowment at the veil. Collectively the individual signs and tokens commemorate all the promises and covenants which we have taken, which together consecrate everything we are and everything we posses to Christ and his kingdom. Nothing of us is meant to be left out. Only in offering it all (every whit) at the altar is the veil removed from our eyes and we can come into God's presence, i.e. until all is given this is not possible. This temple truth is wonderfully illustrated in the Prophet Joseph's favorite song, "A Poor Wayfaring Man of Grief."

> My friendship's utmost zeal to try,
> He asked if I for him would die.
> The flesh was weak; my blood ran chill,
> But my free spirit cried, "I will!"
> Then in a moment to my view
> The stranger started from disguise.
> The tokens in his hands I knew;
> The Savior stood before mine eyes.

Christ, our friend, has asked us to die for Him, which is the gospel's great paradox. From the beginning it has been the plan, not just for Christ, but for all of us – will you die to self and ego so that Christ can live in you? To Peter Christ said, "Except a corn of wheat fall into the ground and die, it abideth alone: but if it die, it bringeth forth much fruit. He that loveth his life shall lose it; and he that hateth his life in this world shall keep it unto life eternal." (Jn 12:24) This resonates in King Benjamin's admonition to yield one's free spirit to the Holy Ghost's promptings and put off or sacrifice the natural man (weak flesh), also found in the hymn's phrase – The flesh was weak; my blood ran chill, But my free spirit cried, "I will!" (Mosiah 3:19). Bruce Porter, of the Seventy, explains it wonderfully, "The Savior's perfect submission to the Eternal Father is the very essence of a broken heart and a contrite spirit. Christ's example teaches us that a broken heart is an eternal attribute of godliness. When our hearts are broken, we are completely open to the Spirit of God and recognize our dependence on Him for all that we have and all that we are. The sacrifice so entailed is a sacrifice of pride in all its forms . . . As we make the sacrifice to Him of all that we have and all that we are, the Lord will fill our hearts with peace. He will "bind up the brokenhearted" (Isaiah 61:1) and grace our lives with the love of God, "sweet above all that is sweet, ... and pure above all that is pure" (Alma 32:42)."[123]

- **Eden's Sacrament**

Whether the Garden of Eden or a sacrament meeting, what is eaten, and what it represents, has present and eternal consequences. When making ancient covenants, eating played a key role just as it does today in our sacrament (covenant renewing) service.[124] Meals to ratify and seal covenants appear in many Bible stories, all the way up to the great wedding supper of the Lamb in Revelation, when those who have been conventally true and faithful will dine in celebration with the Lord (Rev 19:8-9). Subsequently, as we partake of the sacrament and renew our covenants I am reminded of Adam and Eve, who assuredly ate of the tree of life in the first temple, the Garden of Eden, before their fall. As they sampled the many fruits in Eden, their favorite surely must have been the fruit from the tree of life – which was "sweet above all that is sweet." (It is likely the fruit that preserved them in their immortal state while in Eden.) Nephi also tells us that this tree represented the love of God, the fount of living water, who is Jesus Christ. In a way, when we partake of Christ (his emblems) we are a type of Adam and Eve. As they fellowshipped at His tree we can imagine that they (just as we do) tasted the delicious love of God in their hearts. Each week (on the seventh day) as we partake, in a sense we are in the midst of the Garden of Eden, and like our first parents we are given a choice between two trees. As we partake of His emblems we witness our choice to eat solely from the tree of life; i.e. we reject any forbidden fruit which could separate us from God's love, and covenant to give no place in our hearts for the enticings of Satan. In Hebrew we learn that Eden means *pleasure or delight*,[125] which correlates very well to what Nephi tells us about the supernatural tree found in the garden, that its fruit is the most desirable and joyous – or *pleasurable and delightful* – to the soul. Though we are not physically there, nonetheless we can have the joy of Eden in us, shed abroad in our hearts through the Spirit as we faithfully and truly renew our covenants. (See Appendix 3 for information on the sacrament prayer.)

APPENDIX 1

The Prodigal Son's Journey – The Endowment

In scripture, when a journey begins and ends in the same place, it is likely an account of the plan of salvation. Of course, the story of the prodigal son is our story; it represents all of us. Below is the endowment pattern found in this parable:

With Father's love

    Leaves into far country

        Wastes inheritance (famine)   *Telestial*

        Comes to Himself (rebirth), promise of bread *Terrestrial*

        Willing to be Father's servant   *Celestial*

    Returns from far country

Reunited with Father's love (receives all the father has)

The turning point is when the prodigal "comes to his senses" and remembers his Father's love and the loving home from whence he came. This realization is analogous to the mighty change of heart that Alma mentions in Alma 5, or the love of God shed abroad in Nephi's heart as he partakes of the tree of life – both experienced through the Holy Ghost. A new promise of hope, it is also associated with food (partaking). "And he would fain have filled his belly with the husks that the swine did eat: and no man gave unto him. And when he came to himself, he said, How many hired servants of my father's have bread enough and to spare, and I perish with hunger!"

(Lk 15:16-17) The father's bread is contrasted by the husks fed to the swine in the telestial world. It isn't too much to assume that this is an allusion to the saving bread which was promised to Joseph's brothers at the time when Joseph revealed himself as their savior, or to the manna which preserved ancient Israel in Exodus, or the bread of life in John 6 who is Jesus Christ, or the fruit of the tree of life in 1 Nephi.

Assured by the love in his heart, the prodigal resolves to submit to his father (celestial). He expresses this by his willingness to be a servant, which is the celestial quality that Christ talks about in Mat 10:44-45, "And whosoever of you will be the chiefest, shall be servant of all. For even the Son of man came not to be ministered unto, but to minister, and to give his life a ransom for many."

In the end, when the prodigal arrives home our hearts melt as we read of the father's eternal love for his son; that he "had compassion, and ran, and fell on his neck, and kissed him." We are reminded of Nephi's joy as he was "encircled about eternally by the arms of His (Saviors) love" (2 Ne 1:15). We marvel how the father welcomes his son with a feast (a similitude of the celestial wedding feast in Rev 19:7-9). The father also puts his ring on his son's hand, a sign of his authority, reminding us of how Joseph in Egypt was given the ring of Pharaoh (Gen 41:42). Such authority is like that given to Moses, who was told (when he returned to the presence of the Father) that his command would be obeyed "as if thou wert God" (Moses 1:25). The prodigal's father likewise "endows" his son with a kingly robe, a symbol of the robe of salvation in Isaiah 61:10 and the robe of righteousness in Rev 19:8. As well, he is given sandals, which indicate how destitute he has become, walking home without any shoes, which in ancient time was characteristic of a servant.

The following sums up the Father's love so poignantly: "Forgiveness would be empty without restoration to the privileges forfeited by sin. Therefore, if you bear the name son or daughter through having received Jesus as Lord and Savior by the power of the Holy Spirit you have found favor with the Father. The best robe has been placed upon you, a demonstration of the Father's complete approval of you and love and protection for you. A ring has been put on your hand representing the riches you have in Christ, authority you have been given in the name of Jesus and installation into the the office of king and priest to God. Sandals have been put on your feet affirming sonship and all of its benefits, including but not limited to healing, loving kindness, tender mercies and every good thing (Psalm 103). You are a joint heir with Christ Jesus who has been appointed heir of all things (Romans 8:17, Hebrews 1:2). You can join Isaiah in saying as he did in 61:10: "I will greatly rejoice in the Lord, my soul shall be joyful in my God; for He has clothed me with the garments of salvation, as a bridegroom decks himself with ornaments and as a bride adorns herself with her jewels." [126]

APPENDIX 2

Paul's Endowment – A Plan of Mercy and Grace

Paul was there when Stephen was stoned in Acts 7, and likely he also heard Stephen's three patriarchal defenses (the endowment pattern) on the temple mount (ch 5 of this book). It is only fitting that Luke records Paul's conversion in a similar pattern. Below is from Acts 9:

4-8 Sees **Jesus** near Damascus
    9 Three days **without sight, did not eat**
        10 Disciple named **Ananias in Damascus**
            11 Ananias – **Arise** and go into the **street called Straight**
                12 Saul sees Ananias in vision, that he will **lay hands on him**, and he will **receive sight**   *Telestial*
                    13 **How much evil** Saul hath done to saints
                        14 Authority from high priest **to bind** all that call on **thy name**
                            15 **He is a chosen vessel unto me**   *Terrestrial*
                        16 Chosen **to bear Lord's name** to Gentiles, Kings, Israel
                    16 **How much Saul must suffer** for my name's sake
                17 Ananias **lays hands on Paul** to **receive sight** and Holy Ghost   *Celestial*
            18 Paul **Arises** and is **baptized (make his ways straight)**
        19 With disciples **in Damascus**
    19 For certain days **Paul has sight,** and **eats**
20 Preaches that "he is **Christ, the Son of God**"

The way that this story begins and ends is wonderful; verse 5 tells us that Paul sees Jesus, and the parallel verse 20 tells us that

Paul later preaches that he, Jesus, is Christ the Son of God; developing fully the nature of who He is! Another parallel whose meaning is amplified when viewed jointly, is verse 11 which speaks about going "into the street called Straight." The corresponding verse (18) helps us to understand that the street called Straight represents baptism. For context, the word "straight" (*euthus* in Greek) is used in Mat 3:3 and refers to John who was **baptizing** in the wilderness, "Prepare ye the way of the Lord, make his paths straight (*euthus*)." Like baptism, the first side of the chiasmus represents a descent into the grave, while the other side represents the ascent unto eternal life. The center, very much like the endowment, hinges on "bearing the Lord's name." Let's look at some other parallels.

Vs 10 and 19

Ananias, pronounced Hananias, means God is merciful or gracious, and comes from the Hebrew root *chanan*; which is also what this story (and the plan of salvation) is all about. Below I provide some of the wonderful Old Testament scriptures which are referenced in the Lexicon for *chanan:*

> Psa 30:8-10 I cried to thee, O LORD; and unto the LORD I made supplication. What profit [is there] in my blood, when I go down to the pit? Shall the dust praise thee? Shall it declare thy truth? Hear, O LORD, and have **mercy** (chanan) upon me: LORD, be thou my helper.

> Psa 25:16-18 Turn thee unto me, and have **mercy** (chanan) upon me; for I [am] desolate and afflicted. The troubles of my heart are enlarged: [O] bring thou me out of my

distresses. Look upon mine affliction and my pain; and forgive all my sins.

Psa 41: 4 I said, LORD, be **merciful** unto me: heal my soul; for I have sinned against thee.

We can imagine how these verses might have been Paul's prayer as he lay blind for 3 days in Damascus, praying for Ananias (God's mercy) to come. Isn't it also our prayer?

Vs 12 and 17

In verse 12 Paul sees beforehand that he will receive his sight and that the darkness of death will be lifted. Reflectively, in verse 17 Paul receives the anointing of the Holy Ghost when Ananias lays his hands on him. He then "sees" physically and spiritually.

Vs 14 and 16

Verse 14 speaks of the high priest's earthly authority given to Paul to "bind" all those who call on the Lord's name. Verse 16 conversely speaks of the true high priest (the "Lord") and his authority given to Paul to bear the name of the Lord to Israelite and Gentile (breaking the bonds of death).

Vs 15 – The Apex

The apex of the chiasmus is focused in the passage, "for he is a chosen vessel unto me." Paul, in a letter to the Romans, uses the same metaphoric language of vessels and mercy (*chanan*), which he applies to us (we are also chosen vessels). In Romans 9:18-24 Paul encourages:

> . . . that he might make known the riches of his glory on the **vessels of mercy**, which he had afore prepared unto glory, Even us, whom **he hath called**, not of the Jews only, but also of the Gentiles.

As vessels, saved by mercy (*chanan*), like Paul we have been "afore prepared for glory" and chosen to bear the Lord's name (take his name upon us). Hands have also been laid on our head and anointed us with covenant promises and the power of the Holy Ghost whereby we may "know" the riches of his glory.

In the telestial world Paul is blind, denies Christ, is not nourished (does not eat), has done evil to the saints, and possesses only earthly authority; acting in the name of the false high priest. In the terrestrial he is mercifully chosen to bear the Lord's name and is promised true authority. Finally, in the celestial kingdom Paul is healed, can see, is filled with the Holy Ghost, is spiritually nourished, and knows (and with divine authority preaches) that Jesus is the Christ.

APPENDIX 3

The Sacrament Prayer – Chiasmus

If we look at the sacrament prayer with chiastic eyes, we see clear parallels between several elements. Below is a possible chiastic arrangement of the sacrament prayer (parenthesis mine):

A O God, the Eternal Father, we ask thee in the name of thy Son, **Jesus Christ**,
    B to bless and **sanctify** this bread **to the souls** of all those who partake of it;
        C that they may eat in **remembrance** of
            D the body of **thy Son**,
                E and **witness** unto thee,
                    F O God,
                    F' the Eternal Father,
                E' that they are **willing to take upon** them
            D' the name of **thy Son**,
        C' and always **remember him**, and keep his commandments which he hath given them,
    B' that they may always have his **Spirit** (the sanctifier) to be with them.
A' **Amen**.

Arranging the sacrament prayer in this format can be enlightening. You will probably agree that the inner parallels (e.g. thy son, remembrance, God and Eternal Father) are relatively self-evident, but the outer legs, A and B, might need some explanation.

A – A'

It is possible to make a parallel here because we are told a couple of times in scripture that Christ is the Amen (a title meaning faithful or firm in Hebrew[127]), alluding to the fact that he faithfully fulfills the covenant promise of God the Eternal Father. In Revelation 3:14 we read: "These things saith **the Amen**, the faithful and true witness, the beginning of the creation of God." Notice that the Amen is capitalized, indicating a proper name. Also notice that Christ is the faithful and true witness of God's covenant, an exemplary model of our personal covenantal witness in the sacrament prayer. Another and perhaps better example is from 2 Cor 1:20-22: "20 For all the promises of God in him [are] yea, and in him [the] **Amen**, unto the glory of God by us. 21 Now he which stablisheth us with you in Christ, and hath anointed us, [is] God; 22 Who hath also **sealed** us, and given the earnest of the Spirit in our hearts." The "promises of God" (vs 20) refer to the covenant promises which are fulfilled by the Amen, or Christ. Also you may notice that verse 22 repeats what is said in 21, only with slightly different words. Below are these fascinating and instructive parallels:

> Now he which **stablisheth us** with you in Christ,
> and hath **anoint**ed us, [is] God;
> Who hath also **sealed us**,
> and given the earnest of the **Spirit** in our hearts."

According to these parallels we are **established** or **sealed** in Christ by the **anointing** of the **Spirit** in our hearts. Certainly, this also pertains to the sacrament prayer, wherein those who renew their covenants by taking upon themselves His name, remember Him, and keep His commandments – are anointed with the Spirit (always) and are established and sealed in Christ. If we hadn't thought of the sacrament as a sealing ceremony, then we may want to.

B – B'

Most recognize that the sacrament prayer ends with, to "have the Spirit always," but you may not have noticed that it also begins with reference to the Spirit, because sanctification is a process of purification that is done through the Holy Ghost, and in no other way. In B the bread is blessed so as to "sanctify to the soul" of the one who partakes, which as mentioned is a process performed by the Holy Ghost. When we partake of Christ (the bread of life), eat the tokens of Him, we are nourished by Christ. He becomes our source of life (unending and eternal); He is in us and we are in him; there is spiritual at-one-ment.

As the scriptures tell us in Romans 8:9-14, "But ye are not in the flesh, but in the Spirit, if so be that the Spirit of God dwell in you. Now if any man have not the Spirit of Christ, he is none of his. And **if Christ be in you**, the body is dead because of sin; but the Spirit is life because of righteousness. But if **the Spirit** of him that raised up Jesus from the dead **dwell in you**, he that raised up Christ from the dead shall also quicken your mortal bodies by his Spirit that dwelleth in you. Therefore, brethren, we are debtors, not to the flesh, to live after the flesh. For if ye live after the flesh, ye shall die: but if ye through the Spirit do mortify the deeds of the body, ye shall live. For as many as are led by the Spirit of God, they are the sons of God." This last line especially alludes to the sacrament, wherein we renew our covenant to take his name upon us, to be his sons and daughters. Notice that only those "led by the Spirit of God" may claim His name. In these verses "the flesh" and "the body" are mentioned several times as an enemy to the Spirit. In particular we are told that through the Spirit we "mortify the deeds of the body." Of course, this is the same thing that King Benjamin said in the middle of his temple discourse in Mosiah 3:19, that the natural man (the flesh) is an enemy to God until he puts off (mortifies) the natural man and yields to the enticings of the Spirit. King Benjamin adds that thereby we "becometh saints (sanctified) through the atonement. Again, this is the offering that we bring to the sacrament table (altar), the animal within us (pride, natural man), the offering of the broken heart and contrite spirit.

Moreover, it is significant that the prayer begins with the sanctification of our soul, because we cannot truly and faithfully witness that we will take his name upon us unless we have been sanctified through the Holy Ghost. Remember the Holy Ghost (sanctifier) is the personage of the godhead who seals us to Christ (2 Cor 1:20-22), which can only be accorded to his sanctified sons and daughters. Also, there is a chronology established here, which is that that we do not necessarily "keep his commandment" so as to "have his Spirit", but rather we begin with sanctification (to our souls) so that we can keep the commandments. Like Adam, as discussed in the first chapter of this book, our obedience to the commandments must be done in the name of the Only Begotten, enjoined by the Spirit (see pg 7-8). Convental renewal begins and ends with the Spirit.[128]

Finally, consider the clear teachings of Bruce R. McConkie (parenthesis mine): "It is the work and mission and ministry of the Holy Spirit of God to sanctify the souls of men. This is his assigned labor in the Eternal Godhead. How he does it we do not know, except that it is a work that can only be performed by a spirit being, and hence the need for one of his personality, status, and standing in the Supreme Presidency of the universe. Baptism of the Spirit is the way and the means whereby sanctification is made available. Thus, Jesus commands all the "ends of the earth" to be baptized in water "that ye may be sanctified by the reception of the Holy Ghost, that ye may stand spotless before me at the last day" (3 Nephi 27:20.) Truly, the Holy Ghost is a sanctifier, and **the extent to which men receive and enjoy the gift of the Holy Ghost is the extent to which they are sanctified**. In the lives of most of us, sanctification is an ongoing process, and we obtain that glorious status by degrees as we overcome the world (put off the natural man) and become saints in deed as well as in name." (A New Witness for the Articles of Faith, pp. 265-266)

APPENDIX 4

The Holy Spirit of Promise

In chapter 3 we compared the 1st principals and ordinances of the gospel to the temple pattern, assigning each principle to one of three worlds (kingdoms). In particular, the gift of the Holy Ghost is associated with the celestial. Significantly, D&C 88:2-6 not only associates the Holy Ghost with the celestial kingdom, but also reveals an even greater role played by the Holy Ghost within that sphere. Here we read, "your prayers have come up into the ears of the Lord of Sabaoth, and are recorded in the **book of the names of the sanctified, even them of the celestial world.** 3 Wherefore, I now send upon you another Comforter, even upon you my friends, that it **may abide in your hearts**, even the **Holy Spirit of promise**; which other Comforter is the same that I promised unto my disciples, as is recorded in the testimony of John. 4 This Comforter is **the promise which I give unto you of eternal life**, even the glory of the **celestial kingdom**; 5 Which glory is that of the church of the Firstborn, even of God, the holiest of all, through Jesus Christ his Son." The Holy Ghost in these verses is referred to as "the Holy Spirit of promise" which will be sent to those whose names have been recorded in the "book of the sanctified"; i.e. those who have been sanctified through the Holy Ghost (have put off the natural man and yielded to the enticings of the Spirit). [129]

Evidently, when a member of the church has been sufficiently purified by the first comforter (the Holy Ghost) there is a greater endowment of the Spirit which brings that person a promise that they have been sealed "unto eternal life, even the glory of the celestial kingdom." From the LDS Guide to the Scriptures we read: "The Holy Ghost is the Holy Spirit of Promise (Acts 2:33). He confirms as acceptable to God the righteous acts, ordinances, and covenants of men. The Holy Spirit of Promise witnesses to the Father that the saving ordinances have been performed properly and that the covenants associated with them have been kept."

From D&C 76:51-60 we read more of the promises which this higher manifestation of the Spirit may seal upon the righteous after baptism: "52 That by keeping the commandments they might be washed and cleansed from all their sins, and receive the Holy Spirit by the laying on of the hands of him who is ordained and sealed unto this power; 53 And who overcome by faith, and are **sealed by the Holy Spirit of promise**, which the Father sheds forth upon all those who are just and true (righteous). 54 They are they who are the church of the Firstborn. 55 They are they into whose hands the Father has given all things— 56 They are they who are priests and kings, who have received of his fullness, and of his glory; 57 And are priests of the Most High, after the order of Melchizedek, which was after the order of Enoch, which was after the order of the Only Begotten Son. 58 Wherefore, as it is written, they are gods, even the sons of God— 59 Wherefore, all things are theirs, whether life or death, or things present, or things to come, all are theirs and they are Christ's, and Christ is God's. 60 And they shall overcome all things."

Concerning the sealing of the Holy Spirit of promise (vs 53), from the LDS Eternal Marriage Student Manual we find: "Accordingly, the baptism of an unworthy and unrepentant person would not be sealed by the Spirit; it would not be ratified by the Holy Ghost; the unworthy person would not be justified by the Spirit in his actions. If thereafter he became worthy through repentance and obedience, the seal would then be put in force. Similarly, if a worthy person is baptized, with the ratifying approval of the Holy Ghost attending the performance, yet the seal may be broken by subsequent sin.

"These principles also apply to every other ordinance and performance in the Church. Thus if both parties are 'just and true,' if they are worthy, a ratifying seal is placed on their temple marriage; if they are unworthy, they are not justified by the Spirit and the ratification of the Holy Ghost is withheld. Subsequent **worthiness will put the seal in force**, and unrighteousness will break any seal.

"Even if a person progresses to that state of near-perfection in which his calling and election is made sure, in which he is 'sealed up unto eternal life' (D&C 131:5; 132:18–26), in which he receives 'the promise ... of eternal life' (D&C 88:3–4), in which he is 'sealed up unto the day of redemption' (D&C 124:124; Eph. 1:13)—yet with it all, these great promises are secured only if the 'performances' are sealed by the Holy Spirit of Promise" (Mormon Doctrine, 361–62).

APPENDIX 5

President Monson – First Presidency Message, Aug 2015

    A I would like all of **the youth** of the Church **to know** that they are children of light.
       B As such, they have a responsibility to be "as lights in the world" (Philippians 2:15). They have a duty to **share the truths** of the gospel. They have a calling to **stand as a temple beacon, reflecting gospel light** to an increasingly dark world. They have a charge to keep their light aflame and burning brightly. In order for us to be "an example of the believers" (1 Timothy 4:12), we ourselves must believe. We must develop the faith necessary to survive spiritually and to **project a light for others**.
         C We must nurture our testimony until it becomes **an anchor** to our lives.
            D Among the most effective ways to gain and keep the faith we need today is to read and study the scriptures and to **pray frequently and consistently**. To the youth of the Church, I say, if you haven't done so, develop now a habit of daily scripture study and **prayer**. Without these two essential practices, outside influences and the sometimes-harsh realities of life can dim or even extinguish your light.
                E The teenage years are not easy. They are prime years when Satan will **tempt** you and do his utmost to entice you from the path which will lead you back to your heavenly home.

You
Telestial
                    F But as you read and pray and as you **serve and obey**,
                       G you will **come to know better** "the light which shineth in darkness" (D&C 6:21),
                          H our Exemplar and our **strength**—even the Lord Jesus Christ (truth and righteousness).
                             I **He is the Light** we are to hold up to dispel the gathering darkness (see 3 Nephi 18:24).
                               J With a strong testimony of the **Savior** and His restored gospel,
                                  K you have limitless **opportunities to shine**. They **surround** you each day, in whatever

Christ
Terrestrial
                           circumstances you find yourselves.
                              J' As you follow the example of the Savior,
                             K' yours will be the **opportunity to be a light**, as it were, in the lives of those **around** you—whether they be members of your own family, classmates, co-workers, mere acquaintances, or total strangers.
                        I' When **you are a light** to the world, people around you will feel a special spirit that will make them want to associate with you and

Others
Celestial
                      H' follow **your example**. I plead with parents and leaders of our youth to help them **stand firm** for truth and righteousness.
                 G' Help **open wide to their view the gates of learning, of understanding,**
              F' and **of service** in the kingdom of God.
          E' Build within them strength to resist the **temptations** of the world.
       D' Give them the will to walk in virtue and faith, to **be prayerful**,
    C' and to look to heaven as their **constant anchor**.
A' **To our youth**, I say, our Heavenly Father loves you. May **you feel** also the love which Church leaders have for you. May you ever have a desire to serve your Heavenly Father and His Son.
    B' And may you always **walk in truth** and **stand as a light among God's children**.

Alistair Begg (a contemporary Christian preacher) once said that if you are content to go to heaven alone, then you're probably not going. Certainly, this is the sentiment expressed here by President Thomas Monson. In this talk the pattern of the temple and creation is also uniquely amplified. He begins by telling us we are called to be a light, and that it will increase as we nurture our testimony by applying gospel principles such as faith, scripture study, service, and prayer. We could easily associate this initial phase with the telestial; immature until we come to "know better" (G) our Exemplar (H) who is the light (I).

At the center of this talk (the terrestrial) the focus is turned to Jesus Christ (the Savior). We are told that our testimony has become strong (J), because we follow the example of the Savior. (J'). With the Savior as our bridge (from the telestial to the celestial), President Monson wonderfully parallels – "He is the light" (I) to, "you are the light" (I'), and whereas He is the "Exemplar" (H), we become the "example" (H'). Here we discover transformation and rebirth (a sense of taking upon us his name) as we become **His** light. Then, as a type of Christ (having his image in our countenance, engraven in our hearts), the celestial side of this chiasmus emerges wherein we assist others in the same divine process; "opening wide the gates of learning and understanding" (G') allowing the light of Christ to illuminate the minds and hearts of others. Grace for grace, those who also respond to the light receive all that we did – the strength to resist temptation (E, E'), a will to pray (D,D'), an understanding of service (F,F'), and heaven as a constant anchor (C,C').

This pattern should remind us of Lehi's vision of the tree of life, where after Lehi has partaken of the tree of life he desires that his family partake. When we partake of the tree, which represents God's love, the proof of its effect is that we want others to experience the same joy. In fact, if our hearts are not turned to others then it is evident that we never really partook. In 1 John 4:7,8,11 we read, "Beloved, let us love one another: for love is of God; and every **one that loveth is born of God**, and knoweth God. **He that loveth not knoweth not God**; for God is love. Beloved, **if God so loved us**, we ought also to love one another." In other words, if the warmth of God's love has truly touched our lives, then we will necessarily shine that love into the lives of others, effecting change and transformation in their hearts.

At its core, President's Monson's talk is really about the path (a "walk in truth") that leads to eternal life. This is so because life eternal is to "know God and Jesus Christ who he sent," (John 17:3); and, as we have just read, "knowing God" is to love others (1 Jn 4:7-8). Subsequently, only those who have felt His love and shared it are "born of God" and have the promise of eternal life (they are experiencing it right now). Loving those around us is how His light shines. (Can it shine in any other way?) In fact, President Monson ends his talk (A') substituting (or elevating) love for light – "To our youth, I say, our Heavenly Father **loves** you. May you **feel** also the love which Church leaders have for you." This concluding statement is contrasted by his opening statement (A) where he admonishes our youth "**to know** that they are children of light." These are insightful parallels, because our youth can only truly "know" that they are children of light if they have "felt" His divine love in their hearts. If they are children of light then they are born of His love. As Nephi reminds us, it is the most desirable; the most joyous to the soul! (1 Ne 11). Finally, consider how Alma interlaces light and love: "He has brought them into **his everlasting light**, yea, into everlasting salvation; and **they are encircled about with the matchless bounty of his love**; yea, and we have been instruments in his hands of doing this great and marvelous work." (Alma 26:15)

APPENDIX 6
2 Cor 11:2-4, Rom 1:21
Corrupted Mind, Darkened Heart

There are other verses found in scripture which shed additional light on Adam and Eve's experience in the garden. The first is in 2 Cor 11:12-14. Here Paul uses marriage imagery, which, as we have explored (pg 96-97, Chapter 19), is also an important temple theme, symbolizing our deep relationship to our bridegroom and high priest, Jesus Christ. In these verses Paul compares the early saints to Eve, stressing that what happened to Eve's mind in Eden continues to occur. "2 For I am jealous over you with godly jealousy: for I have espoused you to one husband, that I may present you as a chaste virgin to Christ. 3 But I fear, lest by any means, as the serpent beguiled Eve through his subtilty, **so your minds should be corrupted from the simplicity that is in Christ**. 4 For if he that cometh preacheth another Jesus, whom we have not preached, or if ye receive another spirit, which ye have not received, or another gospel, which ye have not accepted, ye might well bear with him."

First of all, notice Paul's zeal to present the saints as a chaste bride to her husband, Christ. This is reminiscent of the temple endowment's center point (terrestrial kingdom), when we (dressed in wedding white) receive greater light and priesthood, along with the law of chastity and a new name. Regarding the first principles and ordinances (also an endowment pattern), this phrase (espoused as a chaste virgin to Christ) also reminds us of when we are baptized and take his name upon us. The verb "espoused" here is *harmozo*, which is the word that the English "harmony" comes from, meaning to join or fit together in one. This word is used once in the New

Testament (here), and perfectly captures not only Adam and Eve's charge to become joined as one (cleave), but also embraces the idea of the Atonement (at-one-ment) for all saints – those espoused to Christ. In addition, "espoused" is a word that in Paul's day was understood exclusively in terms of covenant (The groom paid a bride price and provided a *ketubah* – a contract wherein he consecrated himself to his future wife.[130])

So what happened to Eve's mind (or the mind of any saint) that it became tainted, and from what "simplicity" was it corrupt? As the first married couple, the command to cleave to one another implies that Adam and Eve were to love and care for one another, which also exemplifies the edict to Christ's disciples, to "love one another as I have loved you", which is the heart of Christ's new covenant. John 3:16 is a scripture that conveys the simplicity of God's love for us; that he sent his son, and that whoever believes on him (loves him) will have eternal live.

A chaste (pure) virgin is characterized by her faithfulness, her love, and her covenantal purity. Clearly, a fallen virgin is one whose heart forsakes her lover, which Eve portrays (according to Paul) when she partook of forbidden fruit without consulting God or Adam (her espoused lovers). This idea is supported by the tree of life found in Eden, which Nephi tells us represents the love of God, which also personifies Jesus Christ's sacrifice. When Eve forsakes this tree (representing love) to eat from the other, she effectively forsakes the beauty and simplicity of love; the power which binds man to God, God to man, and man to one another.

It is no coincidence that the words used in the temple to describe our worthiness are "true and faithful". These are words that also express a married couple's commitment to one another. "True and faithful" describes the original condition of creation, just as it is the chosen phrase and criteria whereby we pass through the veil, returning to God – who is love (Jn 4:8). As well, think about verses 13-14 where Paul compares Satan's message in the garden to "another gospel", preached to corrupt Christian minds and lead them astray, even as a different gospel preached by Satan led Eve astray. As we have already considered on page 90 of this book, this different gospel is loveless, requiring no sacrifice of its followers (something which genuine love always inspires). Also, along with this "other gospel" there is another endowment, that of Satan, which darkens the mind and heart of those who receive it (pg 94).

- **Romans 1:20-21**

How the mind is darkened is supported by another verse worthy of our consideration, which is Rom 1:20-21: "For the invisible things of him from the creation of the world are clearly seen, being understood by the things that are made, even his eternal power and Godhead; so that they are without excuse: Because that, when they knew God, they glorified him not as God, neither were thankful; but became vain in their imaginations (*dialogismos*, thinking), and **their foolish heart was darkened.**" Many believe that this verse is an allusion to not just man in general, but specifically Adam and Eve. Whether or not that is the case, we do find here a description of how the "heart was darkened" by a similar process.

Paul uses the phrase that "they knew God", which as discussed previously has a very specific scriptural definition –

meaning to love God and his children. Paul adds that when one knows God he will glorify him (vs. 20), which the scriptures tell us is to bear the fruit of love. "Herein is my Father glorified, that ye bear much fruit; so shall ye be my disciples. As the Father hath loved me, so have I loved you: continue ye in my love." (Jn 15:8-9) Love, then, is what their hearts were darkened to; i.e. their thinking became empty or vain which in turn darkened their hearts. In Gen 3 we see Eve's mind at work, "imagining" that the bad fruit was "pleasant to the eye, good for food, desirable to make one wise." These are vain imaginations because they are not true. To the contrary, love is the truth which Eve already enjoyed in Eden, and anything other than that simplicity ("another gospel") is a dim counterfeit. As mentioned, on pg 93 a reverse endowment pattern is diagrammed which follows exactly the steps given by Paul here in Romans; wherein a "vain imagination" of the mind (telestial) replaces the love of the heart (celestial), darkening it. This process explains how one is ultimately begotten of Satan (the serpent), the father of lies.

APPENDIX 7

The Seven Churches of Asia – The Endowment

John begins his revelation to the churches of Asia, addressing them as "kings and priests unto God and his Father", drawing the temple into focus (Rev 1:6). Such a reference sets the stage for other elements of the temple, immediately introduced by John into this narrative. And, because the endowment is embedded in so many stories of the scriptures, we would especially expect to find it in Revelation, which is a book replete with sevens (the very rhythm of the endowment) – seven candlesticks, seven stars, seven churches, seven bowls, seven seals, seven horns, seven angels, and so on. (In fact, it is reported that there are over 60 uses of seven in this book.) Let's examine chapters two and three where John is commanded to record the instructions given to the seven churches of Asia. Below is an outline of the endowment narrative implanted within these verses.

Ephesus – desired (reflects Eve's desires in Eden)

Smyrna – myrrh (used to anoint for burial)

Pergamos – elevated, height (pride)

Thyatira – sacrifice (love)

Sardis – red (garments once red made white)

Philadelphia – love of a brother (death's door opened)

Laodicea – judgment of the people (lukewarm spued out)

At first glance there may be little to substantiate the notion that these verses are an endowment sequence. In order to support such a perspective, below is more information as it relates to each creation segment. Notice that each church is given an important promise to those that overcome:

Ephesus – thou hast left thy first love, thou art **fallen,** overcomer given to eat of **tree of life**

    Smyrna – be faithful **unto death**, overcomer not hurt by second **death**

        Pergomas – they dwell where Satan's dwell, hold to doctrine of Balaam, overcomer given a **new name**
        (*Telestial*)

            Thyratira – saith the **Son of God**, works are love, service, charge to be chaste, promises of power over the nations, overcomer given **the Morning Star – Christ**   (*Terrestrial*)

        Sardis – works not perfect before God, a few of worthy shall walk with me in white, overcomer clothed in white raiment, and name not blotted out but **confessed before Father**   (*Celestial*)

    Philadelphia – He with Key of David opens **door**, overcomer is made pillar in temple (and go out no more), will **write upon him the name of God (Father)**, and my new name.

Laodicea – These things saith the **faithful and true**, lukewarm spued out, counsel to be clothed in white, no shame of nakedness, overcomer will **sit with Christ in throne of Father.**

While each church is called out for shortcomings, key phrases or events are also given to each one that relate to a specific part of the modern endowment, which I have emboldened. Although some of the elements are slightly out of position, this can easily be accounted for by the fact that they transition from one period to the next; e.g. "faithful and true" are words used to transition from the veil into the presence of God.

Something should also be said about the expression "overcome" which plays such an important role in these verses. John is probably making reference here to what Christ said in John 16:33, "be of good cheer; I have overcome the world." Taken in context, Christ is referring to overcoming the sin and death (spiritual and physical) in the world. In his other writing John enlarges on this: "For whatsoever is born of God overcometh the world: and this is the victory that overcometh the world, even our faith" (1 Jn 5:6). To know that Jesus is the Christ, to have this love shed abroad in our hearts, and to yield to it – this is rebirth, it is eternal life (1 Jn 5:12-13), it is an endowment of the Spirit needed to overcome the natural man who is in the world. This is how one "becometh a saint", overcoming a fallen world through the Atonement (Mos 3:19).

Below are a few Notes.

Ephesus – The first love mentioned here is the "love of God" which one experiences at the tree of life when he\she partakes of its fruit. When Adam and Eve were separated from this love they "art fallen." However, as promised in Genesis, they can return when they overcome the world, i.e. when the serpent has been crushed (the natural man put off). The underlying meaning of the word Ephesus is desire which reflects the conflict in Eden, when Eve's desires changed to hunger after the tree of knowledge of good and evil rather than the tree of love\life. (Notice that we have the tree of life in Ephesus, just as it is present in the first part of our spiritual creation story in the modern endowment.)

Smyrna – "And unto the angel of the church in Smyrna write; These things saith the first and the last, which was dead, and is alive." These abrupt introductory words immediately turn our attention to death, and that it has been overcome through Jesus Christ. Herein is the genius of each of these 7 steps, which is that each also refers to Christ; suggesting that any part of our journey without Christ is incomplete – even (and especially) death.

Pergamos – By virtue of its Greek meaning, Pergamos is elevated or heightened, characterizing prideful man. We are told, it is a land where Satan dwells (Rev 2:13), which if you have been to the temple is especially apropos because it is in the telestial world that Satan makes his claim as its ruler. (Before Adam can advance to the terrestrial world Satan must be cast out.) Balaam is also mentioned here (Rev 2:14), who was a false prophet (Num 22) and represents the false teaching found in the telestial world. (Satan is a type of Balaam in the temple endowment, preaching the philosophies of man mingled with scriptures.)

Thyratira – For the first time we have the mention of the "Son of God"; the name upon which the temple endowment hinges. Those that have been to the temple will recognize its importance at this juncture. As well, Thyratira is from the Greek *thuros,* meaning sacrifice, which reflects the sacrifice of the Son of God. Wonderfully, the overcomer here is given the Morning Star – which refers to the rising "sun" and is another name for Christ. Rev 22:16 tells us: "**I Jesus** have sent mine angel to testify unto you these things in the churches. I am the root and the offspring of David, and the bright and **morning star**." Also, matching perfectly the chronology of the endowment, Jezebel is mentioned in Rev 2:20-23 along with a charge to be chaste (repent from adultery and fornication)! See pg 96 for more info on the terrestrial law of chastity – a remembrance of one's temple marriage.

Sardis – This represents the celestial world. Curiously, it is still a church that is "not perfect", though a very select group is identified; "Thou hast a few names even in Sardis which have not defiled their garments; and they shall walk with me in white: for they are worthy" (Rev 3:4). There is also possibly a play-on-words here because Sardis means red, yet the promise is that the worthy will be clothed in white. In fact the promise of white raiment is repeated in verse 5: "He that overcometh, the same shall be clothed in white raiment; and I will not blot out his name out of the book of life, but I will confess his name before my Father, and before his angels." (Rev 3:5) The overcomer's name is not blotted out, but apparently his\her sins are, which reminds us of Isa 1:18, "though your sins be as scarlet, they shall be as white as snow; though they be red like crimson, they shall be as wool." (The art of dyeing wool is said to have been invented in Sardis.) [131] Sardis (the celestial church) is also associated here (3:5) with the name of the Father, which is mentioned by John for the first time. In the temple endowment this is also where we hear patriarch (of the Father).

Philadelphia – The door revealed to the church in Philadelphia represents the veil. And, as mentioned before, the veil represents Jesus Christ, through whom we have access to the holiest of the temple (Heb 10:19). For this reason, in Rev 3:7 it says – "no man openeth and no man shutteth," but Christ, who "hath the key of David (meaning the beloved)." The name of the church is also very appropriate because it means brotherly love, representing the supreme love of a brother; our brother Jesus Christ who sacrificed his life unto death, that through the shedding of his blood we might have life with the Father. At the veil (door) our name is confessed to the Father (as promised in Sardis). The overcomer in Rev 3:12 is then promised that he "will go no more out", meaning that he is leaving death behind forever and entering a kingdom of life. As well, the temple is mentioned here: "Him that overcometh will I make a pillar in the temple of my God." Pillars supported the structure of the earthly temple, which represents the spiritual basis for standing firm in God's presence – those who are true and faithful (two pillars which support our worthiness). The overcomer is also given a name here, just as a celestial name is reserved for the veil of the modern endowment. "I will write **upon him the name of my God (the Father)**, and the name of the city of my

God, which is new Jerusalem, which cometh down out of heaven from my God: and I will write upon him my new name." (God is Elohim in Hebrew, which comes from *el*, meaning power and strength.)

Laodecia – "And unto the angel of the church of the Laodiceans write; These things saith the Amen, the faithful and true witness, the beginning of the creation of God." Here we are told again that Christ will be the witness to those who are **true and faithful**, confessing their worthiness before the Father. Verse 3:14 tells us that those who are lukewarm will be judged and "spued out of my mouth," which is an image of Christ spueing from his mouth the names of the unworthy, those which he cannot confess to the Father as true and faithful. Moreover, these unworthy are described with the following shortcoming: "thou sayest, I am rich, and increased with goods, and have need of nothing; and knowest not that thou art wretched, and miserable, and poor, and blind, and naked" (Rev 3:17). Nakedness is an allusion back to Eden – the first period (Ehpesus) which is a parallel to the last (seventh). Adding weight to this idea, we then read the remedy for one's nakedness and shame before God; "I counsel thee to buy of me gold tried in the fire, that thou mayest be rich; **and white raiment, that thou mayest be clothed, and that the shame of thy nakedness do not appear**; and anoint thine eyes with eyesalve, that thou mayest see" (Rev 3:18). Adam and Eve's nakedness did not represent shame until they sinned, at which time they needed a covering (kaphar-Atonement) so that they could return to the presence of God. From Rev 19:8 we recognize that the "white raiment" represents the righteousness of those who would be in the Father's presence, the inner substance illustrated by an outward symbol. Moreover, we should realize that the counsel to "buy gold tried (refined) in the fire" is more than a request, but required of all those who wish to enter the Father's kingdom. It symbolizes the process whereby we are purified by the fire of His Spirit; yielding to enticings which test our hearts. Like the virgin's oil (Mat 25) it is purchased a drop at a time over the course of our lives. In addition, gold is the celestial metal which adorned the holy of holies in the temple, covering the mercy seat of God (his throne) representing purity and holiness.

Rev 3:19 also hearkens back to Eden and our first estate. Here Christ says, "As many as **I love**, I rebuke and chasten: be zealous therefore, and repent." The reason for this chastening was cited in Rev 3:3 – a church which "hast left thy first **love**" (reminiscent of Eve in the garden). Falling into a telestial world was part of Adam and Eve's learning and repentance process, as it is for us, but it in no way means that we are unloved, rather that we are deeply loved.

Finally, Rev 3:20 is a clear image to what we see in the modern temple as we pass through the veil. "Behold, **I stand at the door, and knock**: if any man hear my voice, and open the door, I will come in to him, and will sup with him, and he with me." It is interesting that Christ says, "I will come into him," indicating that he will come into the holy of holies of our heart, as much as it means that we will enter into the celestial presence of the Father; i.e. the first determines the reality of the latter.

What are we to make of this – the temple endowment as a prologue to John's Revelation? Significantly, the temple endowment is an "apocalypse," a revelation of what is to happen in our lives, from the beginning to the end; prophetic (predictive) of every man's spiritual journey. The phrase, "hear what the spirit says" is used 7 times (once for each church) which is the Lord's way of saying that we need spiritual eyes to see and understand; i.e. because the Spirit is speaking, it (the temple) can only be perceived and understood by those in tune to the Spirit's voice (revealed by the Spirit).

APPENDIX 8 – A

3 Nephi 11:31-41, "This is my Doctrine"

A 31 Behold, verily, verily, I say unto you, I will **declare unto** you my doctrine.

    *a. and **I bear** record of the Father,*
      b. and the Father beareth
B   *c. record of me,*
          d. and the Holy Ghost
      b. beareth record of the Father
        c. and me;
    *a. and **I bear** record that the Father*

    C commandeth all men, everywhere, **to repent** and believe in me.
33 And whoso **believeth** in me, and is **baptized,** the same shall
be saved; and they are they who shall **inherit the kingdom of God.**
    D 34 And whoso **believeth** not in me, and is not **baptized,** shall **be damned**.
      E 35 Verily, verily, I say unto you, that this is my doctrine, and I **bear record** of it from the Father;
        F and whoso believeth in me believeth in **the Father** also; and unto him will the Father **bear record** of me,

          G for he will visit him with **fire**
          G' and with the **Holy Ghost**.

        F' 36 And thus will the **Father bear record** of me,
      E' and the Holy Ghost will **bear record** unto him of **the Father** and me; for the Father, and I, and the Holy Ghost are one.
    D' 37 And again I say unto you, ye must **repent**, and become as a little child, and be **baptized** in my name, or ye can in **nowise receive these things** (be damned).
    C' 38 And again I say unto you, ye must **repent,** and be **baptized** in my name, and become as a little child, or ye can in nowise **inherit the kingdom of God.**

    *a. 39 Verily, verily, I say unto you, that this **is my doctrine**,*
      b. and whoso buildeth upon this
        c. buildeth upon my rock,
          d. and the gates of hell shall not prevail against them.

B'   *e. 40 And whoso shall declare **more***
          *e' or **less** than this,*

    *a' and establish it for **my doctrine**, the same cometh of evil,*
      b' and is not built upon my rock;
        c' but he buildeth upon a sandy foundation,
          d' and the gates of hell stand open to receive such when the floods come and the winds beat upon them.

A' 41 Therefore, go forth unto this people, and **declare** the words which I have spoken, **unto** the ends of the earth.

The next four appendixes are about 3rd Nephi and present a series of related chiasmi which not only reveal the wonder and beauty of the Book of Mormon, but also help us to better understand the fullness of the everlasting gospel as it relates to the temple. This first chiasmus occurred at the temple on the first day of Christ's visit, at which time he clearly lays out his "doctrine," the essentials of which he repeats many times during his visit to the Nephites. In 3rd Nephi 27 (Appendix 9 – C) Jesus repeats this outline, but instead of "doctrine" he will call it His "gospel."

C,C' Each parallel here repeats the temple\plan-of-salvation formula that we must repent and be baptized in order to "inherit the kingdom of God." However, you will notice that the Holy Ghost is omitted from both. Ingeniously, the center apex (G,G') completes FOR BOTH parallels the requirement after baptism – which is the Holy Ghost! (the feature of the plan whereby we are reborn, sanctified, and celestialized)

B,B' These parallels are two smaller structures – one a chiasmus (C) and the other a series of reflecting parallel ideas with a center point (C'). As you compare them, notice that the first one is the Godhead, centered on the Holy Ghost who bears witness. The second (C') tells us that those who are established on "more or less" than this, which is the witness of the Holy Ghost (C), are built on sand. The rock is Jesus Christ, of whom both the Father and the Holy Ghost witness.

Apex – G,G' It is by the fire of the Holy Ghost that "the Father bears record" (witnesses) of Jesus Christ. This spiritual witness is the foundation upon which we are to be built (B'). The gates, winds, and floods of hell cannot prevail against such a witness of Christ.

We should especially notice the charge given by Christ at the end of this "**message**" (A') which is to declare "the words which I have spoken unto the ends of the earth." Significantly, this message is the very first teaching that Jesus gives upon his appearance (immediately after the multitude feels the prints of the nails in his hands and thrusts their hands into his side). It sets the stage for the events in the hours and days that follow, when Christ will extend the scope of this initial "**message**." In particular, Christ will expand the understanding of what it is to take upon oneself His name at baptism, repeating the beatitudes which he gave on the mount (temple) during his mortal ministry (Mat 5-7). He will also explain how this gospel **message** will be taken to "other sheep" who have been scattered from the covenant fold (3rd Ne 15-16). The last event of the first day is the institution of the sacrament, which celebrates the covenant message of repentance, baptism, and the Holy Ghost (3 Ne 18). What is more, after Christ departs we read that the disciples spread the **message** through the night to "gather" the people, for "Christ was coming again", on the morrow (imagery of Elijah).

On the beginning of the 2nd day (3 Ne 19) we find the disciples, as commissioned, already baptizing. As the Holy Ghost falls upon the newly baptized, Christ appears and prays for his disciples three times, whereupon they again celebrate the sacrament. Jesus then spends roughly two chapters (3rd Ne 20-21) explaining the Lord's vast and expansive plan to gather his people, "as a man gathereth his sheaves into the floor" (3 Ne 20:18, Micah 4:12). An important part of this gathering, we discover, is that liberty must be set up in "this land" (America), so that the **message** of the everlasting gospel might go forth among the gentiles, "that they may repent and come unto me and be baptized in my name and know of the true points of **my doctrine**" (3 Ne 21:6). The gentiles will then take this **message**\doctrine to "my people, the remnant of the house of Jacob, and also as many of the house of Israel as shall come' (3 Ne 21:23).

Christ will end the 2nd day of his visit by repeating all of Isaiah 54 (3 Ne 22), along with Malachi 3 and 4 (3 Ne 24-25). These Old Testament chapters are especially well chosen because they relate events of Israel's gathering. The next appendix covers Malachi 3, whose text is a chapter-wide chiasmus.

APPENDIX 8 – B

Malachi 3 (3 Nephi 24) – Tokens of the Bread and the Wine Opening the Windows of Heaven

A 1 Behold, I will send my messenger, and he shall prepare the way before me, and the Lord whom ye seek **shall suddenly come** to his temple, even the messenger of the covenant, whom ye delight in;

  B behold, he shall come, saith the **Lord of Hosts. 2 But who may abide the day** of his coming, and who shall stand when he appeareth?

    C For he is like a refiner's fire, and like fuller's soap. 3 And he shall sit as a refiner and purifier of silver; and he shall purify the **sons** of **Levi, and purge them as gold and silver**, that they may offer unto the Lord an offering in righteousness. 4 Then shall the offering of Judah and Jerusalem be pleasant unto the Lord, as in the days of old, and as in former years.

      D 5 And I will come near to you to judgment; and I will be a swift witness against the sorcerers, and against the adulterers, and against false swearers, and against those that oppress the hireling in his wages, the widow and the fatherless, and that turn aside the stranger, and **fear not me**, saith **the Lord** of Hosts.

        E 6 For I am **the Lord,** I change not; therefore ye sons of Jacob are not consumed.

          F 7 Even from the days of your fathers ye are **gone away from mine ordinances**, and **have not kept them**. Return unto me and I will return unto you, saith **the Lord of Hosts.**

           G **But ye say**: Wherein shall we return?

             H 8 Will a man rob God? Yet ye have robbed me. **But ye say**: Wherein have we robbed thee? In tithes and offerings.

              I 9 Ye are **cursed with a curse**, for ye have robbed me, even this **whole nation**.

               J 10 Bring ye all the tithes into the storehouse, that there

Bread   May be **meat** in my house; and prove me now herewith, saith the **Lord of Hosts,**

                K if I will not **open you** the windows of heaven,
                K' and **pour you** out a blessing that there shall not be room enough to receive it.

Wine   J' 11 And I will rebuke the devourer for your sakes, and he shall not destroy the fruits of your ground; neither shall your **vine cast her fruit** before the time in the fields, saith the **Lord of Hosts.**

               I' 12 And **all nations** shall call **you blessed**, for ye shall be a delightsome land, saith the Lord of Hosts.

              H' 13 Your words have been stout against me, saith the Lord. **Yet ye say**: What have we spoken against thee?

             G' 14 **Ye have said:** It is vain to serve God, and what doth it profit

           F' that we **have kept his ordinances** and that we have walked mournfully before **the Lord of Hosts?**

      D' 15 And now we call the proud happy; yea, they that work wickedness are set up; yea, they that tempt God are even delivered. 16 Then they **that feared the Lord** spake often one to another,

        E' and **the Lord** hearkened and heard;

  B' 17 and a book of remembrance was written before him for them that feared the Lord, and that thought upon his name. And they shall be mine, saith **the Lord of Hosts**, in **that day**

    C' when **I make up my jewels**; and I will spare them as a man spareth his own **son** that serveth him.

A' 18 Then **shall ye return** and discern between the righteous and the wicked, between him that serveth God (those that seek him) and him that serveth him not.

Perhaps the best place to begin with Malachi 3 is to briefly discuss the significance of the angel Moroni who sits atop today's temples, a "messenger" sent before the day of the Lord (his second coming). Marvelously, "angel" is the same Hebrew word that Malachi comes from – *malach,* which means angel or messenger! The message that Moroni trumps with his horn is the everlasting gospel he received from his own personal messenger (malachi), his father Mormon. As we will see, there are many Malachis and many Elijahs. For instance, in Malachi 3:1 John the Baptist is referenced as a messenger (*malach*) who "shall prepare the way before me," and also in verse 1 we read of Christ who "shall suddenly come to his temple, even the messenger of the covenant." Of course, Elijah himself (Mal 4:5) is also a messenger (*malach*).

Before examining the vibrant and radiant chiastic parallels found in Malachi 3, for important context let's review again the sequence of events which surround this chapter in 3rd Nephi. On the second day of his visit to the Nephites, Jesus uses the words of the ancient prophets Micah and Isaiah as he outlines that, by God's power and wisdom, liberty will be set up in the new world so that the Book of Mormon can come forth, signaling the beginning of God's covenant promise to gather scattered Israel (chapters 20-22). In fact, Christ quotes the entirety of Isaiah 54 (chapter 22) in order to emphasize this promised gathering. Then, in chapter 23 after expounding Isaiah's teachings he commands them to create new scripture by recording the words of their prophet Samuel, whose prophecies of the dead arising were fulfilled at Christ's coming. Christ uses Samuel here to introduce the idea of a messenger, because Samuel was also a messenger and a type of Elijah. Christ then tells his disciples that he has additional new scripture to give them. "And it came to pass that he commanded them that they should write the words which the Father had given unto Malachi, which he should tell unto them. And it came to pass that after they were written he expounded them" (3rd Ne 24:1).

These Malachi verses are important because they point us to the temple and the sealing (gathering) power to be restored by Elijah before the second coming. Malachi is a messenger for Elijah, who is also a messenger sent before the Lord's coming, when the work for the all dead will be done, uniting and gathering the entire covenant family of God. Today, when we perform vicarious work in the temple, we actively participate in this chain of messengers as "saviors on mount Zion" (Oba 1:21) and types of Elijah who bring the message of the gospel to the dead, extending the Father's covenant blessing of gathering to the entire family of man, living and dead. For this reason, when we read the call in Isaiah 54:2 to "enlarge the tent" and strengthen its "cords and stakes", we realize that we are going to need a very big tent indeed, one large enough for the living who accept the gospel as well as those dead who accept its covenant **message** of saving ordinances, becoming Israel.

Sequentially speaking, the Malachi chapters here are part of a finely orchestrated lead-in to 3rd Nephi 27 where we read that the saints must do the works that they have seen Christ do (see 3rd Ne 27:21), part of which is to participate in redeeming the dead (those resurrected at his coming were a sign of this redemptive work). As we know, one of Christ's works was to preach the gospel message to those in spirit prison at the time of his death. "For Christ also hath once suffered for sins, the just for the unjust, that he might bring us to God, being put to death in the flesh, but quickened by the Spirit: By which also **he went and preached unto the spirits in prison.**"

(1 Pet 3:18-19). For this reason we send messengers (missionaries) not just to the living, but we also take the gospel message to those passed on, which we do in the temple. In a very personal way as "messengers of the covenant" we "come to his temple" and perform the vicarious priesthood ordinances, which is the gospel message of faith, repentance, baptism, and the gift of the Holy Ghost, which can then be accepted by those spirits waiting for the associated ordinances of the gospel message.

Like the name Malachi, which we know means my messenger (*malach*), the word "gospel" means good message or good news (*euangelio*), from the Greek for angel or messenger! Indeed, when Christ says this is "my gospel" it could in fact be rendered "this is my message" – repent, be baptized, receive the Holy Ghost; his plan of salvation which endows us with heaven's power, preparing us to return to the Father's presence.

B, B' The question – "who can abide the day of his coming" – is answered in its parallel B', "them that feared the Lord, and that thought upon his name ("always remembered Him"). As just indicated, as gathering messengers to Israel, we are the Elijah that "comes to his temple" with the saving gospel – faith, repentance, baptism, and the Holy Ghost. Those spirits who accept this gospel message (these 1st principle vicarious ordinances) become those who "fear him" and "think on his name (take his name), and they "will stand" in the resurrection. (Rev 6:17 – who shall stand? Rev 7:3 those sealed.)

Also, in verse 17 (B') a "book of remembrance" is mentioned containing the names of those who take His name. Such a book is later mentioned in 3rd Ne 27 where the Lord tells his disciples to record in a book (of life) the names of the righteous, telling them that we will judge and be judged out of this book. Curiously, in the church today we are told to compile a book of remembrance for our families. Compiling such a book may have more far-reaching importance than we realize, a **message** to future generations of our love and concern for them, a history of how we were "gathered" and how they can be also.

C, C' Fascinating parallel. In C we see that the Lord will sit as a refiner and purify his priesthood (the "**sons** of Levi"), and "purge them as gold and silver" so that their offering to the Lord will be righteous. The language here speaks of transformation and new creation, changing something plain into something valuable and beautiful. In its parallel (C') the Lord again is portrayed as an artificer, but in this case setting jewels, which again represent the "**sons**" that serve him in righteousness. Obviously, these "whom he will spare" are those, both living and dead, that have accepted his gospel (see 3rd Ne 27). We should also keep in mind that the Lord here in Malachi 3 is talking to all that have ever held or will hold his priesthood, from whom he desires a righteous offering from a pure heart. These are his beautiful jewels. [132]

Though Christ did not share Malachi 2 with the Nephites, in its verses we learn important context for Malachi 3, which is that the group to whom the Lord is primarily talking is his temple priesthood. Malachi 2 begins with: "And now, O ye priests, this commandment is for you," whereupon the Lord chastises them for becoming lax with their priesthood, telling them that as they are true and faithful to their oath and covenant they become his "godly seed" (Mal 2: 15), which could also be rendered as the "seed of God" or his Godly offspring. (Is this not the purpose of the temple\gospel?)

J,J' K,K' Here at the center we find a celebration of covenant, imagery of the tokens of **eternal life** and endless provision, pointing us to Jesus Christ. In Matthew 26:26-29, when Christ institutes the sacrament, he designates the bread and the wine as symbols to remind us of his sacrifice and new covenant. Using the sacrament tokens to send a message of Christ's coming is done often in the Old Testament (see chapters 10 and 11 on Joseph and Elijah). Jesus certainly did not choose them (bread, wine) haphazardly as they have very ancient tradition – when a covenant was made in ancient Israel it was ratified with a covenant meal. [133] In a sense, the covenantal meal was a sign that the involved parties were in relationship, like a family, "gathered" together in mutual and greater purpose.

Each of these center parallels intimates something supernatural, everlasting, and enduring. J speaks of bringing meat into the Lord's house (temple) which produces a blessing so infinite (eternal) that a room with **endless** boundaries is needed to store it (reminiscent of feeding of the 5,000; bread multiplied). And, it's parallel (J') indicates that Israel's vines will not "cast their fruit before their time," which in Hebrew means that their vines will not be barren, pointing to endless seed and fruitfulness (endless wine). [134] In Hebrew there is also a pun of sorts here, which is, that if you bring your spoils to the temple, God's provision will never spoil.[135]

- **Importance of Messengers in the Temple Endowment**

Messengers also play a significant role in the endowment. Once Adam and Eve leave the garden we hear them say several times that they are waiting for messengers (*malachim*) from their Father. When Satan hears this, he declares that they obviously need someone to preach to them, which he is more than happy to do. However, he is a false messenger (*malach*) with a false gospel – the philosophies of men mingled with scripture. He does not want them to repent, be baptized, or yield to the enticings of the Spirit. When the true messengers Peter, James, and John reveal themselves, they cast out Satan with a sign that we are very familiar with, the same sign used to baptize, the arm to the square. Further, after Satan has been cast out of the telestial world, the messengers Peter, James, and John simultaneously lead Adam and Eve to a body of water (or into the light), indicating that Adam and Eve are prepared for baptism; i.e. readied to enter the terrestrial world.

As the telestial portion of the endowment ends, Adam and Eve encourage us to listen to Peter, James, and John, who they tell us are true messengers, whose words will lead us in the way of life and salvation. We are then given the law of the gospel, which as we know (see 3 Ne 27) is faith, repentance, baptism, and the receiving the Holy Ghost; i.e. the plan of salvation (the way of life and salvation). Curiously, part of that plan is that messengers play an important role in it. Rather than do it all himself, God is using messengers (even his son – the messenger of the covenant) to act in his name, hold his priesthood, to become like him, and to assist in gathering Israel.

These Malachi chapters are an excellent and well-placed introduction to 3rd Ne 27 where Christ explains again, in a detailed chiasmus, his gospel message. However, the next appendix concerns the interim chapter, 3rd Ne 26, where Christ indicates that God's message is given in parallels, and that we should seek these parallels in order to receive a greater portion of his word. To be sure, this is also the underlying premise of this book – e.g. that the story of Joseph's life is parallel to Jacob's, which is parallel to the prodigal son's, all of which are sevenfold creation stories, parallel to the temple endowment and to the 1st principles and ordinances; the original and most ancient paradigm; reprised, created, and comparable to every man's journey, purposed to tell us more about who we truly are and what we can become.

* Note – The messenger of the covenant who "shall suddenly come to his temple" (Mal 3:1) is a picture of Christ who comes to the temple of our hearts. In fact, in order to be gathered into God's covenant family, this message must be personally delivered by his Spirit. Though we may hear the gospel message audibly, or read it visually, it is only by the fire of Holy Ghost that we truly understand it. Alma 32:28 aptly explains (parenthesis mine): "Now, we will compare the word (the gospel message) unto a seed. Now, if ye give place, that a seed may be planted in your heart, behold, if it be a true seed, or a good seed, if ye do not cast it out by your unbelief, that ye will resist **the Spirit of the Lord**, behold, it will begin to swell within your breasts; and when **you feel** these swelling motions, ye will begin to say within yourselves—It must needs be that this is a good seed, or that the word (message) is good, for it beginneth to **enlarge my soul**; yea, it beginneth to **enlighten my understanding**, yea, it beginneth to be delicious to me." This spark ignites the subsequent process of refining and purifying unto righteousness (being set as jewels).

APPENDIX 8 – C

Christ Expounds Malachi – Message on Parallelism
3rd Nephi 26:1-10

A 1 And now it came to pass that when **Jesus had told these things** he expounded them unto the multitude; and he did expound **all things** unto them, both **great** and **small.**

    B 2 And he saith: **These scriptures**, which ye had not with you, the Father commanded that I should give unto you (**to be written**);

        C **for it was wisdom in him that they should be given unto future generations.**

            D 3 And **he** did **expound all things**,

                E even **from the beginning** until the time that he should come in his glory— yea, even all things which should come upon the face of the earth, even until the elements should melt with fervent heat, and the earth should be wrapt together as a scroll, and the heavens and the earth should pass away. 4 And even **unto the great and last day,**

                    F when all people, and all kindreds, and all nations and tongues shall stand before **God**, to be judged of their works, **whether** they be **good** or whether **they be evil**

                      G 5 If they be good, to the resurrection of everlasting life;
                      H and if they be evil, to the resurrection of damnation;

                      I **being on a parallel**,

                      H' the one on the one hand
                      G' and the other on the other hand,

                  F' **according to the mercy**, and **the justice**, and the holiness which is in **Christ,**

              E' who was **before the world began.**

            D' 6 And now there cannot be written in this book even **a hundredth part of the things** which Jesus **did truly teach** (expound) unto the people;

    B' 7 But behold the **plates of Nephi** do contain the more part of the things which he taught the people. 8 And these things **have I written,** which are a lesser part of the things which he taught the people;

        C' and I have written them **to the intent that they may be brought again unto this people,** from the Gentiles,

A' according to **the words which Jesus hath spoken.** 9 And when they shall have received this, which is expedient that they should have **first, to try their faith** (small things) and if it shall so be that they shall believe these things (small things) then shall the **greater things** be made manifest unto them. 10 And if it so be that they will not believe these things, then shall the **greater things** be withheld from them, unto their condemnation.

After giving his Nephite disciples the new Malachi scriptures, we are told that Christ again explains them. As well, we are told that the Savior "expounded all things" (26: 1) great and small, which is very similar to 3rd Ne 23:14 when he "expounded all the scriptures in one". If we wonder how he is able to accomplish this, Christ describes the process using a word that is found **only once** in all of scripture – "parallel." Additionally, Christ teaches this principle by example, because his explanation is a wonderful **parallel** structure, a chiasmus! Significantly, "parallel" is also the nexus of his teaching here in 3 Ne 26, revealing to us a key; how we might better understand "all things," from the beginning of the world, "even unto the great and last day" (vs 3).

In these verses Christ speaks of greater things that will be "made manifest," although we are told that only the lesser part of what he expounded was recorded. In verse 9 we read, "And when they shall have received this, which is expedient that they should have **first, to try their faith** and if it shall so be that they shall believe these things then shall the **greater things** be made manifest unto them." Perhaps part of what is implied here is that the "greater things" spoken of in verse 9 will be "made manifest" by means of this prescribed technique, examining the parallels in scripture.

This method of using the scriptures certainly reminds us of "likening" the scriptures, a term used in the Book of Mormon several times (e.g. 1 Ne 19:23, 2 Ne 11:2). In the Bible Jesus also frequently likened things – using parables to "liken" or parallel the kingdom of heaven. For instance, in Mat 13:24 we read, "Another **parable** put he forth unto them, saying, the kingdom of heaven is **likened** unto a man which sowed good seed in his field." Christ later unfolds for his disciples the meaning of the seed, as well as the parallel meanings of the parable's other elements. (Of course, the seed here represents the **message** of the gospel, the good word of God). In particular, during his mortal ministry Jesus always\only spoke in parables, which by definition are parallels; one idea likened or analogous to another.[136] Again in Mathew we read, "All these things spake Jesus unto the multitude in parables; and without a parable spake he not unto them: That it might be fulfilled which was spoken by the prophet, saying, I will open my mouth in parables; I will utter things which have been kept secret from the foundation of the world." Notice that the parables reveal information which has been "kept secret from the foundation of the world." Again, I believe this signifies that "greater things" are revealed or "made manifest" as we take the time to ponder the variety of ways Christ utilizes parallels in his word (his gospel message). I believe that using this kind of scripture study requires us to linger and ponder more intently, which more fully engages our minds and invites the Spirit's assistance. As we feast upon the words of Christ, we are filled with that which is most desirable and joyous to the soul, a manifestation of the love of God through his Spirit, the knowledge which Nephi tells us (in 2 Ne 31) leads to eternal life (the greatest thing).

Proceeding to the next chapter (3rd Ne 27), which is the third and last day of Christ's visit, we would be remiss to read his ensuing words without looking for parallels or asking for the Spirit's help unfolding them. If the test to "try our faith" has already begun, if we truly desire greater light and knowledge to be "made manifest," then we cannot ignore what Jesus has just taught. As well, keep in mind that Christ used this method (parallels) in order to "expound all things," confirming that there must be elements of the temple which are reciprocal to elements of the gospel's 1st principles and ordinances – that the "things" of one expound the other, and vise versa.

APPENDIX 8 – D

Christ's Chiasmus in 3 Nephi 27 – "This is my Gospel"

A 13 **This is my gospel** which I have given unto you – to do the will of the Father.

    B 14 That **I might be lifted up** on the cross;

        C that ***I might draw all men unto me***
            that as ***I have been lifted*** up by men
                men should ***be lifted up by the Father***, to be judged
            15 for this cause ***have I been lifted up***
        therefore, ***I will draw all men unto me***, that they may be judged

            D 16 whoso **repenteth and is baptized in my name** shall **be filled** if he endureth to the **end** him **will I hold guiltless** before my father

                E 17 **he that endureth not** (unclean) is also hewn down and cast into the fire from whence they can no more return
                    because of the justice of the Father

                      F *18 This is the **word***
                      which he has given unto men
                          *For this cause he **fulfilleth** the **words***
                      ***Which he hath given**,*
                  F' *and he lieth not, but fulfilleth all his **words***

                E' 19 And **no unclean thing** can enter into his kingdom, save it be those who have washed their garments in my blood
                    because of their faith and repentance of all their sins

            D' 20 **Repent,** ye ends of the earth, and come unto me **and be baptized in my name** that ye may **be sanctified** by the Holy Ghost that ye may **stand spotless** before me at the **last** day.

A' 21 Verily, verily, I say unto you, **this is my gospel;**

        C' *and ye know the things that **ye must do** in my church;*
            *for the works ye have **seen me do***
                *that ye **shall also do;***
            *for that which ye have **seen me do***
        *even that **shall ye do***

    B' 22 Therefore, if you do these things blessed are ye, for **ye shall be lifted up** at the last day.

On the beginning of the *third* day the 12 disciples come together uniting in mighty prayer and fasting, at which time Christ again appears. At that time the discussion turns to what they are to call the church, to which Christ explains that it should be called after his name (vs7), built upon his gospel and works (vs10-11). The Savior then unfolds again (as on the first day), the meaning of His gospel, structuring his words in a breathtaking chiasmus. Its structure includes *three* smaller chiasmi, one at the center or apex (D-F), and two others on either end, each paralleling the other (C,C'). At the apex, the Savior uses "word" *three* times, emphasizing its (the word's) creative and transforming power.

- **The First Principles as the Endowment (D, D')**

Applying a temple lens to evaluate the Savior's poetic instruction, let's first review some important concepts. In chapter 2 of this book we compared the chronology of the first principles and ordinances of the gospel to the sequence of the temple (telestial, terrestrial, celestial). We examined Harold B. Lee's words explaining temple covenants – that they "embody" and "unfold" the covenants already taken at baptism. Moreover, we inspected the definition of "gospel" from the LDS bible dictionary, which indicated that it is "God's plan of salvation." We also found a surprising correlation or parallel when we looked at the first lesson from the temple prep manual, which is entitled "The Temple Presents the Plan of Salvation." Remarkably, we discovered a mutual definition between the temple and the gospel, that they are synonymous, both presentations of the plan of salvation.

Consequently, when we talk about the gospel we are speaking of the temple, each embodying and unfolding the other (and the plan of salvation). Since the Savior here is describing his gospel, let's see how he is also outlining his temple. In 3 Ne 27 Christ twice defines the gospel, D and D'. Below is an analysis of these two as they relate to the temple endowment pattern. First is D, verse 16:

16 whoso **repenteth**	*Telestial*
and is baptized in my name	*Terrestrial*
shall **be filled** (with the Holy ghost) if he endureth to the **end** him will I hold **guiltless** before my father	*Celestial*

And its parallel, vs 20:

20 **Repent**, all ye ends of the earth,	*Telestial*
and come unto me and **be baptized** in **my name**,	*Terrestrial*
that ye may be sanctified by **the reception of the Holy Ghost**, that ye may stand **spotless** before me at the **last** day.	*Celestial*

Notice how both of these describe a progression whereby we are brought "spotless" or "guiltless" into the presence of "my father," which is also what the temple endowment celebrates – the process of spiritual creation whereby we return to our Heavenly Father. D&C 45:12 tells us that the Book of Mormon contains a **fullness of the gospel**. "And again, the elders, priests and teachers of this church shall teach the principles of my gospel, which are in the Bible and the Book of Mormon, in the which is the **fulness of the gospel**." (This is repeated in D&C 20:9, 27:3, 135:3) Many ponder how it can contain the fullness and make no specific mention of the temple endowment. However, in order to see the gospel's fullness we must understand how the first principles and ordinances, which Christ calls his gospel, follow the pattern of the temple endowment, both illustrating the plan leading to salvation. For instance, making a celestial temple covenant to <u>consecrate</u> all that we possess means yielding (consecrating) our hearts and minds (all that we are) to the influence of the Holy Ghost, who sanctifies and purifies (celestializes) us. We are not "true and faithful" to this covenant when we withhold any part of our being, disqualifying us for exaltation with the Father (its all or nothing). As the Spirit fills those who "hunger and thirst after righteousness" (3 Ne 11:6), all vestiges of the natural man are eliminated, and we <u>become</u> (suggests newness\creation) pure, prepared to see God (3 Ne 11:8).[137]

- **Apex – The power of his word, nothing more powerful**

Alma aptly exclaimed, "Behold, how many thousands of our brethren has he loosed from the pains of hell; and they are brought to sing redeeming love, and **this because of the *power of his word which is in us***, therefore have we not great reason to rejoice?" (Alma 26:13) Is there anything more powerful than God's revelatory and creative word! At the center (F,F') we read that the word of the Father will assuredly be fulfilled. This "word" upon which everything pivots in one sense refers to God's covenant promises to man. (You might also remember how the word is the center of

Stephen's temple\plan of salvation stories; e.g. the **promise** represented by the olive branch in Noah's story; the **revelation** of Joseph to his brothers as their savior; Moses receiving revelation [word] on Sinai. The implications of this are myriad. Yes, God will fulfill his corporate covenant promises, but we should also keep in mind that salvation is a process done by changing\transforming the heart of the individual. In 2 Ne 33:1 we find that the word (which contains the gospel promises and covenant) is heard and then carried to an individual's heart by the Holy Ghost. Its inseparable relationship to the Spirit is especially evident in Eph 6:17 where we are told the word of God is the sword of the Spirit. And in D&C 84:24 we read that God's word is truth, and whatsoever is truth is Spirit, even the Spirit of Jesus Christ. Consider some additional examples which illustrate the creative power of God's word:

> **Psa 33:6** By the word of the LORD were the heavens made; and all the host of them by the breath of his mouth.9 For he spake, and it was done; he commanded, and it stood fast.
>
> **Jacob 4:9** For behold, by the power of his word man came upon the face of the earth, which earth was created by the power of his word.
>
> **2 Pet 3:5** For this they willingly are ignorant of, that by the word of God the heavens were of old, and the earth standing out of the water and in the water:

As important we also have scriptures which illustrate the power of His word to create us spiritually.

> **James 1:8** Of his own will begat he us (created) with the word of truth, that we should be a kind of firstfruits of his creatures.
>
> **1 Pet 1:23** Being born again (created), not of corruptible seed, but of incorruptible, by the word of God, which liveth and abideth for ever.

Combining both of these creations – the physical in Genesis as well as the spiritual – in 2 Cor 4:6 we read of their common source, "For God, who commanded the light to shine out of darkness, hath shined in our hearts, to give the light of the knowledge of the glory of God in the face of Jesus Christ."

Many times in the Book of Mormon the narrative pivots on the word, a promise, or Christ himself. A great example of this is at the center of 1 Nephi, in chapter 11, where Nephi describes what its like to partake of the fruit of the tree of life, which is to feel through the Holy Ghost the love of God <u>spoken</u> to his heart. You will recall that it is the word (iron rod) that leads to the sacred tree; i.e. without the word we cannot come to know the love of God. The consequence of this experience is life changing for Nephi. In Alma 32 we read a variation of this and learn that if the word is planted in ones heart it takes root and grows into a tree of life (love of God\Jesus Christ). We are told that once it has grown we can partake of its fruit – which is eternal life (exaltation with the Father). Here we grasp that unless we personally grow the tree we cannot partake.

Curiously, there is a connected idea in 3 Ne 27:17 where "hewn" is uniquely used to describe those who have grown a different tree, whose "works (fruit) are evil". Of this group we read, "and they are hewn down and cast into the fire, from whence there is no return" (E). Like the tree of life this metaphor gives us the image of a tree, only this one is hewn down and burned. This lesser tree is obviously grown from the word (seed) of another variety, that of Satan's, whose tainted message can also be planted and grow a less desirable fruit within our hearts. In fact, there is even a comparison here to the tree of life, whose fruit is described by Nephi as "most joyous to the soul" (1 Ne 11). Christ tells us in verse 10 that those who have grown their tree from the evil word, "have joy in their works for a season, and by and by the end cometh." Like the false word from which it grows, the joy that it produces is corrupted and short-lived. Fittingly, in ancient Hebrew trees were used as metaphors for men, good and bad.[138]

- **C,C' – He will be lifted up and so shall we, two meanings**

Thus, at the apex the word, or promise of the Father to bring to pass the Atonement, convinces us of his 100% commitment and reliability to do so. The giving of his son tells of his love – nothing held back. God's covenant is preserved by this total commitment, and so is ours, and only in this way. With that in mind let's next look at two fascinating parallel chiasmi which (if we pay attention) shed light on how the gospel or plan of salvation works. The first mentions that Christ should be lifted up, which is a reference to His crucifixion; his complete and total sacrifice.

> C that **I might draw all men unto me**
>   that as **I have been lifted** up by men
>   men should **be lifted up by the father**, to be judged
>   for this cause **have I been lifted up**
> therefore, **I will draw all men unto me**, that they may be judged

Remarkably, in its parallel (C'), we are told that we must do the same work that we have seen him do, and that by this (doing his works) we will be judged.

> *C' and ye know the things that **ye must do** in my church;*
> *for the works ye have **seen me do***
> *that ye **shall also do**;*
> *for that which ye have **seen me do***
> *even that **shall ye do***

Immediately after this chiasmus we are told that, "**if you do** these things blessed are ye, for **ye shall be lifted up**," which is surely a reference to our being resurrected (as He was). However, there is also a secondary meaning, suggesting that in order to do His work we must also be lifted up – to sacrifice (offer) all, inferring that only when we "do" that will we then be "lifted up" into the presence of the Father, judged worthy to be in his presence. Commenting on these parallel verses (14-21), Andrew Skinner writes: "And so the meaning of the cross for us personally comes down to this: we can ignore it or we can embrace it and die upon it—meaning we can be transformed by it, crucify the natural man, and yield to the enticings of the Holy Spirit (see Mosiah 3:19). The Apostle Paul put it this way: "And they that are Christ's have crucified the flesh with the affections and lusts" (Galatians 5:24). This was Paul's personal experience; he stated, "I am crucified with Christ: nevertheless I live; yet not I, but Christ liveth in me: and the life which I now live in the flesh I live by the faith of the Son of God, who loved me, and gave himself for me" (Galatians 2:20).[139]

- **What kind of man? – Even as I am.**

3 Nephi 27 begins with a question and ends with a question, presenting us with another interesting parallel. At the beginning of this gospel discourse the disciples are disputing over a question - what the name of the church should be called. Christ tells the disciples:

> 5 Have they not read the scriptures, which say ye must take upon you the <u>name</u> of Christ, which is my <u>name</u>? For by this <u>name</u> shall ye be called at the last day; 6 And whoso taketh upon him my <u>name</u>, and endureth to the end, the same shall be saved at the last day. 7 Therefore, whatsoever ye shall do, ye shall do it in my <u>name</u>; therefore ye shall call the church in my name; and ye shall call upon the Father in my <u>name</u> that he will bless the church for my sake. 8 And how be it my church save it be called in my <u>name</u>? For if a church be called in Moses' name then it be Moses' church; or if it be called in the name of a man then it be the church of a man; but if it be called in my <u>name</u> then it is my church, if it so be that they are built upon my gospel.

Of this, Brandt Gardner has written: "The Lord answered the Nephites' question not by merely telling them what name should be given to the church, but what name they should take upon themselves: "Ye must take upon you the name of Christ." Jesus came when the twelve "called" him in prayer; similarly, when he "calls us by our name at the last day, his believers will come. The name is the key to our entry into the kingdom, <u>a point of particular significance to temple-endowed modern Saints</u>. The essential issue is not just the naming of the church, but also the naming of the person: "And whoso taketh upon him my name, and endureth to the end, the same shall be saved at the last day." (Brant Gardner, Second Witness, 5:575)

At the end of his instruction Jesus will ask another question, one directly related to Bro Gardner remarks, and parallel to the first. In 3 Nephi 27:27 we read, "Therefore, what manner of men ought ye to be? Verily I say unto you, even as I am." Clearly, when we take upon us the name of Christ we are expected to be as Christ, who is like the Father. On the first day of his visit to the Nephites, Christ taught the beatitudes at the temple and instructed something very similar, "Therefore I would that ye should be perfect even as I (am), or your Father who is in heaven is perfect" (3 Ne 12:48). This was the culmination of his teaching then, just as it is here in 3 Ne 27. Moreover, it is the purpose of the gospel, the temple, and God's plan, that we should be as he is – holy, pure, full of love and charity. This idea is reprised for us in the modern temple endowment. There we learn that Michael, who helped create the world, is also Adam. We learned in chapter 8 of this book that Michael (in Hebrew) means – who is like God. (it is actually a question – who is like God?) Michael later becomes Adam, which in Hebrew means – man. Therefore, who is like God – man. This is the premise of the gospel and the temple message, to instruct us in our spiritual creation, so that we (man) might become like God.

What manner of **man** – ought ye to be?	as I am (God)	*1 Ne 27:27*
Man	– who is like God	*Adam-Michael*

- **E, E'**

These interesting parallels are antithetical. Either we will be cleansed by the blood of Christ or we will be destroyed by fire. Curiously, in scripture both fire and blood are cleansing agents.

- **A Larger Chiasmus**

Finally, analysis of this chapter would be incomplete without examining the additional parallels that exist in 3 Nephi 27. In fact, the chiasmus here is larger than just verses 13-22. Below is an extended chiasmus formed from 3 Ne 27:1-12, which is parallel to verses 23-33.

Extension of Chiasmus in 3 Ne 27, verses 1-12 parallel to 23-33

A 1 And it came to pass that as the **disciples** of Jesus were **journeying** and were preaching the things which they had both heard and seen, and were **baptizing** in the name of Jesus, it came to pass that the disciples were gathered together and were united in mighty prayer and fasting.
B 2 **And Jesus again showed himself unto them,** for they were praying unto the Father in his name; and Jesus came and stood in the midst of them, and said unto them: What will ye that I shall give unto you?
C 3 And they said unto him: Lord, we will that thou wouldst tell us the name whereby we shall call this church; for there are **disputations** among the **people** concerning this matter.
D 4 And the Lord said unto them: Verily, verily, I say unto you, why is it that the people should murmur and dispute because of this thing? 5 Have they not read the scriptures, which say **ye must take upon you the name of Christ**, which is my name? For by this name shall ye be called at the last day; 6 And whoso taketh upon him my name, and endureth to the end, the same shall be saved at the last day.
E 7 Therefore, whatsoever ye shall do, ye shall do it in **my name**; therefore ye shall call the church in my name; **and ye shall call upon the Father in my name that he will bless the church for my sake.** 8 And how be it my church save it be called in my name? For if a church be called in Moses' name then it be Moses' church; or if it be called in the name of a man then it be the church of a man; but if it be called in my name then it is my church, if it so be that they are built upon my gospel.
F 9 Verily I say unto you, that ye are built upon my gospel; **therefore ye shall call whatsoever things ye do call,** in my name; therefore **if ye call upon the Father,** for the church, **if it be in my name the Father will hear you;**
G 10 And if it so be that the church is built upon my gospel then will the Father show forth **his own works** in it. 11 But if it be not built upon my gospel, and is built upon the **works of men,** or upon the works of the devil, verily I say unto you they have joy in their works for a season, and by and by the end cometh, and they are hewn down and cast into the fire, from whence there is no return (judged).
H 12 **For their works do follow them,** for it is because of their works that they are hewn down;
I. therefore **remember the things that I have told you**.

Apex – vs 13-22 (see pg 294)

I 23 **Write the things which ye have seen and heard**, save it be those which are forbidden
H 24 Write the **works of this people**, which shall be, even as hath been written, of that which hath been.
G 25 For behold, out of the books which have been written, and which shall be written, **shall this people be judged,** for by them shall **their works** be known unto men. 26 And behold, all things are written by the Father; therefore out of the books which shall be written **shall the world be judged**
D 27 And know ye that ye shall be judges of this people, according to the judgment which I shall give unto you, which shall be just. Therefore, what manner of men ought ye to be? Verily I say unto you, **even as I am.**
E 28 And now I go unto the Father. And verily I say unto you, **whatsoever things ye shall ask the Father in my name shall be given unto you.**
F 29 Therefore, **ask, and ye shall receive; knock, and it shall be opened unto you**; for he that asketh, receiveth; and unto him that knocketh, it shall be opened.
C 30 And now, behold, **my joy is great, even unto fulness**, because of you, and also this generation; yea, and even the Father rejoiceth, and also all the holy angels, because of you and this generation; for none of them are lost. 31 Behold, I would that ye should understand; for **I mean them who are now alive of this generation**; and none of them are lost; and in them I have **fulness of joy**. 32 But behold, it sorroweth me because of the fourth generation from this generation, for they are led away captive by him even as was the son of perdition; for they will sell me for silver and for gold, and for that which moth doth corrupt and which thieves can break through and steal.
B And in that day **will I visit them**, even in turning their works upon their own heads.
A 33 And it came to pass that when Jesus had ended these sayings he said unto **his disciples: Enter ye in at the strait gate (baptism);** for strait is the gate, and narrow is the way that leads to life, and few there be that find it; but wide is the gate, and broad the way which leads to death, and many there be that **travel** therein, until the night cometh, wherein no man can work

D, D' – This is the parallel that was just discussed on pages 302-305. Again, notice that "taking his name" (D) is parallel to "what manner of man ought ye to be" (D'). And, as we examined, in order to be the manner of Him we must do the work that we have seen him do, which is to sacrifice all, even our lives.

F, F' – Here we are told in both parallels that whatever we ask of the Father, in the name of Christ, we will receive. The caveats to this are that we must be "built upon his gospel" (F), have taken his name, and that we must be "even as I am" (F'). Also, notice that the Lord is reprising here a verse from the sermon of the first day (the beatitudes) found in 3 Ne 14:7-8, which is that if we "knock it shall be opened." We might also take note that the imagery of knocking appears at the end of this sermon even as knocking occurs at the end of the temple endowment. Here, as in the temple, the patron must be true and faithful, after the manner of Christ, in order to converse with the Lord through the veil.

C, C' – Towards the fringes of the chiasmus the parallels become less exact. Nonetheless, we can see that these parallels are antithetical. In C the <u>people</u> are disputing, whereas in C' the Savior celebrates his great joy because of the people, which he refers to as "this generation." Apparently, if there is a good thing to have a disputation over, it's the name of the church.

- **Review of temple items mentioned in 3 Nephi 27**

The telestial, terrestrial, and celestial vs 16, 20
Required <u>garment</u> washed in blood of Lamb vs 19

Standing spotless, reference to white linen vs 20

Taking Christ's name vs 5-8

Consecration – "even as I am" vs 27, lifted up in sacrifice vs 14

Praying (in the true order having consecrated all) vs 28

Afterwards knocking and asking the Father vs 29

Entering the kingdom of the Father (celestial room) vs 19

Allusion to the tree of good and evil – to be "hewn" vs 17

At the apex is God's <u>covenant</u> word – that a Savior will be provided ("lifted up") so that man can return back into their presence vs 18

Regarding the last (and central) item – God's covenant word which "he fulfilleth" – we should remember that the Hebrew for covenant is *berith*, from the root *bara*, which means to create (see pg 72-74), which is God's intention for us – to be spiritually created through covenant, words spoken as promises by God to man, and man to God. While we fulfill our covenant promises (words) to repent, be baptized, and follow the Holy Ghost, the Lord "fulfilleth" his promised word to be "lifted up" and atone for our sins, so that we might be "sanctified by the Holy Ghost and stand spotless" before the Father. This covenantal collaboration has the power to spiritually beautify us, a type of physical creation and how the earth is beautified in the temple endowment. (See 3 Ne 26, Appendix 8-C, where the Savior tells us that he teaches all things on a parallel.)

Additional Note: Throughout his visit to the Nephites Christ brings a heightened awareness of baptism. In fact, "baptize" or baptized is used 34 times in the book of 3rd Nephi, twice as many as any other book. Moreover, the "Holy Ghost" is used 26 times in 3rd Nephi (2nd Nephi and Moroni are the next closest with 15 uses each.)

- **Mormon as Malachi (A Messenger) – 3rd Nephi 30**

Finally, Mormon, who has been compiling the events of the Savior's visit, is very in-tune to the overriding focus of Christ's teaching. In his editorial, which is the last chapter of Nephi 3, he succinctly sums up the covenant gospel message which Christ brought to the Nephites. Two verses comprise the entirety of 3rd Nephi 30, making it the shortest chapter in the Book of Mormon. Mormon writes: "1 Hearken, O ye Gentiles, and hear the words of Jesus Christ, the Son of the living God, which he hath commanded me that I should speak concerning you, for, behold he commandeth me that I should write, saying: 2 Turn, all ye Gentiles, from your wicked ways; and **repent** of your evil doings, of your lyings and deceivings, and of your whoredoms, and of your secret abominations, and your idolatries, and of your murders, and your priestcrafts, and your envyings, and your strifes, and from all your wickedness and abominations, and come unto me, and **be baptized** in my name, that ye may receive a remission of your sins, and **be filled with the Holy Ghost**, that ye may be numbered with my people who are of the house of Israel."

Again we might recognize familiar temple elements "enfolded" within this message – a progression whereby we come to the Lord, are saved and become "numbered with (gathered with) my people who are of the house of Israel."

2 Turn, all ye Gentiles, from your wicked ways;
and **repent** of your evil doings, of your lyings
and deceivings, and of your whoredoms, and *Telestial*
of your secret abominations, and your idolatries,
and of your murders, and your priestcrafts, and
your envyings, and your strifes, and from all your
wickedness and abominations,

and come unto me, and **be baptized** in my name, *Terestrial*

that ye may receive a remission of your sins,
and **be filled with the Holy Ghost**, that ye may *Celestial*
be numbered with my people who are of the house
of Israel.

How high the temple exalts us depends on how well we observe these basic purifying principles and ordinances – the fundamental gospel message. Our temple possibilities, including our eternal temple marriage, must be **sealed** by the Holy Spirit of Promise, which we will never enjoy unless we repent when we fall, remember his name (as at baptism), and yield continually to the Holy Ghost. Through this sanctification process our covenant temple blessings are sealed.

In D&C 76 we read of the promises which this higher manifestation of the Spirit may seal upon the righteous after baptism: "52 That by keeping the commandments they might be washed and cleansed from all their sins, and receive the Holy Spirit by the laying on of the hands of him who is ordained and sealed unto this power; 53 And who overcome by faith, and are **sealed by the Holy Spirit of promise**, which the Father sheds forth upon all those who are just and true (righteous). 54 They are they who are the church of the Firstborn. 55 They are they into whose hands the Father has given all things— 56 They are **they who are priests and**

kings, who have received of his fullness, and of his glory; 57 And are priests of the Most High, after the order of Melchizedek, which was after the order of Enoch, which was after the order of the Only Begotten Son. 58 Wherefore, as it is written, **they are gods, even the sons of God—** 59 Wherefore, all things are theirs, whether life or death, or things present, or things to come, all are theirs and they are Christ's, and Christ is God's. 60 And they shall overcome all things."

These verses, which make mention of sealing, becoming kings and priests, and becoming "gods, even the sons of God" so that "all things are theirs," were revealed nearly a year before the command to build the Kirtland temple was received. Though the language here seems to denote temple ideas, at the time this revelation was given it would have applied only to the principles and ordinances already received, which were repentance, baptism, and the gift of the Holy Ghost.

Appendix 9 – Mosiah 15

AA 1 **God himself shall come down,** 2 **dwell in the flesh,** being the Father and the Son, 3 The Father because he was conceived by power of God, the Son because of the flesh, 4 They are one God, 5 Suffers temptation, mocked scourged, but yields not.
    BB 6 After working mighty miracles, he shall be led, yea, even **as Isaiah said,** as a sheep before the shearer is dumb, so he opened not his mouth. **(Isaiah 53:7)**

A 7 Yea, even so he shall be led, crucified, and slain, the flesh becoming subject even unto death, the will of the Son being swallowed up in the will of the Father.
    B 8 And thus God **breaketh the bands of death,** having gained the victory over death;
        C giving the Son **power to make intercession**
            D for the **children of men**—
a   E 9 Having ascended into heaven, having the bowels of mercy;
                E' being filled with compassion
            D' towards the **children of men;**
        C' standing **betwixt them and justice;**
    B' having **broken the bands of death,**
A' taken upon himself their iniquity and their transgressions, having redeemed them, and satisfied the demands of justice.

A 10 And now I say unto you, who shall declare his generation? Behold, I say unto you, that when his soul has been made an offering for sin he shall see his seed. And now what say ye? And **who shall be his seed**?
    B 11 Behold I say unto you, that whosoever has heard the words of the prophets, yea, all the holy prophets who have prophesied concerning the coming of the Lord—I say unto you, that all those who have hearkened unto their words, and believed that the Lord would redeem his people, and have looked forward to that day for a remission of their sins, I say unto you, that **these are his seed,** or they are the heirs of the kingdom of God.
        C 12 For these are they whose sins he has borne; these are they for whom he has died, to redeem them from their transgressions. And now, are they not **his seed**?
            D 13 Yea, and are not the prophets, every one that has opened his mouth to prophesy, that has not fallen into transgression, I mean all the holy prophets ever since the world began? I say unto you that **they are his seed.**
                E 14 And these are they who have **published** peace,
b   F who have brought good tidings of good,
                E' who have **published** salvation;
                    F' and said unto Zion: Thy God reigneth!
            D' 15 And O **how beautiful upon the mountains were their feet**!
        C' 16 And again, **how beautiful upon the mountains are the feet** of those that are still publishing peace!
    B' 17 And again, **how beautiful upon the mountains are the feet** of those who shall hereafter publish peace, yea, from this time henceforth and forever!
A' 18 And behold, I say unto you, this is not all. For O **how beautiful upon the mountains are the feet of him** that bringeth good tidings, that is the founder of peace, yea, even the Lord, who has redeemed his people; yea, him who has granted salvation unto his people;

311

A 20 But behold, the **bands of death shall be broken**
   B and **the Son** reigneth,
      C and hath **power over the dead**;
         D therefore, he bringeth to pass the **resurrection** of the dead.
         21 And there cometh a resurrection,
            E even a **first resurrection**; yea, even a resurrection
               F of **those that have** been,
                  G and **who are**,
                     H and **who** shall be,
                        I even until the resurrection
      b'   J of **Christ**—for so shall **he** be called.
                        I' 22 And now, the resurrection
                     H' of **all** the prophets,
                  G' and **all** those that have believed in their words,
                F' or **all those that have** kept the commandments of God,
             E' shall come forth in the **first resurrection**; therefore,
         D' they are the first **resurrection**.
      C' 23 They are raised to dwell with God who has redeemed them; thus they have **eternal life**
   B' through **Christ,**
A' who has **broken the bands of death**.

A 24 And these are those who have part in the first resurrection; and these are they that have died before Christ came, in their ignorance, **not having salvation declared** unto them.
   B And thus the Lord bringeth about the restoration of these; and they **have a part in the first resurrection**, or have eternal life,
      C **being redeemed** by the Lord. 25 And **little children** also have eternal life (not claimed by justice).
         D 26 But behold, and **fear, and tremble** before God, for **ye ought to tremble**;
            E for **the Lord redeemeth none such**
               F that **rebel against** him and die in their sins; yea,
                  G even all those **that have** perished in their sins ever
      a'   since the world began,
               F that have wilfully **rebelled against** God,
                  G **that have** known the commandments of God, and would not keep them;
   B these are they that have **no part in the first resurrection**.
         D 27 Therefore **ought ye not to tremble?**
            E For salvation cometh **to none such**; for the Lord **hath redeemed none such;**
      C yea, **neither can the Lord redeem** such; for he cannot deny himself; for he cannot deny justice when it has its claim (but not **little children**).
A 28 And now I say unto you that the time shall come that **the salvation** of the Lord shall be **declared to every nation**, kindred, tongue, and people.

- -

   BB '28-30 Yea Lord, thy watchmen shall **lift their voice, shall they sing**, they shall see eye to eye when the Lord shall bring forth Zion. Break forth into joy, **sing** together; for the Lord had comforted his people. (**Isa 52:9**)
AA' 31 The Lord has made **bare his holy arm in the eyes of all** the nations; and **all shall see the salvation** (Yeshua – Jesus) **of our God.** (Isaiah 52:10)

As mentioned in chapter 15 of this book, "redeem" is used more times in Mosiah 15 than anywhere else in the Book of Mormon (11 times). You might recall that in the temple, as the physical creation is completed, and just as Adam is about to be formed, Elohim introduces the plan of salvation\redemption. He states that if Adam yields to temptation then a plan is prepared whereby a Savior will be sent and that by the power of the redemption Adam can come again into God's presence and partake of eternal life. Therefore, one of the keys to understanding the temple, or Abinadi's explanation of Isa 52:7, is a clear understanding of what it means to be redeemed (the power of redemption). Indeed, this plan of redemption is the "good tidings" being published by the incarnate God (Jesus Christ) and his spiritually created offspring – all of whom are described as beautiful upon the mount (the temple).

Rightly so, Alma (the only hearer to accept Abinadi's message) later explains redemption as he baptizes at the waters of Mormon (Mos 18:13-14). "And when he had said these words, the Spirit of the Lord was upon him, and he said: Helam, I baptize thee, having authority from the Almighty God, as a testimony that ye have entered into a covenant to serve him until you are dead as to the mortal body; and may **the Spirit of the Lord be poured out upon you; and may he grant unto you eternal life, through the redemption of Christ**, whom he has prepared from the foundation of the world. And after Alma had said these words, both Alma and Helam were buried in the water; and they arose and came forth out of the water rejoicing, being filled with the Spirit."

Here we find the telestial man Helam being baptized in the name of Christ (terrestrial) and the Spirit of the Lord poured out upon him (celestial), so that "he may grant unto you eternal life." Notice that Alma then mentions a Savior which was "prepared from the foundation of the world," which is exactly what Elohim says as he introduces the plan of redemption in the temple.

Later, father Alma has a son, also named Alma, who is living telestially. In Mosiah 27 we read of his redemption, which follows the same pattern just examined. "23 And it came to pass after they had fasted and prayed for the space of two days and two nights, the limbs of Alma received their strength, and he stood up and began to speak unto them, bidding them to be of good comfort: 24 For, said he, I have repented of my sins, and **have been redeemed of the Lord; behold I am born of the Spirit.** 25 And the Lord said unto me: Marvel not that all mankind, yea, men and women, all nations, kindreds, tongues and people, must be born again; yea, born of God, **changed from their carnal and fallen state**, to a state of righteousness, **being redeemed of God**, becoming his sons and daughters; 26 And thus they become new creatures; and unless they do this, they can in nowise inherit the kingdom of God."

Here it is especially apparent that we must be "born of the Spirit" in order to be redeemed – the critical celestializing key of the plan. We must know the love of God "shed abroad" in our heart, feasting upon that which is "most desirable and joyous to the soul" (1 Ne 11) As a consequence of this new birth, we are "redeemed of God, becoming his sons and daughters," and inheriting "the kingdom of God" (eternal life). Moreover, notice how both accounts, Helam's and Alma the Younger's, use language which alludes back to Mosiah 15. Indeed, Christ the beautiful is the Father of beautiful seed, those who have experienced the "power of redemption" and now declare its "glad tidings."

On the same occasion the sons of Mosiah also experienced a mighty change of heart and rebirth. In a wonderful tribute to Abinadi and Isa 52:7, though many years later, we read in Mosiah 27:36-37 "And thus they were instruments in the hands of God in bringing many to the knowledge of the truth, yea, to the knowledge of their Redeemer. 37 And **how blessed are they! For they did publish peace; they did publish good tidings of good; and they did declare unto the people that the Lord reigneth**. (See also Mosiah 18:30)

APPENDIX 10

Sod – Mysterion – Sacramentum – Sacrament

What do the four words above have in common? The first is Hebrew, the second is Greek, the third is the Latin rendering of the first two, and the fourth is the English equivalent. Because the sacrament is the centerpiece of our church services each week, perhaps we should know a little more about these ancient words and the ideas that "sacrament" comes from. Its oldest meaning is very interesting, particularly as it also relates to the temple and the plan of salvation. The following is a brief history of our English word *sacrament*.

> "Historically, the word 'sacrament' developed from the Greek word 'mysterion' and the Latin word 'sacramentum'. 'Mysterion' means 'something hidden or secret' – our word 'mystery'. The language surrounding 'sacraments' did not develop in the Church for some time. . . . It was not until the third century that the word 'mysterion', a word that the pagans used to describe rites of initiation, began to be used to describe Christian rites. In order to avoid any confusion with pagan thinking the theologian Tertullian began to use the Latin word, 'sacramentum' for 'mysterion' particularly in explaining baptism. The sacramentum was a sacred oath of allegiance to the emperor taken by a Roman soldier. Tertullian suggested that just as the soldier's oath was a sign of the beginning of a new life, so too was initiation into the Christian community through baptism and eucharist. 'Sacramentum' then became a general term for the rites of Christian initiation."[140]

Here the sacrament is called a mystery – something hidden or secret. In addition, it is referred to as a rite of initiation. In terms of the gospel, it (the sacrament) is a mystery because it is knowable only by those who have been initiated by the Holy Ghost, a revelation of God's love to those with spiritual ears to hear and eyes to see. Moreover, we read above that it is considered a "sign", something that we often associate with the temple rite. In this regard (as it relates to the temple), the words of the sacrament prayer must be actualized in our lives, which is a true sign that we are prepared to pass by the angels into the presence of the Father. This is possible because the intended purpose of the sacrament is to sanctify or purify the souls of those who partake, accomplished by "always having His Spirit to be with them." As with the 1st principles and ordinances, this is also the stated purpose of the temple, to endow a people (with power from on high) so that their lives personify the principle inscribed upon its walls – Holiness to the Lord. Of this pursuit – sanctification – from the same source as before we read:

> "A more detailed reflection on the sacraments came from St Augustine of Hippo in the 5th century. Augustine developed the notion that a sacramentum is **a sign that sanctifies – makes holy** – because it is efficacious – produces the intended effect."[141]

If we apply this meaning to other rites and occasions within the church, we might classify many of them as sacraments because of their capacity to sanctify us. For instance, Malachi 3 is recognized as the great tithing scripture wherein the Lord promises his saints that the windows of heaven will be opened and a blessing poured out upon those who bring their tithe to the storehouse. However, we also find that the intent of this commandment is to purify (refine) the sons of Levi as purest gold – to sanctify them. Thus, tithing by definition is a sacrament – a holy and cleansing sign, a symbol of an inner reality.[142] In this same regard, Exodus 31:13 tells us that those who observe the Sabbath will be sanctified ("**a sign** between me and you throughout your generations; that ye may know that I am the LORD that doth sanctify you") clearly implying its sacramental nature. Indeed, only those who are initiated and observe it can know its mystery – God's love shed abroad in their hearts through the Holy Ghost.

- **Sod**

Finally, let's consider the Hebrew equivalent of these ancient words – *sod*, the word used in the Old Testament as the translation of mysterion (sacrament). If we look in the lexicon we find a definition:

>1.council, counsel, assembly
>>a.council (of familiar conversation)
>>>i.divan, circle (of familiar friends)
>>>ii.assembly, company
>>
>>b.counsel
>>>i.counsel (itself)
>>>ii.secret counsel
>>>iii.familiar converse, intimacy (with God)[143]

On the night of the last supper, when Christ broke the bread and distributed the wine, his apostles were gathered in a banquet sharing intimate counsel together (*sod*). The secret revealed to them at this time was that through His death, as symbolized by the tokens of His flesh and blood, those who believed on His name could receive eternal life. The truth of this secret (mysterion) was revealed to them by the Spirit (the only way to become an initiate). You might also see temple imagery in the definition above because a "circle" is mentioned, calling to mind the circle of initiates who assemble to pray at the temple altar (reviewing covenants and counsel) in the temple – a reflection of those who also pray in covenant renewal before (around) the altar of the sacrament table. Also, the word *sod* carries with it the notion of how they were sitting at this intimate banquet, suggesting in Hebrew to be reclined on pillows or cushions, as was the custom when eating in ancient Israel.[144] This would have been how the Seder or Passover meal was observed by Christ and his apostles, pointing forward to the great end-time feast in Revelation 19:9-10 when the saints in their white linen (which represents their righteousness, purity, and holiness), attend the great supper of the Lamb. (In Rev 3:21 the overcomers are promised that they will sit with him in his throne – no doubt taking counsel.)

In a similar vein, there has been much written by LDS authors about *sod* in relationship to the council in heaven – suggesting that the heavenly council in the preexistence was mirrored in temple rites through the ages, and also often alluded to in scripture. For example, Psalm 25:14 is one place where the *sod* is the central subject of the psalm. "The secret (*sod*) of the LORD is with them that fear him; and he will shew them his covenant." In other words, only those that take secret counsel (through the Spirit) of the Lord will be given his covenants. In his book "Who Shall Ascend into the Hill of Lord," LeGrand Baker writes:

"The Hebrew word *sode* as it is used in many parts of the Old Testament is a reference to the secret deliberations and decisions of the Council in Heaven. They were not secret before we came to this earth, but because we have lost our memory of them, they are secret now. A "*sode* experience" is when one is called, in vision, back to the Council to review one's covenants and assignment. . . The ancient Israelite temple rites were a kind of stage performance of a *sode* experience that assured all the participants that they had been foreordained in the Council in Heaven. It was designed to teach them how to fulfill the covenants they had made then, so that after this life they could return again to their Father in Heaven."[145]

Clearly, the temple description above also has distinct parallels to the sacrament – "when one is called into the Council to review one's covenants," and to be taught "how to fulfill the covenants they have made, so that after this life they can return again into their Father in Heaven." Also, because the temple endowment empowers us from on high (an allusion to Acts 2 and Pentecost, when the Holy Ghost came in power), it is also a sacrament. And, even though the temple endowment supremely illustrates God's plan of redemption for man, relatively speaking, no new covenants are received outside of those taken at baptism – which also require the new member (initiate) to ultimately consecrate all to the Lord (the price of discipleship).
[146]

In conclusion, though we don't go to the temple to partake of the sacrament, there are apparent correlations between the two ceremonies.[147] Both are sacred occasions to commune with, and take counsel (*sod*) from, the Spirit; to be purified from sin; be instructed from on high and reaffirm our covenant promises. And, because the temple and the gospel both teach the plan of salvation (how we return to our Father) – one an overlay of the other – they are both blueprints for spiritual development – to learn (be counseled) of Christ (Mat 11:28), be perfected in Him (see Moroni 10:32).

APPENDIX 11

Alma's Three Sons – Three Endowments

In Alma 36-42, Alma gives final instructions to his three sons – Helaman, Shiblon, and Corianton. Like the seven days of creation, here we find seven chapters which reflect the spiritual creation of Alma's' sons. Helaman represents the celestial son, Shiblon the terrestrial, and Corianton the telestial. This reverse order mirrors the sequence of the resurrection, which Alma discusses in chapter 40.

In these chapters Alma teaches various aspects of the gospel and plan of salvation, which as we know, is what the temple also teaches (see pg 9-10). In fact, Alma 42 has the highest concentration of the phrase "plan of salvation," or a variant, in the Book of Mormon (7 x's). Using a variety of parallelistic forms, Alma outlines a journey back into God's presence (a plan of salvation) for each of his three sons.

Let's begin with Chapter 36, a well known chapter-wide chiasmus[148] which outlines Alma's spiritual metamorphosis – his passing from a rebellious telestial condition, to a terrestrial nexus in which the Spirit reveals the love which is "most desirable and joyous to the soul," to a celestial state of fruitfulness where he works without ceasing to bring to pass the joy of others, all the while supported in trials, and delivered and "raised up" to dwell with God in glory (Alma 36:24-28).

Alma 36 – Chiasmus of Rebirth, a Tree of Life

a) My son give ear to my words (v 1)
  b) Keep the commandments and ye shall prosper in the land (v 1)
    c) Do as I have done (v 2)
      d) Remember the captivity of our fathers (v 2)
        e) They were in bondage (v 2)
          f) He surely did deliver them (v 2) LIFTED UP AT LAST DAY
            g) Trust in God (v 3)
              h) Supported in trials, troubles and afflictions (v 3)
                i) I know this not of myself but of God (v 4)
                  j) Born of God (v 5)
                    k) I sought to destroy the church (v 6-9)   *Telestial*
                      l) My limbs were paralyzed (v 10)
                        m) Fear of the presence of God (v 14-15)
                          n) Pains of a damned soul (v 16)
                            o) Harrowed up by memory of sins (v 17)
                              p) I remembered Jesus Christ, a son of God (v 17)   *Terrestrial*
                              p) I cried, Jesus, thou son of God (v 18)
                            o) Harrowed up by memory of sins no more (v 19)
                        n) Joy as exceeding as was the pain (v 20)
                      m) Long to be in the presence of God (v 22)
                  l) My limbs received strength again (v 23)   *Celestial*
                k) I labored to bring souls to repentance (v 24)
              j) Born of God (v 26)
            i) Therefore my knowledge is of God (26)
          h) Supported under trials and troubles and afflictions (v 27)
        g) Trust in him (v 27)
      f) He will deliver me (v 27) RAISE ME UP AT THE LAST DAY
    e) As God brought our fathers out of bondage and captivity (v 28-29)
    d) Retain in remembrance their captivity (v 28-29) our fathers
    c) Know as I do know (v 30)
  b) Keep the commandments and ye shall prosper in the land (v 30)
a) This according to his word (v 30)

The center of Alma's chiasmus is Jesus Christ (vs 17). On either side of this hinge-point, Alma tells us that he has been reborn (j, j'), at the same time using language which indicates that he has partaken of the fruit of the tree of life.[149] In Alma 36:24 he says, "Yea, and from that time even until now, I have labored without ceasing, that I might bring souls unto repentance; that I might bring them to **taste of the exceeding joy of which I did taste**; that they might also be **born of God**, and be **filled with the Holy Ghost**." Wonderfully, Alma equates the joy of *tasting* the fruit of the tree of life to being "born of God and *filled* with the Holy Ghost." Alternately, Nephi described this experience as "the love of God *shed abroad* in the hearts of the children of men" (1 Ne 11:22). As previously observed, the preeminent endowment pattern is seven parts, however, this abbreviated presentation of the three kingdoms is often substituted in scripture.[150]

- **Chapter 37 – Helaman given sacred tokens**

Alma also entrusts Helaman with the plates (of Nephi, of brass, of Jared), the seer stone Gazelam, and the Liahona. His instructions to Helaman at this time emphasize the "sacred" nature of these items, that the plates were "small means" by which the Lord accomplishes great things, and that because of their preservation many will be brought "to the knowledge of their God unto the salvation of their souls" (vs 7-8). Alma also speaks about the Liahona in similar terms, saying that following its instructions was the "small means" which led Lehi's family to a promised land (37:42). Moreover, Alma tells Helaman that the Liahona was a "type" and a "shadow" of the word of God, which he (Helaman) now possesses. Alma calls Lehi's journey a "type" of our mortality, saying that "the words of Christ, if we follow their course, carry us beyond **this vale of sorrow** into a far better land of promise." Indeed, as discussed in chapter 9 of this book (pg 114-120) Lehi's journey is a sevenfold endowment pattern. Alma seems aware of this sacred model, using various aspects of it to teach his sons.

The articles given to Helaman are reminiscent of the three sacred tokens or oracles kept in the Israelite ark of the covenant, in the holy of holies of the ancient temple – the stone tablets (word), the budded rod of Aaron which represented the authority of God's living word,[151] and the manna (the word of God). These sacred articles are associated with God's promises to Israel; their covenant "means" of deliverance. In particular, the seer stone or Urim and Thummin given to Helaman are associated with the high priest of the temple, a type of Christ, intercessing for His people. In ancient times only the high priest had access to the third level (celestial) of the temple. Urim and Thummin in Hebrew mean *lights and perfections,* and were worn by the high priest on his ephod. They were "the means" whereby God would provide divine instruction (his word) to his covenant people. We know that Helaman was made a high priest at this time, or soon thereafter (see Alma 46); and possessing Gazelam certainly represents attainment to that temple office, and ensuing access into God's presence.

Did the Nephites also have an ark in which to put these oracles? Did their temple have a holy of holies? Though not mentioned in the Book of Mormon, others have speculated that they did. Don Bradley, for instance, supports this notion: "How could the Nephites keep the Law of Moses without access to the Ark of the Covenant? And with what, if not the miraculous relics of the Exodus, including their literal touchstones with Deity, would sufficiently sanctify their Holy of Holies to make it an appropriate dwelling place for God? . . . Whether it (the temple) was like Solomon's here, at its heart, the Holy of Holies, was vital.

Something remarkable would have to sit in the Ark's place. But what did the Nephites have that could stand in for the sacred relics of the Exodus kept in Solomon's temple? They had their own sacred relics, including those of their exodus to the new Promised Land, relics handed down through the line of kings and then that of prophets and ultimately recovered by Joseph Smith on the Hill Cumorah. In the stone box—which Martin Harris reportedly called an 'ark'—Joseph found a set of Nephite sacred treasures that paralleled the relics associated with the Ark and its custodian, the High Priest. Cumorah's 'ark' contained the plates, the breastplate and interpreters, the Liahona, and the sword of Laban."[152]

Alma clearly demonstrates an understanding of the spiritual or figurative nature of the temple and its "relics." On two occasions, prior to blessing his sons, he compared the physical temple to the human heart, the place where the oracles are spiritually kept; the sacrifices of the mosaic law pointing forward to the covenant sacrifice of the broken heart and contrite spirit (3 Ne 9:21-22). As you examine the following verses, notice that this spiritual temple (just like the type it fulfills) is preparatory to "sitting down" or "being received" into God's kingdom.

1. Alma 7:21 – In the city of Gideon, Alma teaches faith, repentance, baptism, and the Holy Ghost (plan of salvation). Then, drawing comparisons to the temple, he adds: "And he (God) doth not **dwell in unholy temples**; neither can filthiness or anything which is unclean be received into the kingdom of God."

2. Alma 34:36 – Amulek (Alma's co-teacher) compares the temple sacrifice to the temple of the heart: "36 And this I know, because the Lord hath said he **dwelleth not in unholy**

temples, but in the hearts of the righteous doth he dwell; yea, and he has also said that the righteous shall sit down in his kingdom, to go no more out; but their garments should be made white through the blood of the Lamb."

In a figurative and real sense, we also have access to God's purifying oracles, his covenant word, the very scriptures given long ago to Helaman. Planted in our hearts, much as the ancient ark stored the tokens of God's covenant promises, we can *divine* His will for our lives, and by the Spirit's *perfect light* we grow a tree of life. "Sanctified through the word" (Jn 17:17) our garments become "white through the blood of the lamb," preparing us to enter His presence. Deuteronomy 6:6 provides an early comparison of *ark* to *heart*. Referring to the stone tablets (the word of God) kept in the temple Ark, the Lord told Moses, "And these words, which I command thee this day, shall be in thine heart."

Finally, returning to Alma 37, Alma continues his use of types, comparing the brass Liahona, to yet another sacred "relic" – the brass Serpent (an even earlier token of Christ)[153] to which the ancient Israelites looked for deliverance and eternal life (Num 21:8-9). He says, "do not let us be slothful because of the **easiness of the way**; for so was it with our fathers; for so was it prepared for them, that if they would look they might live; even so it is with us. The way is prepared, and if we will look we may live forever." This is the same reference that Alma used a few chapters earlier as he taught the Zoramites about the tree of life, explaining that casting one's eyes to the serpent was a *sign* of belief in the Son of God, and that, "he shall rise again from the dead, which shall bring to pass the resurrection; that all men shall stand before him, to be judged at the last and judgment day, according to their works" (Alma 33:22).

Importantly, this last sentence is also Alma's definition of "the word" to be planted in the heart and grown into a tree of life. Alma continues, "And now, my brethren, I desire that ye shall plant this word in your hearts, and as it beginneth to swell even so nourish it by your faith. And behold, it will become a tree, springing up in you unto everlasting life." (Alma 33:23) Alma here removes any confusion concerning "the word" to be planted, which he specifies as the Atonement (death and resurrection) of Jesus Christ. It is "the means" Helaman now holds literally (the oracles), and spiritually in his heart.

- **Alma 38 – Rebirth Retold to Shiblon**

Alma next admonishes his son Shiblon, who represents the terrestrial. Below is a chiastic outline of this instruction:

A 1 **My son**, give ear to my words, for I say unto you, even as I said unto Helaman, that inasmuch as ye shall keep the commandments of God ye shall prosper in the land; and inasmuch as ye will not keep the commandments of God ye shall be **cut off from his presence**.

B 2 And now, my son, I trust that I shall have great joy in you, because of your steadiness and your faithfulness unto God; for as you have commenced in your youth to look to the Lord your God, even so I hope that you **will continue** in keeping his commandments; for **blessed** is he **that endureth to the end**.

C 3 I say unto you, my son, that I have had great joy in thee already, because of thy faithfulness and thy **diligence**, and thy **patience** and thy long-suffering

    D among the people of the **Zoramites.** 4 For I know that thou wast in bonds; yea, and I also know that thou wast stoned for the word's sake; and thou didst bear all these things with patience because the Lord was with thee; and now thou knowest that the Lord did deliver thee.

        E 5 . And now my son Shiblon, I would that **ye** should remember, that as much as **ye** shall put **your** trust in God even so much **ye** shall be delivered out of **your** trials, and **your** troubles, and **your** afflictions, and ye **shall be lifted up** at the last day.

           6 Now, my son, I would not that ye should think that I **know these things** of myself,
              but it is the **Spirit of God** which is in me
     F   which maketh these **things known** unto me;
            for if I had not been **born of God**
          I should not have **known these things**.

             7 But behold, the Lord in his great mercy sent his **angel**
                to declare unto **me**
     G   that I must stop the work of **destruction** among his people
            and I have seen an **angel** face to face,
                and he **spake** with **me**,
                      and his voice was as thunder, and it **shook** the whole earth .

         H 8 And it came to pass that I was three days and three nights

               in the most bitter **pain and anguish of soul**;
               and never, until **I did cry** out
                  unto the Lord **Jesus Christ**
                    for **mercy**,
     G'   did I receive
                  a **remission** of my sins.
               But behold, I **did cry**
                  unto him and
               I did find **peace to my soul**.

          9 And now, my son, I have told you this that ye may **learn wisdom**,
              that ye **may learn of me** that there is no other way or whereby man can be saved,
                  only in and through **Christ**.
                  Behold,
     F'   he is **the life**
                    and **the light** of the world.
               Behold,
              he is the word of truth and righteousness.
           10 And now, as ye have begun to **teach the word**
         even so I would that ye should continue **to teach**;

C and I would that ye would be **diligent** and **temperate** in all things.

    E 11 See that ye **are not lifted up** unto pride; yea, see that ye do not boast in **your own** wisdom, nor of **your** much strength. 12 Use boldness, but not overbearance; and also see that ye bridle all your passions, that **ye** may be filled with love; see that **ye** refrain from idleness.

    D 13 Do not pray as the **Zoramites** do, for ye have seen that they pray to be heard of men, and to be praised for their wisdom.14 Do not say: O God, I thank thee that we are better than our brethren; but rather say: O Lord, forgive my unworthiness, and remember my brethren in mercy—

B yea, acknowledge your unworthiness before God at **all times**. 15 And may the Lord **bless** your soul, and receive you **at the last day**

A **into his kingdom, to sit down** in peace. Now go, my son, and teach the word unto this people. Be sober. **My son,** farewell.

329

Shiblon is only given one chapter, which, upon inspection, is an adaptation of Alma 36, Alma's rebirth experience; his spiritual awakening when the light suddenly flooded into his heart and the mystery that was previously unknown was revealed – God's love. This chapter begins with the phrase "being cut off from the presence of God," but ends with the blessing of entering "into his kingdom;" the path back to our Father's presence outlined in-between. At the center of the chapter (H) Alma emphasizes the "three days" that he was unable to move or speak, when his soul was "racked with the pains of a damned soul," calling to mind the Atonement, when Christ emerged after three days in the tomb. As in the temple, creation is the preeminent theme represented here – the rebirth or spiritual resurrection of Alma's anguished and fallen soul. The shaking of the earth (vs 7) is prophetic imagery accompanying Christ's crucifixion, which Alma wonderfully interweaves into his personal experience, the trembling of his soul before awakening to new life. And, though Shiblon does not receive the 3 physical tokens\signs – the plates, Gazelem, and Liahona – Alma calls attention to the importance of God's word (his oracles), spoken personally by the Spirit (vs 6) or by an angel (vs 7); knowledge to be learned and then taught to others (vs 9,10). In verse 9 he even clarifies that Christ is "**the word** of truth and righteousness."

- **Corianton – The Telestial, Chapters 39-42**

Alma's final instruction is to his less obedient son Corianton, who has fallen into sexual transgression. Let's look at chapter 42, verses 13-26, which form an interesting parallelistic structure.

Fall from Tree of Life, verses 3-12

A
13 Therefore, according to **justice,**
    the plan of REDEMPTION could not be **brought about,**
        only on conditions of repentance of men
            in this probationary state,
                yea, this preparatory state;
            for except it were for these conditions,
    mercy could not **take effect**
except it should destroy the work of **justice.**

Now the **work of justice** could not be destroyed; **if so, God would cease to be God.** 14 And thus we see that all mankind were fallen,

b
        and they were in the grasp of **justice**; yea, the justice of God,
            which consigned them forever to be cut off from his presence.
                15 And now, the plan of mercy could not be brought about
                      except an **atonement** should be made;
                therefore God himself **atoneth** for the sins of the world,
            to bring about the plan of mercy,
        to appease the demands of justice,
that God might be a perfect, **just** God, and a merciful God also.

c
        16 Now, repentance could not come unto men except there were a **punishment,**
            which also was eternal
                as the life of the soul
        should be, affixed opposite to the plan of **happiness,**
            which was as eternal
                also as the life of the soul.

c
    17 Now, how could a **man repent** except he should sin?
        How could he sin if there was no law?
            How could there be a law save there was a punishment?
                18 Now, there was a punishment affixed,
        and a just law given, which
brought **remorse of conscience unto man.**

c'
    19 Now, if there was no law given
        —if a man murdered he should die
        —would he be afraid he would die if he should murder?
    20 And also, if there was no law given against sin
        men (who murdered)
                would not be afraid to sin (such as murder).

c'
    21 And if there was no law given,
        if men sinned what could justice do, or mercy either,
            for they (mercy and justice) would have no **claim** upon **the creature**?
    22 But there is a law given,
        and a punishment affixed, and repentance granted;
            which repentance, mercy **claimeth**; otherwise, justice **claimeth the**
        creature and executeth the law, and the law inflicteth the punishment;
if not so, **the works of justice** would be destroyed, and **God would cease to be God.**

b'
23 But God ceaseth not to be God,
    and mercy claimeth the **penitent,**
    and mercy cometh
        because of the **atonement;**
        and the **atonement**
            bringeth to pass the resurrection of the dead;
        and the resurrection of the dead
            bringeth back men into the presence of God;
            and thus they are restored into his presence,
        to be judged according to their works,
        according to the law and justice.
    24 For behold, justice exerciseth all his demands,
    and also mercy claimeth all which is her own;
and thus, none but the truly **penitent** are saved.
    25 What, do ye suppose that **mercy** can rob justice? I say unto you, Nay; not one whit.
If so, **God would cease to be God.**

A
26 And thus God bringeth about his great and eternal purposes,
    which were prepared from the foundation of the world.
And thus cometh about the salvation and the REDEMPTION of men,
    and also their destruction and misery.

Return to Waters of Life, verse 27

Notice how this instruction is poetically sandwiched between the tree of life (vs 3-12) and the waters of life (vs 27), both representations of the love of God. In between these two symbols of Jesus Christ is a plan for Corianton's redemption from the fall; how through mercy a transgressor like him might return to the "Waters of Life." Alma indicates that unless Corianton repents he will not be claimed by mercy, but instead justice will be executed and punishment "inflicted" (vs 22). Alma is clear that God would cease to be God if this weren't the case – he is bound according to law. Exploring the dynamics of this, in chapter 42 Alma creates multiple parallels, repeating in a variety of ways the relationship between justice and mercy, painting for us an intricate portrayal of its various associated principles. And, whereas the two other brothers (who represent the new covenant) received no instruction pertaining to the law, Corianton (as a representation of the old or telestial covenant) is told multiple times how it (the law) functions. In fact, "law" is not mentioned at all to the other bothers, but to Corianton it is mentioned 11 times. Other related terms are also reserved exclusively for Corianton – justice 17 times, and punishment 6 times. And, whereas mercy is used 11 times in this chapter, it is used only once with Helaman and twice with Shiblon.

As we begin to appreciate the foregoing – that Alma's teaching parallels the temple's three tiers of progression – then our awareness expands regarding other temple elements, in particular, the symbolism of the ancient temple veil, embroidered with cherubims facing each other (Ex 26:31). In fact, Alma is the only person to mention cherubim in the Book of Mormon, once in chapter twelve when he was teaching about the high priesthood (an event that Jack Welch calls a temple text[154]), and again here in Alma 42.

As described in Genesis and the modern temple, the cherubim guard the way back to the tree of life and God's presence. Alma 42, however, also tells us that God's justice will keep us from the tree of life just as surely as the cherubim. A reasonable conclusion is that they represent the same thing. Understandably, if the tree of life can figuratively represent an abstract such as God's love, then a cherub can represent his justice (also an intangible ideal). Similarly, mercy is also personified by a cherub, because it subsequently allows assess to the tree of life.[155] Indeed, justice and mercy unavoidably intersect and must be sorted out before a holy God will allow man (through the veil) into his holy presence. As others have observed, justice and mercy are really two sides of the same coin, or the same veil (as is the case here in Alma 42). In fact, as we read Alma's instructions to Corianton, his style of rapidly repeating parallels impresses upon our minds their close connection.

Two Cherubim (winged Phoenician sphinxes with lion bodies) flank a sacred tree (Lotus/Palmette) on an ivory Prixis found at Nimrud from ca. the 9th-8th century BCE (p. 86, Abb. 38. Wolfgang Zwickel. Der Salomonische Tempel. Mainz Am Rhein. Verlag Philipp Von Zabern. 1999. ISBN 3-8053-2466-9)

Bruce R. McConkie has written: "As justice is the child of the fall, mercy is the offspring of the atonement."[156] R. Whitson Seaman is credited with saying that, "It is at the cross where justice and mercy meet."[157] And, superbly summing up the perfect connectedness or "harmony" of these two seemingly incompatible principles is the 6th verse in our LDS Hymn, "How Great the Wisdom and the Love":

> How great, how glorious, how complete,
> Redemption's grand design,
> Where justice, love, and mercy meet
> In harmony divine!

The forgoing lines poetically reveal several layers of vital understanding, because the veil (as discussed on pg 79-80) also represents the **atoning sacrifice of Christ** (Heb 10:19) – God's love fully expressed – by which the demands of **justice** are fulfilled and **mercy** claims her own.

Though we may not be in the temple, Alma delightfully transports us to its ritual through his temple teaching, learning with each son a pattern of eternal truths purposed to bring us back to the Father. And, because the gospel and the temple share the same heartbeat, examining one will ultimately reveal the other. All temples today depict this idea, where fundamental gospel principles such as faith, repentance, baptism and the Holy Ghost are encountered in the temple baptistery (in the basement), supporting the endowment practiced above, providing the foundational rhythm\pattern upon which the temple endowment stands.

- **Nibley's temple list**

Hugh Nibley provides a listing of characteristics which he says "are often embodied in the texts of the Book of Mormon, which **may reflect the doctrines taught and the ordinances administered in the Nephite temple during the time of Alma**."[158] Upon examination, most of the qualifications are met in Alma 36-42. The following section identifies where Nibley's criteria are found in Alma's teaching to his three sons:

the plan of salvation – Alma 36, 38, and 42

the promise of heavenly treasures – Alma 37 a heavenly promised land; Alma 38 "receive you at the last day into his kingdom, to sit down in peace"; Alma 40:25 righteous shine forth in Kingdom; 41:4 "raised to endless happiness to inherit the kingdom of God": Alma 42 the tree of life and the waters of life

premortality – Alma 36:1,30 chiastic pattern illustrates premortality; Alma 42

creation motifs – Alma 36 and 38 explore spiritual creation, 42 relates temporal and spiritual creation

instructions given to Adam and Eve – Alma 42

the tree of life – Alma 36 parallel to Nephi's tree of life, tasting its fruit. Alma 42 temporal tree of life

ritual combat against the powers of evil – Alma 36 is Alma's personal battle; 37:25-31 secret combinations that battle against light; Alma 37 three items (found in ark of temple) to battle darkness; 41:4 Lord vs Satan

purification – Alma 36 sins forgiven; also 38 and 42 teach cleansing through atonement.

the road back to God – Alma 36, 38, 42.

apocalyptic and ritual imagery – Alma 37 outlines items in ark; Alma 42 portrays veil with cherubim. The ark and the veil were part of temple ritual imagery. Fiery indignation and wrath 40:14; the last day 37:2, 28; 41:3

335

ordinances – the endowment pattern in 36, 38, 42 demonstrates the progressive gospel ordinances of repentance, baptism, Holy Ghost.

the right and left hand – N/A

the white garment – Alma 34:36, just prior to Alma 36-42

the strait way – Alma 37:12, 44

covenant making – Alma 36:22 keep commandments and prosper, Alma 37:13, 17, 18, 20 keep commandments or be cut off

petition for admission – Cries out for Christ in Alma 36 and 38; Alma 37:34 look to serpent (Christ) and live forever.

the entrance into God's presence – Alma 36:22, sees God's throne; Alma 38 "receive you at the last day into his kingdom, to sit down in peace"; Alma 40:25 righteous shine forth in Kingdom; 41:4 "raised to endless happiness to inherit the kingdom of God"

APPENDIX 12

Noah's Temple Pattern

The story of Noah in Genesis 6-9 is a remarkable retelling of creation, modeled after the initial creation story found in Genesis 1-3. And, because Eden is considered to be God's first temple,[159] we might also expect an intermingling of temple elements in Noah's parallel story. In particular, there is a pivotal scene in Noah's creation account which is better understood when examined through the lens of the temple and its presentation of the plan of salvation.

Upon leaving the ark, Noah is told to be fruitful, and to multiply and replenish the earth (Gen 9:1). Like Adam and Eve, he is also given dominion over the earth (Gen 9:2-3), as well as dietary restrictions – what he can and cannot partake (Gen 9:4-5). Further paralleling Adam and Eve, an incident then occurs which involves fruit, nakedness, shame, a covering, and subsequent curses or blessings.

> 18 And the sons of Noah, that went forth of the ark, were Shem, and Ham, and Japheth: and Ham is the father of Canaan. 19 These are the three sons of Noah: and of them was the whole earth overspread. 20 And Noah began to be an husbandman, and he planted a vineyard: 21 And he drank of the wine, and was drunken; and he was uncovered within his tent. 22 And Ham, the father of Canaan, saw the nakedness of his father, and told his two brethren without. 23 And Shem and Japheth took a garment, and laid it upon both their shoulders, and went backward, and covered the nakedness of their father; and their faces were backward, and they saw not their father's nakedness. 24 And Noah awoke from his wine, and knew what his younger son had done unto him. 25 And he said, Cursed be

Canaan; a servant of servants shall he be unto his brethren. 26 And he said, Blessed be the Lord God of Shem; and Canaan shall be his servant. 27 God shall enlarge Japheth, and he shall dwell in the tents of Shem; and Canaan shall be his servant.

Below is a list of the common elements between these two stories or Edens.

Eden	New Eden	
be fruitful	be fruitful (Gen 9:1)	
forbidden fruit	dietary restrictions (Gen 9:3-4)	
Adam – garden	Noah – vineyard	
perfect, innocent	perfect in his generation (Gen 6:9)	
naked	naked	
trees	vines	
fruit	grape	
partook	partook	
Satan – points out shame	Ham – points out shame	
covered	covered	
3 blessings, curses	3 blessings, curses	
Satan – crawl on belly	Ham - servant of servants	*Telestial*
Eve – by her seed, Christ	Shem – by his name, Christ	*Terrestrial*
Adam – "rule over"	Japheth – rule over	*Celestial*

Though the participants have different names, the storyline is surprisingly similar – both histories portray the first incidence of shame in their respective creation narratives. In both cases the main character(s) are working in a garden, they are innocent or perfect, there is fruit that is eaten that causes an accusation of shame to be leveled, in one case by Satan and in the other by Ham. In both stories a garment is then provided to cover this shame. Afterwards, in each story three blessings or curses are given. In addition, there is a clear hierarchy to these blessings, foretelling of three kingdoms – the telestial, terrestrial, and celestial. The Satan\Ham comparison is apparent, including the somewhat disparaging meaning of Ham's name in Hebrew\Coptic, which is hot or dark.[160] Both Satan and Ham ultimately receive a similar malediction, Satan cursed to crawl on his belly, and Ham's descendants (through Canaan) to be a "servant of servants", in other words, the lowest of the low.

Eve's parallel to Shem is also significant. Eve means life - "the mother of all living," and by her seed, who is Christ, all shall live. In particular, Eve's seed (Jesus) was foreordained to bruise (crush) the serpent's head, who is Satan (Gen 3:15). Jesus will come through Shem's seed or lineage, preserving God's promise to Eve. In fact, "Semite" comes from shemite, the descendants of Shem (Israel). In Hebrew, Shem means "name" or "sign,"[161] pointing us forward to the saving name of Jesus.

Last of all, Japheth is also given a very distinguished blessing – "God shall enlarge (multiply, expand) Japheth, and he shall dwell in the tents of Shem; and Canaan (Ham's posterity) shall be his servant." Like Adam, who was told that he shall "rule over" Eve (Gen 3:16), Japheth is given preeminence over his brothers. His blessing to be "enlarged" is a play on the Hebrew meaning of his name, which comes from the Hebrew root *patah*, meaning to be opened.[162] However, some etymologies dispute that his name comes from the Hebrew root *yafah*, which means fair or beautiful. Such a designation parallels physical and spiritual creation in the temple, ultimately beautified and fruitful. Japheth's posterity is understood to be the gentile nations, to whom the gospel will go after the "Semites" reject it.[163] He is promised that his descendents will dwell in the tents of Shem (the temples of Shem). As we know, the Semite remnant will eventually be gathered by the gentiles – fulfilling God's covenant. Below is a side-by-side comparison of how each story parallels the pattern of salvation set forth in the temple:

Satan	Ham	*Telestial*
Eve	Shem	*Terrestrial*
Adam	Japeth	*Celestial*

In the modern temple we are told that an animal (lamb) is sacrificed to provide Adam and Eve with a garment (covering) for their shame (nakedness). In Hebrew the word for Atonement is *kaphar*, which means to cover.[164] Accordingly, Noah's covering is also a story about Atonement, reinforcing similar aspects of the first Eden story. Shem and Japheth illustrate how the Atonement is a gift, because Noah, in his unconscious state, was unable to provide a covering for himself, much as Adam and Eve ineffectively covered their shame with fig leafs. Unlike Ham, who intended to bring disgrace and condemnation upon his drunken father, Shem and Japheth intercede with mercy, extending unmerited grace, capturing the loving character and nature of the Atonement. (See appendix 11, Alma's discussion on justice and mercy – Pg 330-334.)

In addition, the entirety of Noah's story has been arranged as a chiasmus. Against the backdrop of the modern temple endowment we can easily identify the three kingdoms which represent our earthly spiritual growth, and which also make up the heavenly world. Genesis 6:10 -7:24 portrays a telestial world and its utter destruction. Subsequently, Genesis 8:1-2 is the pivot when God changes course, he remembers his promise\covenant with Noah (terrestrial), while Genesis 8:3-9:19 represents the new celestial world, washed from sin as the waters abate, new land appears, and God covenants anew with man.

The Chiastic Structure of the Genesis Flood
(Genesis 6:9–9:19)

A Noah (6:10a)
  B Shem, Ham and Japheth (10b)
    C Ark to be built (14-16)
      D Flood announced (17)
        E Covenant with Noah (18-20)
          F Food in the ark (21)
            G Command to enter ark (7:1-3)
              H 7 days waiting for flood (4-5)
                I 7 days waiting for flood (7-10)
                  J Entry to ark (11-15)   *Telestial*
                    K Yahweh shuts Noah in (16)
                      L 40 days flood (17a)
                        M Waters increase (17b-18)
                          N Mountains covered (19-20)
                            O 150 days waters prevails ((21)-24)
                              P GOD REMEMBERS NOAH (8:1)   *Terrestrial*
                          O' 150 days waters abate (3)
                        N' Mountains tops visible (4-5)
                      M' Waters abate (5)
                  L' 40 days (end of) (6a)
                K' Noah opens window of ark (6b)
              J' Raven and dove leave ark (7-9)
            I' 7 days waiting for waters to subside (12-13)   *Celestial*
          H' 7 days waiting for waters to subside (12-13)
        G' Command to leave ark (15-17 (22))
      F' Food outside ark (9:1-4)
    E' Covenant with all flesh (8-10)
      D' No flood in future (11-17)
    C' Ark (18a)
  B' Shem, Ham and Japheth (18b)
A' Noah (19)

Source: Gordon Wenham, "The coherence of the Flood narrative", Vetus Testamentum 28 (1978): 336-48.

*Remember that Stephen also alludes to Noah's dove in the middle of his presentation of Abraham, a plan of salvation, presenting the temple pattern within a temple pattern (pg 54-57).

Plan of Salvation
Preach my Gospel (Pg 54)

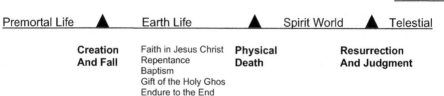

Plan of Salvation
Temple Adaptation

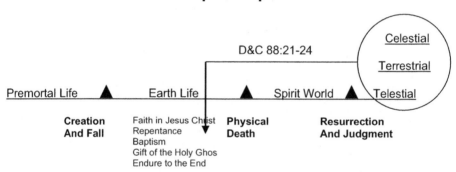

Earth Life – New Paradigm (combined)

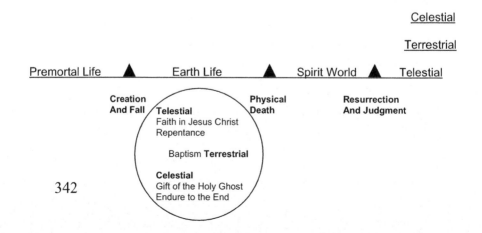

NOTES

1 Hugh W. Nibley, Temple and Cosmos: Beyond This Ignorant Present (Vol. 12 of the Collected Works of Hugh Nibley), edited by Don E. Norton, (Salt Lake City, Utah: Deseret Book Company; Provo, Utah: Foundation for Ancient Research and Mormon Studies, 1992), 31

2 Margaret Barker, Creation Theology, Wakefield 2004, http://www.margaretbarker.com/Papers/CreationTheology.pdf

3 Michael Bull, The Bible in 3D, p 33

4 Andrew Ehat, 'Who Shall Ascend into the Hill of the Lord?' Sesquicentennial Reflections of a Sacred Day: 4 May 1842," *Temples of the Ancient World,* edited by Donald W. Parry (Salt Lake City: Deseret Book Company, 1994), 58-59.

5 "Temple Worship,"*Utah Genealogical and Historical Magazine,* Apr. 1921, p. 62.

6 Teachings of Presidents of the Church: Harold B. Lee, *p.99*

7 https://www.lds.org/scriptures/gs/gospel, Feb 2, 2015

8 "The Salt Lake Temple," *Ensign,* Mar. 1993, 5–6

9 "The Temple was a model of the creation, and the liturgy of the temple preserved the creation. Genesis 1 was not an account of the historical process of creation, but a record of the great vision granted to Moses and others of how the world is made. In the six days when Moses was on Sinai, before the LORD called to him (Exod. 24.16), he saw the six days of creation, and was then told to replicate these when he built the tabernacle. A few ancient sources say that Moses saw the heavenly temple; but most assume that he saw the process of creation, and that the tabernacle represented this." Margaret Barker, Creation Theology, http://www.margaretbarker.com/Papers/CreationTheology.pdf, May 2015

10 Elder Bruce D. Porter , "The First Principles and Ordinances of the Gospel", Ensign, Oct 2000

11 The Discourses of Wilford Woodruff, ed. G. Homer Durham (1946), pg 20

12 General Conference, Honorably Hold a Name and Standing, Elder David A. Bednar, April 2009. In this talk Elder Bednar connects baptism to a sort of greater baptism in the temple. "These scriptures help us understand that the process of taking upon ourselves the name of Jesus Christ that is commenced in the waters of baptism is continued and enlarged in the house of the Lord. As we stand in the waters of baptism, we look to the temple. As we partake of the sacrament, we look to the temple. We pledge to always remember the Savior and to keep His commandments as preparation to participate in the sacred ordinances of the temple and receive the highest blessings available through the name and by the authority of the Lord Jesus Christ. Thus, in the ordinances of the holy temple we more completely and fully take upon us the name of Jesus Christ."

[13] Interestingly, Paul concludes his remarks in 1 Cor 3 with a temple analogy, comparing the works of the telestial membership to materials that cannot withstand the fire of God. He also lists materials used in temple construction, like gold, silver, and precious stones, which could survive the fire. Then he says, "Know ye not that ye are the temple of God, and that the Spirit of God dwelleth in you? If any man defile the temple of God, him shall God destroy; for the temple of God is holy, which temple ye are."

[14] There may be a question concerning faith's designation as an element of the telestial world. To answer these possible concerns I would refer you to Joseph's Smith's Lectures on faith. In his seventh and final lecture (#7) he sums up that the plan of salvation is "a system of faith — it begins with faith, and continues by faith; and every blessing which is obtained, in relation to it, is the effect of faith, whether it pertains to this life or that which is to come." However, in the next section Joseph tells us that through faith the early saints obtained something even greater – knowledge or God. "For there is a great difference between believing in God and knowing him: knowledge implies more than faith. And notice, that all things that pertain to life and godliness, were given through the knowledge of God; the answer is given, through faith they were to obtain this knowledge; and having power by faith to obtain the knowledge of God, they could with it obtain all other things which pertain to life and godliness." Subsequently, if we were to ascribe "knowledge of God" a kingdom it would be the celestial. In fact, 1 Cor 13 also tells us of something greater than faith; "and though I have all faith, so that I could remove mountains, and have not charity (love), I am nothing. And now abideth **faith,** hope, charity (love), these three; but the greatest of these is charity" (1 Cor 13:2,13). In these verses Paul refers to faith as "seeing in part" or "seeing through a glass darkly." However, he compares love to "that which is perfect", and states that when it comes, "that which is in part (faith) shall be done away." Of course, love is a fruit of the Spirit (Gal 5:22), and in our temple model the Holy Ghost (Spirit) is associated with the celestial world. By the power of the Holy Ghost we feel the love of God shed abroad in our hearts (Rom 5:5), and by this power (love) we are celestialized. See 1 Jn 4:4-8 for more on love as the definition of knowing God.

¹⁵ If we place this "journey" into our seven-part creation archetype it might look like this:

Standing in temple

    Sin separates you from God – leave temple

        Repent – struggle with desire to
        place ego (**natural man**) on altar *(telestial)*

            Call upon the name of the Son of God,
            feel His loving forgiveness   *(terrestrial)*

        Filled with power of Atonement,
        led by Spirit, reconcile with your *(celestial)*
        fellow man

    Present yourself at the veil of the temple – having been true and faithful

Return into His holy presence, stand worthily in His temple

¹⁶ Choose You This Day, Elder Dale G Renlund, Oct Conference 2018

¹⁷ Shon D. Hopkin, "Representing the Divine Ascent: The Day of Atonement in Christian and Nephite Scripture and Practice," in *The Temple: Ancient and Restored*, ed. Stephen D. Ricks and Donald W. Parry (Salt Lake and Orem, UT: Eborn Books and Interpreter Foundation, 2016), 347

¹⁸ Joseph M. Spencer, *An Other Testament: On Typology*, 2nd ed. (Provo, UT: Neal A. Maxwell Institute for Religious Scholarship, 2016), 46.

¹⁹ Hugh Nibley, *Temple and Cosmos*, The Collected Works of Hugh Nibley, Volume 12 (Salt Lake City and Provo, UT: Deseret Book and FARMS, 1992), accessed online.

²⁰ Not too surprising, a fractal image of this creation\template is provided "again" in D&C 52. In verses 9-10 the Lord gives his saints the pattern as they prepare to do successful missionary work – which he describes as preaching repentance, baptism, and the laying on of hands (for the Holy Ghost) – the pattern, sequence, template in all things.

²¹ The Three Pillars of Eternity, Bruce R. McConkie, BYU Devotional Feb 17, 1981

²² Old Testament: Gospel Doctrine Teacher's Manual, "Lesson 4: Because of my Transgression my Eyes are Opened," pg 12-16

²³ Ibid.

[24] Chiasmus in the Book of Mormon, John W. Welch, http://maxwellinstitute .byu.edu/ publications/ books/?bookid=111&chapid=1292, 21 Jan 2011

[25] Teachings of the Prophet Joseph Smith, Joseph Fielding Smith, pg 187-88

[26] Christ's instructions in 3 Nephi 9:19 are also chiastic:

> 19 And ye shall **offer** up unto me no more **the shedding of blood**;
>   yea, your sacrifices and your burnt offerings
>   shall be done away,
>   for I will accept none
>   of your sacrifices and your burnt offerings.
> 20 And ye shall **offer** for a sacrifice unto me **a broken heart and a contrite spirit**.

Notice how the "shedding of blood" is parallel to the new sacrifice of the broken heart.

[27] Neal A. Maxwell, "'Deny Yourselves of All Ungodliness'," *Ensign*, May 1995, 66

[28] Peter B. Rawlins, "Covenants, Sacraments, and Vows: The Active Pathway to Mercy," Religious Educator 13, no. 3 (2012): 205–219

[29] Right from "the beginning" we find parallel poetry in scripture. Genesis 1:1-5 can easily be arranged in a chiasmus:

a In **the beginning**
  b God created (bara-divided)
    c the heaven
      d and the earth.
        e And the earth was without form, and **void**;
          f and **darkness** [was] upon the face of the deep.
            g And the **Spirit** of God moved upon the face of the waters.
            g And God said, Let there be **light**: and there was light.
          f And God saw the **light**,
        e that [it was] **good**:
  b and God divided
    c the light
      d from the darkness.
a And God called the light Day, and the darkness he called Night. And the evening and the morning were **the first day**.

Notice how the Hebrew for "created" is bara, which by definition means "divided", and that heaven is parallel to light and earth is parallel to darkness. Of course, the center is a comparison of the Spirit to light, both of which are the hinge for the first day. The earth is void until the Spirit moves and light appears. Notice that f and f' are antithetical (darkness, light), as are e and e', (void and good).

[30] Blue Letter Bible. "Dictionary and Word Search for *rachaph (Strong's 7363)*". Blue Letter Bible. 1996-2011. 30 Oct 2011

[31] Blue Letter Bible. "Dictionary and Word Search for *Gethsēmani (Strong's 1068)*". Blue Letter Bible. 1996-2008. 7 Sep 2008

[32] If we take a closer look at Jonah's story we will see that there are many other parallels that resonate with the Savior's life and Atonement:

- Jonah from Gathhepher (the wine press) in Galilee, and Jesus from Galilee will tread the winepress alone (Isa 63:3)
- Jonah swallowed by whale for three days, and Christ in the heart of the earth for three days. Both result in impossible and miraculous re-births.
- Jonah pays a price to "go down" into the ship on the chaotic sea, Christ pays a price to go down into a chaotic mortality
- Jonah freely offers himself as sacrifice to bring peace to the chaotic sea, Christ freely offers himself to bring peace to a chaotic world
- Lots are cast at the time of Jonah's sacrifice; lots are cast when Jesus was sacrificed
- Jonah prayed for "salvation" while in the depths of the sea, Jesus (whose name means salvation) secures salvation for all men while in the heart of the earth.
- Jonah preached repentance to Nineveh, as did Jesus to Judea and mankind
- All Nineveh turns to the Lord; all mankind will confess that Jesus is Lord.

[33] "From Talmudic references it would appear that reading from the prophetic books had become a well-established custom long before the destruction of the Second Temple. There are also early Christian allusions to the "reading of the Law and the Prophets" (Luke 4:17; Acts 13:15)." Encyclopedia of Judaism, http://www.answers.com /topic/haftarah

[34] Encyclopedia Judaica Jr.

[35] Joseph Smith, History of the Church, 5:260-261

[36] "The human body contains from 55% to 78% water, depending on body size. To function properly, the body requires between one and seven liters of water per day to avoid dehydration; the precise amount depends on the level of activity, temperature, humidity, and other factors." What percentage of the human body is composed of water? Jeffrey Utz, M.D., The MadSci Network. http://en.wikipedia.org/wiki/ Water#cite_note-45, 16 Dec 2011

[37] Blue Letter Bible. "Dictionary and Word Search for *pneuma (Strong's 4151)*". Blue Letter Bible. 1996-2011. 27 Sep 2011.

[38] "God's Love," Children's Songbook of The Church of Jesus Christ of Latter-day Saints, 97

[39] Bruce R. McConkie, "Promises Made to the Fathers," in Genesis to 2 Samuel, vol. 3 of Studies in Scripture, ed. Kent P. Jackson and Robert L. Millet (Salt Lake City: Deseret Book, 1989), 3:51–52.

[40] *M. Catherine Thomas,* Alma the Younger Covenants with the Fathers (Part 1), Maxwell Institute, http://www.farms.byu.edu/publications/transcripts/?id=43#19, 28 Oct 2008

[41] Blue Letter Bible. "Dictionary and Word Search for *'Aram Naharayim (Strong's 0763)*". Blue Letter Bible. 1996-2008. 7 Sep 2008

[42] Blue Letter Bible. "Dictionary and Word Search for *Charan (Strong's 2771)*". Blue Letter Bible. 1996-2011. 23 May 2011

[43] The account in Genesis 15 also tells us that Abraham's seed will be in Egypt for four generations. Four is commonly thought of to be a symbol of the earth or created world; i.e. the four winds. The Lost Language of Symbolism, Alonzo L Gaskill, 2003, p 119

[44] "What is concealed in [the Old Testament] under the veil of earthly promises is clearly revealed in the preaching of the New Testament. Our Lord Himself briefly demonstrated and defined the use of the Old Testament writings, when He said that it was necessary that what had been written concerning Himself in the Law, and the Prophets, and the Psalms, should be fulfilled, and that this was that Christ must suffer, and rise from the dead the third day, and that repentance and remission of sins should be preached in His name among all nations, beginning at Jerusalem." Augustine, On the Merits and Forgiveness of Sins, and on the Baptism of Infants," Book 1, Chapter 53, "The Utility of the Books of the Old Testament"

[45] Walter Eichrodt gives us the following definition of type: "The so-called types . . . are persons, institutions, and events of the Old Testament which are regarded as divinely established models or presentations of corresponding realities in the New Testament salvation history." (Claus Westermann, ed., Essays on Old Testament Hermeneutics, p. 17)

The entire Bible is typical "because it presents examples and patterns of the experience of men and women." (David L. Baker, "Typology and the Christian Use of the Old Testament," SJT 29, April 1976, 141) The Flood, Exodus and Restoration are examples of the salvation everyone must experience; Noah, Job, Moses and David give us patterns for Christian behavior; the Temple is typical of the church as God's dwelling-place. Keith Poysti, The Typological Interpretation of Scripture, July 1983, Vol. 12 No. 3, pp. 3–11

[46] Later, Jacob builds an altar in Shechem when he first returns to Canaan. Also, as a scriptural crossroads, 500 years after that Joshua is instructed to renew Israel's covenant there, upon returning from Egypt. During his ministry, Christ will come to the well in Shechem to offer the Samaritan woman living water. In the Hebrew Shechem means shoulder portion, which signifies strength.

[47] Blue Letter Bible. "Dictionary and Word Search for *Mosheh (Strong's 4872)*". Blue Letter Bible. 1996-2010. 27 Dec 2010

[48] LDS Bible Dictionary, Pg 718

[49] Whereas 1 Cor 6:19-20 speaks about individuals as temples, 2 Cor 6:16-18 is talking about yet another variation of the temple, the church collectively as a temple. "And what agreement hath the temple of God with idols? for ye are the temple of the living God; as God hath said, I will dwell in them, and walk in them; and I will be their God, and they shall be my people. Wherefore come out from among them, and be ye separate, saith the Lord, and touch not the unclean thing; and I will receive you, And will be a Father unto you, and ye shall be my sons and daughters, saith the Lord Almighty." Here Paul quotes verses from Ezekiel, Isaiah, and Jeremiah to support this idea. From Ezekiel 37:27-28 we read, "yea, I will be their God, and they shall be my people. I the LORD do sanctify Israel, when my sanctuary shall be in the midst of them for evermore." And, in Isaiah 52:11 we find, "depart ye, go ye out from thence, touch no unclean thing; go ye out of the midst of her; be ye clean, that bear the vessels of the LORD." The "vessels" referred to here are those that the priesthood used to perform atoning ordinances in the temple, which only the clean (pure) were worthy to handle. As Isaiah points out, one must "depart" or separate themselves from the world (put off the natural man) in order to be clean for this service. In his commentary on 2 Cor 6, David Guzik quotes Alan Redpath concerning how one separates him\herself from the world. "It is not a question simply of trying to empty your heart and life of every worldly desire - what an awful impossibility! It is rather opening your heart wide to all the love of God in Christ, and letting that love just sweep through you and exercise its expulsive power till your heart is filled with love." I would add that this love is shed abroad in our hearts "by the Holy Ghost" (Rom 5:5).

[50] Neal A. Maxwell, Settle This in Your Hearts, Ensign, Oct 1992. "These comments are for the essentially, "honorable" members who are skimming

over the surface instead of deepening their discipleship and who are casually engaged rather than "anxiously engaged." (D&C 76:75; D&C 58:27.) Though nominal in their participation, their reservations and hesitations inevitably show through. They may even pass through our holy temples, but, alas, they do not let the holy temples pass through them."

[51] "Thus the Savior has become the great High Priest, the only source of the blessings of the Father for this earth. When we receive the priesthood it is the Savior's authority we receive. That's why it is called "The Holy Priesthood, after the Order of the Son of God." (See D&C 107:3.) Father to Son: A Dialogue on Priesthood, Chauncey C. Riddle, Ensign, April 1976

[52] http://www.blueletterbible.org/lang/lexicon/lexicon.cfm?strongs=H2896, Mar 1 2015

[53] Because of sin we are separated from God. The veil represents the justice of God which was required to pay for sin, which price Christ paid through his atoning sacrificial blood. The third verse of the LDS hymn, "While of These Emblems We Partake," reflects this truth. "The law was broken **Jesus died, that justice might be satisfied**, that man might not remain a slave, of death of hell, or of the grave."

[54] "We received the priesthood first in the premortal existence and then again as mortals. Adam held the keys and used the priesthood when he participated in the creation of the earth." The Doctrine of the Priesthood, Bruce R McConkie, General Conference, April 1982

[55] Alex Douglas, The Garden of Eden, the Ancient Temple, and Receiving a New Name, Ascending the Mountain of the Lord: Temple, Praise, and Worship in the Old Testament, pg 36-48. "Both within and without the Bible, Eden is presented as a type of temple where God's presence dwells, and in this temple Adam is depicted as a priest. But given the intimate connection between these two spheres, it would be insufficient to say that the temple was a "representation" of Eden, or even that it was a "recreation" of it. In the ancient mind, the temple was the Garden of Eden, and Eden was the world's first temple."

[56] The Doctrine of the Priesthood, Bruce R McConkie, General Conference, April 1982, https://www.lds.org/general-conference/1982/04/the-doctrine-of-the-priesthood?lang=eng

[57] "You Are My Hands," President Dieter F. Uchtdorf, Liahona, May 2010

[58] Interestingly, if we examine the meaning of the word conscious (which means to be aware) we find that it is a compound latin word meaning "with knowledge," likely coming from the Greek *syneidos*, which means the same thing.

[59] What was the first command given to mankind in Eden? There is some confusion because of the two creation accounts given in Genesis. In Gen 1:28 (the general account of creation) God tells "them" that they should multiply and replenish the earth. This command is given to "them" (plural), which assumes that Eve was already created when it is given. However,

there was a previous command. In Gen 2: 16-17, which retells the creation of man in more detail, the first command given there is - not to partake of the fruit of the tree of good and evil, which is given only to Adam. Eve is subsequently created several verses later (Gen 2:22). Since Gen 1:28 indicates that the command to be fruitful was given to both Adam and Eve ("them"), then it must have been given after Eve was created, and after the command given to Adam to not partake of the tree of good and evil. Though Eve apparently wasn't present when this command was given, we know that she was able to repeat it to Satan when he tempts her in Genesis 3. The LDS Old Testament Instructors Manual explains these two accounts:

> "Some have been confused by the account of the creation of man being in both Genesis 1:26-27 and Genesis 2:7. Both passages are accounts of the physical creation of Adam. Use the accompanying chalkboard illustration to help students understand why both accounts are given."

Overlapping Accounts of the Creation of Man

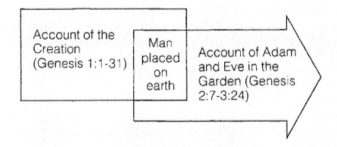

> "Explain that an account of the creation of man was included **as part of** the account of the Creation (see Genesis 1:26-27). When the Lord began telling of the experience of Adam and Eve in the Garden, he started at their placement on the earth (see Genesis 2:7)."

Genesis 1-2, Old Testament Instructor's Guide, Religion 301-2, (1994), Pg 3–4, https://www.lds.org/manual/old-testament-instructors-guide-religion-301-2/genesis-1-2?lang=eng, 1 Jan 2016.

Moses 3:5, clarifies that the initial creation account was "spiritual", done "in heaven" before Adam was "placed" in the garden. If this is the case, then the command to be fruitful would have been veiled from Adam and Eve's recollection, because it was given "in heaven"; pre-Eden. The creation account in Abraham 4-5 also confirms this.

[60] "All people are born with the capacity to distinguish between right and wrong. This ability, called conscience, is a manifestation of the Light of

Christ (see Moroni 7:15–19). A person's conscience is a defense against situations that are spiritually harmful." Gospel Topics, LDS.org website, 5 Feb, 2015

[61] "Wherefore, it came to pass that the devil tempted Adam, and he partook of the forbidden fruit and transgressed the commandment, wherein he became subject to the will of the devil, because **he yielded unto temptation**. Wherefore, I, the Lord God, caused that he should be cast out from the Garden of Eden, from my presence, because of his transgression, wherein **he became spiritually dead**, which is the first death, even that same death which is the last death, which is spiritual, which shall be pronounced upon **the wicked** when I shall say: Depart, ye cursed." (D&C 29:40-41) Not in these verses, nor in any others, does the Lord praise Adam and Eve for their actions. Rather, Adam is harshly categorized here with the cursed and the wicked; i.e. he became "subject to the will of the devil because he yielded to temptation" to not obey God.

[62] Harold B Lee, "The Fall of Man," Lecture Given to Seminary and Institute Teachers, June 23, 1954, Brigham Young University)

[63] James Talmage, Articles of Faith, Pg 63-65.

[64] "The degree of our love for the Lord and for our fellowman can be measured by what we are willing to sacrifice for them. Sacrifice is a demonstration of pure love." Elder M. Russell Ballard, "The Law of Sacrifice," Ensign, Oct. 1998, pg 11.

[65] Skip Moen, http://skipmoen.com/2014/04/09/seduced/, 14 Nov 2015. "Seduction is a matter of inner justification. Eve sins before she ever touched the fruit of the tree. She sinned as soon as she decided it was acceptable for her. She sinned the instant she determined to listen to her own ethical justification rather than follow the directions of the words of Jehovah. We are no less seduced in the same moment; that moment we determine that this act, this thought, this intention is beneficial for me in spite of the fact that it is not God's direction. The craftiness of the one who walks, talks and has a hidden agenda is not unknown to us. In fact, we are ourselves the less-than-transparent seducers of our own souls. That serpent in the Garden is a lot more like me than any snake I have ever known."

[66] Neal A. Maxwell, According to the Desire of [Our] Hearts, Ensign, Oct 1996. "Therefore, what we insistently desire, over time, is what we will eventually become and what we will receive in eternity . . . Mostly, brothers and sisters, we become the victims of our own wrong desires . . . Even when the light of Christ flickers only faintly in the darkness, it flickers nevertheless. If one averts his gaze therefrom, it is because he so desires . . . Like it or not, therefore, reality requires that we acknowledge our responsibility for our desires. Brothers and sisters, which do we really desire, God's plans for us or Satan's? . . . Remember, it is our own desires which determine the sizing and the attractiveness of various temptations. We set our thermostats as to temptations. . . knowing gospel truths and doctrines is profoundly important, but we must also come to love them. When we love them, they will move us and help our desires and outward

works to become more holy ... Said the Prophet Joseph: "The nearer man approaches perfection, the clearer are his views, and the greater his enjoyments, till he has overcome the evils of his life and lost every desire for sin; and like the ancients, arrives at that point of faith where he is wrapped in the power and glory of his Maker and is caught up to dwell with Him (Teachings of the Prophet Joseph Smith, 51)."

[67] " In the temple <u>we are taught by symbols and examples; but that is not the fullness of the gospel.</u> One very popular argument today says, 'Look, you say the Book of Mormon contains the fullness of the gospel, but it doesn't contain any of the temple ordinances in it, does it?' Ordinances (of the temple) are not the fullness of the gospel. <u>Going to the temple is like entering into a laboratory to confirm what you have already learned in the classroom and from the text. The fullness of the gospel is the understanding of what the plan is all about—the knowledge necessary to salvation.</u> You know the whys and wherefores; for the fullness of the gospel you go to Nephi, to Alma, to Moroni. Then you will enter into the lab, but not in total ignorance. The (temple) ordinances are mere forms. They do not exalt us; they merely prepare us to be ready, in case we ever become eligible." Hugh Nibley, *Temple and Cosmos*, The Collected Works of Hugh Nibley, Volume 12 (Salt Lake City and Provo, UT: Deseret Book and FARMS, 1992)

[68] https://www.churchofjesuschrist.org/study/manual/the-gospel/baptism-and-the-holy-ghost, Apr 7, 2019

[69] https://history.churchofjesuschrist.org/faq/joseph-smith/quote-index?lang=eng

[70] The Great Plan of Happiness," address to seminary and institute instructors, 10 Aug. 1993, Pg 3.

[71] The Book of Mormon and the Doctrine and Covenants," Ensign, May 1987, 84.

[72] Thomas R. Valletta, "The True Bread of Life," Ensign, Mar 1999, 7

[73] Nibley, *Approaching Zion*, p. 566-67

[74] Barnes Notes on the Bible, https://biblehub.com/commentaries/matthew/16-20.htm, Dec 12, 2015

[75] Hugh Nibley, Lehi in the Desert [Salt Lake City, Utah: Bookcraft, 1952], p 90

[76] Joseph F. McConkie, Gospel Symbolism, p 274

[77] Blue Letter Bible. "Dictionary and Word Search for *'Eylim (Strong's 362)*". Blue Letter Bible. 1996-2011. 7 Nov 2011

[78] In chapter 12 of the book "And He Spake Unto Me," I outline a lengthy chiasmus found in Nephi 17. Notice how it begins with Nephi discussing the hard hearts of those who complained about building the **Ship** (A), and how it concludes with a comparison of those in Moses' group who hardened their hearts and would not look upon the **Serpent** – who is Christ (A'). A task "so great" in A, and a task too simple in A'.

A 17-19 Ship to **cross** the great waters, Did **complain against** me, Desired **not to labor** on ship, Sorrowful over the **hardness of their hearts,** Saying: Thou canst not accomplish **so great** a work

    B 20 Like unto our **father**, wandered in wilderness, women have born children, toiled, suffered, afflictions, came **out of Jerusalem**

        C 21 We might have enjoyed our **possessions** and our **land**

            D 22 We know that the people in the land of Jerusalem are **a righteous people** for **they kept the statutes and judgments of the Lord**

                E 23 **Do ye believe our fathers** would have been led away if not hearkened?

                    F 24 **Do ye suppose** that had the Lord not commanded Moses that he would **lead** them **(fathers)** out of bondage?

                        G 25 The children of Israel were in **bondage**, they were **brought out** of bondage

                            H 26 ye know that **by his word the waters of the Red Sea were divided**

                                I 27 Egyptians were **drowned** in the Red Sea, the armies of Pharaoh

                                  J 28 They were **fed manna** in the wilderness

                                    29 Yea, And we know that Moses, **by his word** according to the **power of God** which was in him, smote the rock, and there came forth **water**, that the children of Israel might quench their **thirst**.

                                  J 30 They being led … **leading them by day, giving light unto them by night**

                                I 31 And it came to pass that according to his word he led and he did **destroy** them. (Israelites)

                            H 31-32 Not anything done save **by his word**. And after **they crossed the river Jordan**

                        G 32 he did make them **mighty** unto the **driving out** of the children of the land, scattering them to destruction

                    F 33 **Do ye suppose** that the children of this land who were **driven** out by our **fathers** were righteous?

                E 34 **Do ye suppose our fathers** more choice if not righteous?

            D 35 He that is **righteous** is favored of God, but **this people has rejected every word of God.**

        C 36 God created **the earth** and his children that they should **possess** it

    B 40 Loved our **fathers**, Abraham, Isaac, Jacob, remembered covenants made. Did bring them **out of Egypt**

A 41-42 Because of the **simpleness or the easiness** of it – many perished, Did **harden their hearts, Labor** which they had to perform was to look upon Serpent, Did **revile against** Moses, They were **led forth** by his matchless power into the land of promise

[79] Jeffrey R. Holland and Patricia T. Holland, *On Earth As It Is in Heaven*, p. 139.

[80] John W Welch, Chiasmus in the Book of Mormon, New Era, Feb 1972, pg 6

[81] Blue Letter Bible. "Dictionary and Word Search for *keriyth (Strong's 3747)*". Blue Letter Bible. 1996-2010. 6 Oct 2010

[82] Blue Letter Bible. "Dictionary and Word Search for *bara' (Strong's 1254)*". Blue Letter Bible. 1996-2011. 16 May 2011

[83] Blue Letter Bible. "Dictionary and Word Search for *qadash (Strong's 6942)*". Blue Letter Bible. 1996-2013. 15 Jan 2011

[84] John W. Welch, Stephen D. Ricks, King Benjamin's Speech Made Simple, http://publications.mi.byu.edu/fullscreen/?pub=1087 &index=13, Mar 2015

[85] Chiasmus in the Book of Mormon, John W. Welch, BYU Studies, Autumn 1969 (I have modified the center, adding a singular apex, "how beautiful upon the mountains.")

[86] https://onoma.lib.byu.edu/index.php/MOSIAH, 15, Nov 2015

[87] ibid.

[88] "Where did Joseph Smith get the idea that "Navuoo" means "beautiful" in Hebrew? Is that idea correct?", James B. Allen, http://www.nauvoo.com/nauvoo_beautiful.html, 14 Dec 2011

[89] http://www.fairlds.org/Misc/Is_Nauvoo_a_Hebrew_Word.html

[90] Millennial Star 15, no. 41 (Oct. 8, 1853): 661. and Millennial Star 15, no. 41 (Oct. 8, 1853): 662.

[91] http://users.marshall.edu/~brown/nauvoo/symbols.html, 15 Oct 2009

[92] ibid.

[93] Blue Letter Bible. "Dictionary and Word Search for *na'ah (Strong's 4998)*". Blue Letter Bible. 1996-2011. 15 Dec 2011

[94] Blue Letter Bible. "Dictionary and Word Search for *naos (Strong's 3485)*". Blue Letter Bible. 1996-2011. 15 Dec 2011

[95] Similarly, the coal from off the Lord's holy altar touches the lips of Isaiah, which cleanses him and allows him into the Lord's presence. (Isa 6:6-7)

[96] The Music of the Gospel, Wilford W Andersen, Ensign, May 2015, pg 54

[97] "The Odes of Solomon are some of the most beautiful songs of peace and joy that the world possesses. Yet their origin, the date of their writing, and the exact meaning of many of the verses remain one of the great literary mysteries.
They have come down to us in a single and very ancient document in Syriac language. Evidently that document is a translation from the original Greek. Critical debate has raged around these Odes; one of the most

plausible explanations is that they are songs of newly baptized Christians of the First Century.
They are strangely lacking in historical allusions. Their radiance is no reflection of other days. They do not borrow from either the Old Testament or the Gospels. The inspiration of these verses is first-hand. They remind you of Aristides' remark, "A new people with whom something Divine is mingled." Here is vigor and insight to which we can find parallels only in the most exalted parts of the Scriptures.
J. Rendel Harris, MA., Hon. Fellow of Clare College, Cambridge says about them: There does not seem to be anything about which everyone seem agreed unless it be that the Odes are of singular beauty and high spiritual value."
http://www.sacred-texts.com/bib/fbe/fbe195.htm, July 13 2015

בָּגַד fut. יִבְגֹּד; once יִבְגָּד (Mal. 2:10), properly to cover (whence בֶּגֶד covering, garment); hence—
(1) TO ACT COVERTLY, FRAUDULENTLY, PERFIDIOUSLY. (For verbs of covering, hiding are often

[98] applied to fraud and perfidy; compare لبس to cover,

The noun for covering *(beged)* comes from this verb.

[99] When you refer to the creation, day 6 is when man and woman were created and instructed to be as one (put under covenant). This intimate relationship of selfless service and love is purposed to make one's heart pure. Its parallel, the beatitudes which were taught by Christ at the temple in Bountiful, also have the pure seeing God on day six, preceded by mercy (a touchstone fruit of the Spirit). The implication is that if one's heart is pure he will see God in others. One's purity therefore seems relative to the love abounding in one's marriage covenant, and covenants are predicated upon mercy (loving kindness). Neal Maxwell said that how we treat others is a good barometer of the state of one's discipleship.

[100] Ensign, May 2009

[101] "Olive oil is sometimes a symbol for purity and for the Holy Spirit and its influence." Guide to the Scriptures, pg 182

[102] Spencer Kimball, Faith Precedes the Miracle, pg 253-256

[103] Verse 9 informs us that the oil (light) can't be shared. Each virgin had to have their own supply.

[104] "The scriptures are a veritable smorgasbord of symbolism. But we miss the feast if we aren't familiar with the symbolic figures of speech used. One intriguing and appealing symbol, which may be called the marriage metaphor (although the scattered references taken together actually comprise an analogy), is found repeatedly throughout the scriptures. Beginning early in the Old Testament, this metaphor is woven throughout

the saga of the house of Israel like a colorful thread in a tapestry. The marriage metaphor testifies of the great love the Savior feels for all mankind and of the blessings that await those who accept his invitation to become his spiritual sons and daughters." Marriage Metaphor, Richard K Hart, Ensign, Jan 1995

[105] Ibid

[106] Dictionary of Bible Themes Scripture index copyright Martin H. Manser, 2009., The *NIV Thematic Study Bible,* *http://www.biblegateway.com/resources/dictionary-of-bible-themes/*, July 14, 2014

[107] The Christian writer, S.J. Hill tells us, "According to Jewish tradition, the covenant God initiated with His people at Mount Sinai was really a covenant of marriage. In fact, rabbis have believed for centuries that the Jewish wedding ceremony was not only a re-enactment of what happened at Sinai, but it also reflected the primary features of God's covenant with Israel." S.J. Hill, *Burning Desire*, p.42.

[108] www.blueletterbible.org/lang/lexicon/lexicon.cfm?strongs=H3618, July 17 2014

[109] www.blueletterbible.org/lang/lexicon/lexicon.cfm?t=KJV&strongs=H3634, July 17 2014

[110] http://www.judaica-guide.com/jewish_wedding/, July30 2014

[111] www. biblehub.com/isaiah/52-1.htm, July 17, 2014

[112] 2 Cor 11:2 "for I have espoused you to one husband, that I may present you as a chaste virgin to Messiah"

[113] "46 Therefore those things which were of old time, which were under the law, in me are all fulfilled. 47 Old things are done away, and all things have become new. 48 Therefore I would that ye should **be perfect** even as I, or your Father who is in heaven **is perfect**." These verses from 3 Nephi 12 are part of Christ's sermon at the temple (on the mount). Notice how the *new* law or covenant (inward, Spiritual) is opposed to the old (outward), and brings newness and rebirth – making way for the possibility of being perfect like Christ. Which begs the question, how was Christ able to be perfect, and how can we be perfect? When Christ arrived in Gethsemane he was without spot because there was a daily pattern to his life – he always did the Father's will as directed by the Spirit, to which he always yielded. In fact, Christ in Greek, and Messiah in Hebrew, means the Anointed One. Specifically, the anointing that Christ had was an anointing of fullness of the Spirit (Isa 61:1, Jn 3:34). Without this anointing Christ could not have "overcome the world" (natural man). Likewise, we cannot be perfected (put off the natural man or deny ourselves ungodliness) without this anointing.

[114] "Therefore they were called after this holy order, and were sanctified, and their garments were washed white through the blood of the Lamb. Now, they, after being sanctified by the Holy Ghost, having their garments made white, being pure and spotless before God, could not look upon sin save it were with abhorrence; and there were many, exceedingly great

many, who were made pure and entered into the rest of the Lord their God" Alma 13:11-12

[115] This covenant is reprised again in Deut 7:6-12 "For thou *art* an **holy** people unto the LORD thy God: the LORD thy God hath chosen thee to be a special people (peculiar treasure) unto himself, above all people that *are* upon the face of the earth. The LORD did not set his love upon you, nor choose you, because ye were more in number than any people; for ye *were* the fewest of all people: But because the LORD loved you, and because he would keep the oath which he had sworn unto your fathers, hath the LORD brought you out with a mighty hand, and redeemed you out of the house of bondmen, from the hand of Pharaoh king of Egypt. Know therefore that the LORD thy God, he *is* God, the faithful God, which **keepeth covenant** and mercy with them that love him and keep his commandments to a thousand generations; Thou shalt therefore keep the commandments, and the statutes, and the judgments, which I command thee this day, to do them. Wherefore it shall come to pass, **if ye** hearken to these judgments, and keep, and do them, that the LORD **thy God shall keep unto thee the covenant** and the mercy which he sware unto thy fathers." Notice that Moses uses the if\then dependent clause here, even connecting the Abrahamic covenant to the success of the Sinai covenant (as well as connecting it to those "that love him").

[116] In Moroni 7:31-32 we read how the covenant of the Father is fulfilled corporately, and most important, personally.

> "31 And the office of their ministry is to call men unto repentance, and to fulfil and to do the work of the **covenants of the Father**, which he hath made unto the children of men, to prepare the way among the children of men, by declaring the word of Christ unto the chosen vessels of the Lord, that they may bear testimony of him. 32 And by so doing, the Lord God prepareth the way that the residue of men may have faith in Christ, **that the Holy Ghost may have place in their hearts, according to the power thereof; and after this manner bringeth to pass the Father, the covenants which he hath made** unto the children of men."

Note how the covenants of the Father are brought to pass according to the power of the Holy Ghost which works in the heart of those endeavoring to be true and faithful. In fact, without this spiritual power we cannot truly keep our covenants (it is done "after this manner"). This is God's sufficient and enabling grace.

[117] In Romans 12:1-2 we again find the pattern of God's grace - how we spiritually contend with and overcome the world. He reminds us to not be "conformed to this world" (the natural man), but rather to offer ourselves as "living sacrifices," which is an allusion to the temple sacrifices (which were an allusion to blood of the sacrificial Lamb), whereby Israel was convantally cleansed and atoned for. He then tells us how this is done,

which is also very similar to what we just read from King Benjamin and Moroni - to be "**transformed by the renewing** of your mind, that ye may prove what [is] that good, and acceptable, and **perfect, will of God**." Paul contends that when our minds and hearts are "transformed" and renewed by the Holy Ghost (the only power able to change and transform us spiritually) we can know and act in concert (obediently) to "that good and acceptable, and perfect will of God." Paul calls this obedient response to the Spirit, "proving" God's "perfect will." Isn't this also being perfected in Christ? It makes sense, that when we follow the Spirit's voice (no matter the cost), and unite our will with the Father's, there is at-one-ment? (Importantly, the rest of Romans 12 summarizes how those with "one mind", who are "many members in one body" and "one body in Christ," will conduct their lives according to God's *perfect* will, serving and loving one another [fruit of the Spirit],)

[118] http://www.merriam-webster.com/dictionary/grace, July 1, 2014

[119] *The Gospel According to the Apostles* © 2000, John MacArthur, http://www.biblestudytools.com/bible-study/tips/what-is-grace-11649523.html, July 9, 2014

[120] ttp://www.blueletterbible.org/lang/lexicon/lexicon.cfm?Strongs=G1981&t=KJV, July 4 2014

[121] In Eph 3:14-21 Paul beautifully writes of God's love, and how we comprehend it "by his Spirit in the inner man" and "the power that worketh in us":

A 14 For this cause **I bow my knees** unto the Father of our Lord **Jesus Christ**,
  B 15 Of whom the whole **family in heaven and earth** is named,
    C 16 That he would grant you,
      D according to **the riches** of his glory,
        E to be strengthened with might by his **Spirit in the inner man**;
          F 17 That **Christ** may dwell in your hearts by **faith**;
            G that ye, being rooted and grounded in love,
              H18 May be able **to comprehend** with all saints
                what [is] the breadth, and length,
                and depth, and height;
              H'19 And **to know**
          F' the love of **Christ**, which passeth **knowledge**,
            G' that ye might be filled with all the fulness of God.
    C' 20 Now unto him that is able
      D' to do **exceeding abundantly** above all that we ask or think,
        E' according to the **power that worketh in us**,
  B' 21 Unto him [be] glory in **the church**
A' by **Christ Jesus** throughout all ages, world without end. **Amen.**

Most have heard these eloquent verses and never realized that part of what makes them beautiful and so appealing to our ear, is their structure. Because all of the elements are repeated twice, we get a double portion of exquisite teaching, which (just as the verses say) lifts our soul and helps us to comprehend the breadth, and length, and depth, and height, of the love of

Christ. Most especially, notice that "all saints" are able to do the impossible, which is to comprehend that which passes knowledge, because Christ (the tree of life) and his love "dwells in our hearts" by faith. Comparing this to 1 Nephi 11, you might remember that the tree of life (Christ) represented the love of God which "sheddeth itself abroad in the hearts of the children of men" (1 Ne 11:22). Curiously, Nephi also gives dimension to that "which passeth knowledge", explaining the love he felt in his heart as best he could, exalting with the angel, that it is the "most desirable above all things" and "most joyful to the soul" (1 Ne 11:22-23).

[122] Ephesians 4 tells of how we "learn of Christ," and how it is done only by those that are reborn of the Spirit. In verses 23-28 we read, "But ye have not so learned Christ; If so be that ye have heard him, and have been taught by him, as the truth is in Jesus: That ye put off concerning the former conversation (behavior is better Greek translation) the old man, which is corrupt according to the deceitful lusts; And that ye put on (endowed in Greek) the new man, which after God is **created** in righteousness and true holiness. And be renewed in the spirit of your mind." These verses are so rich with gospel imagery. Notice how they speak of (like King Benjamin and Moroni) putting off the natural man (old man) and putting on the newly created man (one who yields to the Holy Ghost). Again, being "renewed in the spirit of your mind" (Rom 12:1-2) refers to regeneration, which is something the Holy Ghost does. Also, notice how Paul says that this new man is "created" as he "puts on" (is endowed with) newness of life. In fact, like Moroni 10:32, Paul tells us that such a man is righteous (Melchizedek – king of righteousness) and holy (see Rev 19:8). These references are especially enlightening in view of the temple "endowment", wherein we are spiritually created as we make and keep covenants. Though the word covenant is not mentioned here (Eph 4), its actions and precepts are evident.

[123] Liahona, "A Broken Heart and a Contrite Spirit," Elder Bruce D. Porter, Nov. 2007

[124] BYU Speeches, Covenant Teachings of the Scriptures, Robert L Ludlow, Oct 13, 1998, https://speeches.byu.edu/talks/victor-l-ludlow_covenant-teachings-scriptures/, Nov 3, 2016

[125] http://www.blueletterbible.org/lang/lexicon/lexicon.cfm?Strongs=H5731&t=KJV, May 18, 2015

[126] The Robe, The Ring and the Sandals, Sandra Micelotti, http://www.sandramministries.com/golden-nuggets.php?dev_id=6, May 20 2015

[127] Blue Letter Bible. "Dictionary and Word Search for *amen (Strong's G281)*". Blue Letter Bible. 1996-2011. 15 June 2014

[128] The sacrament prayer on the water or wine (Moroni 5) also has chiastic elements, yet arranged slightly different than the prayer on the bread:

A O God, the Eternal Father, we ask thee, in the name of thy Son, Jesus Christ,

> B to bless and sanctify this wine to the souls of all those who drink of it,
>> C that they may do it in remembrance of the
>>> D **blood** of thy **Son,**
>>> D which was **shed** for them;
>>>> E that they may witness unto thee,
>>> D' O **God,**
>>> D' the **Eternal Father,**
>> C' that they do always remember him,
> B' that they may have his Spirit (sanctifier) to be with them.

A' Amen.

In this prayer we find all of the members of the Godhead; the Eternal Father and Son in the middle, and the Holy Ghost on either side (B,B'). At the center, surrounded by deity, we are found witnessing. In the Bible the Greek word for witness is *martus,* the word that "martyr" comes from. Martyrs are those who witness of Christ by laying down their lives. Such an idea seems very consistent with what we covenant to do in this baptismal renewal, which is to lay aside our pride and ego so that Christ may dwell and abound in us. It is noteworthy that here we renew all of our covenants, including our enfolded temple covenants, which culminate in the law of consecration – dedicating all that we possess, laying down our lives if necessary (at the very heart of a martyr or "witness").

[129] "Some have thought that the phrase 'another Comforter' in Doctrine and Covenants 88:3 refers to the Second Comforter, or a personal visit from the Savior. However, the Lord in this verse promised that this Comforter would 'abide in your hearts.' The scriptures tell us elsewhere that the "appearing of the Father and the Son [referred to in John 14:23] is a personal appearance; and the idea that the Father and the Son dwell in a man's heart is an old sectarian notion, and is false' (D&C 130:3). The Comforter promised in Doctrine and Covenants 88 is 'the Holy Spirit of promise' (v. 3), 'the promise which I give unto you of eternal life' (v. 4)."
Doctrine and Covenants Student Manual, Section 88 The Olive Leaf (2002), 197–206

[130] Donna B. Nelson, Beloved Bridegroom, pg 18

[131] Smith, William, Dr. "Entry for 'Sardis,'". "Smith's Bible Dictionary", http://www.biblestudytools.com/dictionary/sardis/, 7 Jul 2015

[132] There is a marvelous reference here to Exodus 19:5, when the Lord made a covenant with Israel at Mt Sinai, which is often considered her marriage covenant with God. All of the notable priesthood discourses in

scripture (Heb 3, Alma 13, D&C 84) make reference to this event. It was the time when Israel "provoked" the Lord because they feared to see him face to face (which is the purpose of the high priesthood.) For this they received a lesser (Levite) priesthood. The offering in righteousness that Malachi mentions in Malachi 3 refers to a time when the outward performance becomes the inner reality, when the priest is illuminated with the true understanding of his sacrifice, pointing to Christ's consecrated priestly sacrifice (the priest is the sacrifice). In Hebrew the word "jewel" (found in Malachi 3:17) is *segullah*, which is also rendered as peculiar treasure, and is the Hebrew word used in Exo 19:5,6 – "If ye will obey my voice indeed, and keep my covenant, then ye shall be a **peculiar treasure** unto me above all people: for all the earth is mine: And ye shall be unto me a kingdom of priests, and an holy nation." Peter later refers to this event in his oft-cited verses in 1 Peter2 "5 Ye also, as lively stones, are built up a spiritual house, an holy priesthood, **to offer up spiritual sacrifices**, acceptable to God by Jesus Christ. 9 But ye are a chosen generation, a royal priesthood, an holy nation, **a peculiar people**; that ye should shew forth the praises of him who hath called you out of darkness into his marvellous light:" Here Peter points out that the sacrifice now offered by the holy priesthood (Gods peculiar *segullah* people) is a "spiritual" one, that of yielding one's heart to the enticing of the Holy Ghost, through which God purifies and refines his "sons" (Mal 3 2) and Godly offspring (Mal 2:15).

[133] "Ancient covenants were always very solemn and serious agreements. Animal sacrifices were almost always included. Covenants were accompanied by the promise of blessings for obedience and the warning of curses for disobedience. In pagan societies, the participants almost always invoked their false gods as witnesses to secure the agreement. Finally, a sign of the covenant would usually accompany the sealing of the agreement. From historical information, we see the following eight steps commonly used in ancient covenant ceremonies:"

The Pre-Ceremony Actions
The Selection of the Covenant Representatives and the Cutting of the Covenant Sacrifice
The Exchange of Robes, Belts, and Weapons
The Walk unto Death
The Pronouncement of Blessings and Curses
The Seal of the Covenant Mark
The Exchange of Names
The Covenant Meal

Steps of Ancient Covenant Making, http://www.thectp.org/Notes/Inheritance /Inheritance_2.pdf, Dec 12, 2016
[134] The Hebrew word used here is *shacol*, meaning to be bereaved of children, childless, or to miscarry.

https://www.blueletterbible.org/lang/lexicon/lexicon.cfm?Strongs=H7921&t=KJV, Nov 16, 2016

[135] In Hebrew, the words for "meat" (*tereph*) and "cast fruit" (*shacol*) are both rendered in other instances as spoil.

[136] 1. a placing of one thing by the side of another 2. metaph. a comparing, comparison of one thing with another, likeness, similitude. https://www.blueletterbible.org/lang/lexicon/lexicon.cfm?strongs=G3850, Nov 30, 2016

[137] This obviously alludes back the Savior's first day and his discourse at the temple which contain the beatitudes, a progression leading to perfection. "They describe certain elements that go to form the refined and spiritual character, all of which will be present whenever that character exists in its perfection. Rather than being isolated statements, the Beatitudes are interrelated and progressive in their arrangement." (see the LDS Bible Dictionary). Just prior to the beatitudes Christ states the same "doctrine" of his gospel that we see in 3 Nephi 27. (This "doctrine" is repeated another time in 3 Ne 11:31-41.)

[138] "Trees are the symbol for man: Trees represent men: green trees are the righteous, dry trees the wicked (Luke 23:31; D&C 135:6)." [138] Joseph F. McConkie, Gospel Symbolism, p 274

[139] Andrew C. Skinner, "'This Is My Gospel": Jesus' Discourse in 3 Nephi,' in Religious Educator 11, no. 3 (2010): 123–143. https://rsc.byu.edu/archived/volume-11-number-3-2010/my-gospel-jesus-discourse-3-nephi, Nov 11, 2016

[140] Diocese of Westminster, http://rcdow.org.uk/att/files/faith/catechesis/baptism/sacraments.pdf, Jan 24, 2017

[141] ibid.

[142] ibid. "We, as human beings, need signs and symbols often to express what cannot be expressed in words... Sacraments, particularly, depend on signs and symbols which signify a sacred reality. . .To look at sacraments simply as a series of signs and rituals that alone produce a guaranteed effect would be to ignore their importance for our lives. They are celebrations of our journey of faith . . . They are moments relating to, and enriching our human experience, that make present the mystery and the actions of God in Christ, and are celebrated within the Body of Christ, the Church. God became visible in Christ, Christ is visible in the Church, communicating himself in the sacraments. Thus the Church, as the visible sign of Christ, is also sacrament. The sacraments are the signs and instruments by which the Holy Spirit spreads the grace of Christ the head throughout the Church which is his Body. . . And because we are members of the Body of Christ, we too can be the sacrament of Christ in the world. When we act as Jesus did we embody the presence of Christ in the world, we are living sacraments."

[143] www.blueletterbible.org/lang/lexicon/lexicon.cfm?strongs=H5475, Jan 24, 2017

[144] Sod is a noun derived from the Hebrew verb yasad – "used of men reclining on a couch or cushion, especially as deliberating and consulting together; hence to take counsel together."
https://www.blueletterbible.org/lang/lexicon/lexicon.cfm?t=KJV&strongs=H3245, Jan 27, 2017

[145] http://www.legrandlbaker.org/wp-content/uploads/2012/11/sode-decisions-of-the-Council-in-Heaven-LeGrand-Baker.pdf, Jan 24, 2017

[146] "The receiving of the endowment requires the assuming of obligations by covenants which in reality are but an embodiment or an unfolding of the covenants each person should have assumed at baptism, as explained by the prophet Alma to the effect that "ye are desirous to come into the fold of God, and to be called his people, and are willing to bear one another's burdens, that they may be light; Yea, and are willing to mourn with those that mourn; yea, and comfort those that stand in need of comfort, and to stand as witnesses of God at all times and in all things, and in all places that ye may be in, even until death" (Mosiah 18:8–9). Any [people] who [are] prepared to assume those obligations declared by Alma and "who humble themselves before God … and come forth with broken hearts and contrite spirits … and are willing to take upon them the name of Jesus Christ, having a determination to serve him to the end" (D&C 20:37), need have no hesitancy in going to a holy temple and receiving, in connection with the covenants taken, promises of great blessings predicated upon compliance therewith." (Teachings of Presidents of the Church: Harold B. Lee)

[147] "Ancient altars were not only places of sacrifice and covenant making but also places marked by God's presence. Sister Fronk reminds us that 'the Sabbath and the sacrament are some of the great times that God can teach us (counsel with us), and when He does, we stand on sacred ground. When we enter the chapel for sacrament meeting, are we aware that we are on holy ground and have the opportunity to enter into God's presence?' … If given with a pure heart, our offerings become holy and acceptable to the Lord (see D&C 124:75). Rather than being cut off from God, we are again worthy to enter His presence and can bask in the fulness of His glory." Adrian Juchau, "Sabbath Sanctification: A Tithing of Our Time, an Offering unto the Lord," in Selections from the Religious Education Student Symposium, 2004 (Provo, UT: Religious Studies Center, Brigham Young University, 2004), 47–61.

[148] John W. Welch, Chiasmus in the Book of Mormon, *New Era*, Feb 1972, pg 6

[149] "The love of God for His children is most profoundly expressed in His gift of Jesus as our Redeemer: "God so loved the world, that he gave his only begotten Son" (John 3:16). To partake of the love of God is to partake of Jesus' Atonement and the emancipations and joys which it can bring." Lessons from Laman and Lemuel, Neal A. Maxwell, LDS General Conference, October 1999

[150] In these verses Alma states several times that he has been given an endowment of special knowledge; mysteries of God that can only be known through an endowment of the Spirit. "4 And I would not that ye think that I know of myself—not of the temporal but of the spiritual, not of the carnal mind but of God. 5 Now, behold, I say unto you, if I had not been born of God I should not have known these things; but God has, by the mouth of his holy angel, made these things known unto me." The eternal possibilities of this revealed mystery are stated in verse 26, "And **I know** that he will raise me up at the last day, to dwell with him in glory."

[151] "The instant the feet of the priests carrying the ark enter the river, the waters part, dry land appears, and the children of Israel cross over to inherit their promised land (see Josh. 3:15–17). There are other evidences of the spiritual significance of this event. Among other things, preserved within the ark of covenant was manna. Christ himself testified that manna was a witness of him (see John 6:31–33). The ark also bore the rod of Aaron, the same rod which, **though cut off from a living tree, nevertheless in death budded, blossomed, and brought forth fruit** (see Num. 17). It is this same rod which Moses used to help deliver his people from Egypt with great and powerful miracles. In fact, it was when this rod was lifted up over the Red Sea (see Ex. 14:16) that its waters parted, dry land appeared, and the Israelites crossed over—while the pursuing Egyptians found death in those same waters." L. H. Read, The Ark of the Covenant, Ensign, June 1980

[152] Piercing the Veil: Temple Worship in the Lost 116 Pages, Don Bradley, a presentation at the 2012 FairMormon Conference

[153] "When Alma sought to teach Helaman of the spiritual significance of these events, he referred to the Liahona but not to the (Nephi's) ship. Yet, it seems to me that it was the Liahona and the ark together which accomplished the attainment of the promised land. The Liahona guided them and the ark carried them. In doing so, both represent Christ, just as several elements (the ark, Joshua, manna, the rod) typified Christ in the Israelites' crossing of the Jordan." L. H. Read, The Ark of the Covenant, Ensign, June 1980

[154] John Welch, The Temple in the Book of Mormon, Temples of the Ancient World, Donald W. Parry, p 363

[155] The mercy seat on the Ark of the Covenant, in the most holy place, also had two cherubim facing each other. Clearly the cherubim here are associated with mercy by virtue of the name "mercy seat."

[156] Bruce R McConkie, The Promised Messiah, p. 245

[157] Christian Clippings, Holiday, FL, 34692 February, 2000

[158] John Welch, The Temple in the Book of Mormon, Temples of the Ancient World, Donald W. Parry, p 367

[159] Parry, "Garden of Eden: Prototype Sanctuary," *Temples of the Ancient World,* p. 127.

[160] www.blueletterbible.org/lang/lexicon/lexicon.cfm?strongs=H2526, Mar 11, 2018
[161] www.blueletterbible.org/lang/lexicon/lexicon.cfm?strongs=H8034, Mar 11, 2018
[162] www.blueletterbible.org/lang/lexicon/lexicon.cfm?strongs=H3314, Mar 11, 2018
[163] "The root of yapht is pathach, 'to make wide.' This etymology, however, is not universally accepted, as the word-play is so obvious, and the association of Japheth with Shem ("dark") and Ham ("black") suggests a name on similar lines-either gentilic, or descriptive of race. Japheth has therefore been explained as meaning "fair," from yaphah, the non-Sem and non-Hamitic races known to the Jews being all more or less white skinned. The Targum of Onkelos agrees with the English Versions of the Bible, but that of Jonathan has "God shall beautify Japheth," as though from yaphah." International Standard Bible Encyclopedia, http://biblehub.com/topical/j/japheth.htm, Mar 12, 2018
[164] www.blueletterbible.org/lang/lexicon/lexicon.cfm?strongs=H3722, Mar 11, 2018

Made in the USA
Las Vegas, NV
07 February 2021